A PASSING GAME

FIFTY YEARS
OF
NORTHAMPTONSHIRE FOOTBALL
PART 1
1945-1970

by

IAN ADDIS

Foreword
by
George Swindin

JEMA PUBLICATIONS

Published by:
Jema Publications
40 Ashley Lane
Moulton
Northampton
NN3 7TJ

ISBN: 1 871468 33 7

Particular thanks are given to:
The Chronicle and Echo and The Evening Telegraph for their permission to
reproduce many of the photographs, cuttings and cartoons, without which
the production of the book would not have been possible.
The quality of reproduction of the more dated newspaper cuttings does not
always comply with the high standard of reproduced archive material within
the publication. It is hoped, however, that their inclusion will serve to
rekindle memories and contribute further to your enjoyment of the book.

DEDICATION

"For my brother Peter, who would surely have made his mark."

ACKNOWLEDGEMENTS

The following are thanked for their invaluable assistance in the compilation of this book: Terry Bly, Jim Walker, Ollie Conmy, Chris Turner, Joe Kiernan, Frank Grande, Bob Tebbutt, Steve Gammon, Bobby Wyldes, John Lawman, Barry Stanley, Gordon Livsey, Paul Harris, Tony Jones, Ken Ambridge, Dick Munns, Ian Young, Barry Daldy, Ernie Drage, John Lee, Gordon Linnett, Spencer Kettley, Joe Childs, Ernie Middlemiss, Maurice Goodall, J Hill, Derek Waugh, Nev Tingle, Gordon Inwood, Dave Walden, Reg Abbott, Brian Walden, Leigh Edwards, Ian Holliday, Andy Goldsmith, Walter Morris, Mike Spooner, Dave Holland, Nancy Bellamy, Brian Barron, the late George Hair, Northants Evening Telegraph, Peterborough Evening Telegraph, The Chronicle and Echo, Dave Twydell of Yore Publications, Alan Castle for the expert reproduction of photographs, Jeremy Biggs for copious statistical information, George Swindin for the splendid foreword, Robert Mercer for his evocative line drawings, Mick Dean for his diligent proof reading, Dave Thurland, Graham Russ, John Sellers and John Sewell for their constant encouragement and support, and Tony Noble, whose dedication and determination ensured that the project came to fruition.

The above list should be exhaustive, but sincere apologies are extended to those inadvertently omitted.

Ian Addis

FOREWORD
by
George Swindin

It is my pleasure to have been asked to write a foreword for this book reflecting on Northamptonshire football, having enjoyed associations with Peterborough United, Kettering and Corby Town football clubs.

My first contact locally goes back many years when, as a schoolboy, I played for England v The Rest at Kettering Town ground. Another triallist that day was later to become an international star - Stanley Matthews.

At the end of a 20 year playing career in the Football League with Bradford City and Arsenal, I was offered the player-managership at Peterborough United, then a Midland League club. At Peterborough I found a club with ambitions to be elected to the Football League, backed by an equally keen Board of Directors, and set about building a team to fulfil those aspirations.

Norman Rigby was already at the club as player and captain, and my task was to build the team around him. I brought in young players like Denis Emery from Eynesbury Rovers, Peter McNamee, a Scottish junior doing his National Service , Billy Hails, Bernard Shaw and Roy Killen from Lincoln City and Ellis Stafford from Sheffield junior football.
The team moulded exceptionally well and there were famous FA Cup matches against Lincoln City, Alf Ramsey's Ipswich Town, Swindon, and Huddersfield, then a Second Division club.

Public enthusiasm in Peterborough was reflected in increased attendances and, after winning the Midland League for the first time, the Directors realised the necessity to increase the ground's capacity.

Plans were put in hand to provide an up to date stadium, which involved constructing a new grandstand behind the old decrepit building currently in use. When this was completed, the old stand was demolished and the playing area moved 50 yards towards the new grandstand. The pitch was levelled with soil provided by British Sugar Corporation's Peterborough factory from the sugar beet washings. Local farmers, including a later director of the football club, Pat Terrell, provided transport for the soil free of charge. A slope on the original pitch of 12 feet was eliminated, so today the city has a stadium worthy of its place in football.

After 4 years at Peterborough I returned to Arsenal as manager, moving later to Norwich City and Cardiff, where players included future Kettering favourites, Steve Gammon and Trevor Peck and Peterborough and Northampton centre half, Frank Rankmore.

I realised that football management was becoming a risky career, so when I was sacked by Cardiff I decided to look elsewhere for my livelihood. Hence my return to Northamptonshire as the tenant of a Service Station in Corby.

Football now became a secondary interest, my prime objective being to build up a successful business. However, in 1965 I was approached by John Nash, then Chairman of Kettering Town, and invited to become part-time manager of the 'Poppies'. The club was reasonably successful, but I found the task of combining business and football was causing a clash of priorities. Long Saturday Southern League journeys meant the burden of running the garage business fell on my wife, so I resigned.

Finally, Corby Chairman, John Singlehurst, asked me to help the club on a part-time basis. I really didn't want to, but his enthusiasm persuaded me to accept, and although we had some success, particularly in local FA cup matches, it all became too demanding. With the growth of the garage business I decided the time had arrived to retire from my football activity.

I enjoyed many happy and eventful years in football, memorable occasions locally, and I am certain as you read this book, you too will reflect on the many good times football in this area has provided for its huge band of supporters.

I wish the author every success with his venture, and I am certain it will be of great interest.

George Swindin

September 1995

v

INTRODUCTION

When I mentioned to a friend that I was writing a book recalling the highlights of fifty years of County football, he remarked, "Well that won't take long then!"

How wrong he was. Enough material has accumulated to fill the two volumes planned twice over, and the most difficult task has been in deciding what to leave out. Yet, while the more assiduous reader may successfully locate essential facts and statistics, the result is hardly a definitive history of the period.

Rather, it comprises a selective if indulgent trawl through half a century of a Northamptonshire life which, like Sports writer Hugh McIlvanney's, "has, since childhood and adolescence, been permanently impregnated with the mythology of football."

I recently discovered lying on the cloakroom floor at the Primary school where I was headteacher, what I thought at first to be an artificial limb. Closer examination revealed it was, in fact, a shin-pad of the modern hi-tech variety. A complicated sock-like device which appeared to envelope the entire lower leg, from knee to toe, in plastic and elastic.
Forty five years were shed in an instant as I immediately recalled the 'Radio Times'. The magazine was highly prized in our house during the early fifties because it served two most useful purposes, neither of which involved looking up details of radio or television programmes. At the end of the week, the substantial wad of papers was either hung from a nail on the lavatory door by my mother, or purloined by me, to fold and shove down my football sock - as a shin-pad.

The changing times are reflected in what is essentially a football book. A humble liturgy to the greatest of games, whose creed was expressed so succinctly in Desborough player-manager Bobby Wyldes' oft repeated team-talk.

> "Keep the high balls high
> And the low balls low
> If we score first
> We're one up".

Ian Addis
September 1995

CONTENTS

"And it's sad to know that those days, win or lose, can't return. Nor those remembered faces be gathered into one place again."

J L Carr
'How Steeple Sinderby Wanderers Won the F A Cup'

GROWN MEN CHASING
A BAG OF WIND

My earliest memory of Britannia Road, Kettering is not a happy one. Dad was an insurance agent, who always carried out his rounds on a bike. Sometimes he took me along, perched precariously on a saddle fixed to the crossbar.

One evening, as the bicycle gathered speed racing down the considerable slope towards Rockingham Road, I was suddenly consumed by overwhelming fear. Lifting a sandalled foot from its rest on the frame, I thrust it forward in a desperate attempt to halt the runaway machine. The shoe wedged in the spokes of the front wheel, bringing riders and cycle crashing heavily to the ground.

Miraculously my father escaped unscathed. The bike and I were not so lucky. Both the damaged machine, its front wheel completely buckled out of shape, and I were propped against the great wooden fence that stretched from Cowper Street to Rockingham Road, while a kindly neighbour bathed my bleeding leg. Painful contact with a loosely gritted road surface had removed most of the skin from knee to ankle.

Although barely four years old, I was already aware that on the other side of the fence was a field where, in my mother's words, "twenty two grown men ran about like silly beggars chasing a bag of wind."

While reporting an FA cup replay against Crystal Palace in 1938, journalist Peter Wilson of the Sunday Pictorial had described Kettering's ground as a disgrace, likening the sloping pitch to Porlock Hill. So pronounced was this notorious local incline that my father often recalled being able to stand at the bar in the Athletic Club, (known familiarly as the Tin Hat), situated at the Rockingham Road end of the ground, and watching matches through the windows with a clear view of both goal areas.

In the summer of 1946, however, the club completed the major task of levelling the pitch, which involved transporting 11,500 tons of earth from the top to the bottom of the field.

One of the last matches played before the mammoth construction work was undertaken was the Maunsell Cup Final between Kettering and Northampton.

Kettering, taking advantage of the slope, built up a two goal lead at half-time. In the second half however, the Cobblers fierce downhill onslaught brought four goals in reply.

KETTERING TOWN FOOTBALL CLUB
••••••••••••••••
GRAND FOOTBALL MATCH
Thursday, May 2nd, 1946.
ON THE ROCKINGHAM ROAD GROUND
Kick off—6-30. p.m.

MAUNSELL CUP FINAL
KETTERING TOWN
v.
NORTHAMPTON

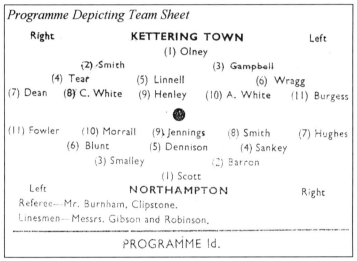

Programme Depicting Team Sheet

Right   **KETTERING TOWN**   Left
(1) Olney
(2) Smith   (3) Gampbell
(4) Tear   (5) Linnell   (6) Wragg
(7) Dean   (8) C. White   (9) Henley   (10) A. White   (11) Burgess

(11) Fowler   (10) Morrall   (9) Jennings   (8) Smith   (7) Hughes
(6) Blunt   (5) Dennison   (4) Sankey
(3) Smalley   (2) Barron
(1) Scott
Left   **NORTHAMPTON**   Right
Referee—Mr. Burnham, Clipstone.
Linesmen—Messrs. Gibson and Robinson.

PROGRAMME !d.

Cobblers winger Tommy 'Flash' Fowler who would make 521 league appearances for Northampton between 1945 and 1962

Northampton Town Football Club 1946

2

Kettering Town Football Club 1946

Back Row: Whitwell, Mansfield, Tear, Campbell, Linnell, Barton, Maddocks, Smith, Skinner Mabelson. Front Row: Joell, Burt, Henley, White, Brown

Skinner Mabelson (pictured extreme right in the back row) had played for the Poppies between the wars and was a member of a remarkable footballing dynasty. His father, 'Smiler', had played in Kettering's Midland League championship winning side of 1895-96, son Don, for Birmingham and Southern League teams between 1948 and 1953, and grandson Gordon made several appearances in Ron Atkinson's side during the early seventies.

ALEC LINNELL

Alec Linnell, Kettering's captain and centre half.
Alec's football experience began with Walgrave School. After leaving school he joined Walgrave Amber and played for them for two seasons. Manager of Kettering Town, Bill Collier, signed Alec in 1929 and he scored 54 goals in his first season, 41 with his head!
After a short spell with Wellingborough during the 1937-38 season he returned to Kettering Town as a centre half. Called up in 1941 he joined the RAF and played regularly for its Service XI. In 1946 he rejoined the Poppies as centre half.

On Monday September 16th 1946 Peter Wilson returned to Rockingham Road to officially open the remodelled ground. The local press reported the occasion with articles and photographs.

"LOOKS LIKE ARSENAL"
—PETER WILSON
Poppies' £2,500 Ground Officially Opened

By PETER WILSON

ONCE the most-talked-of man in Kettering football circles because of his scathing criticism of the "Porlock Hill" slope of the old pitch, Mr. Peter Wilson, the London sports writer, finally buried the hatchet to-day when, before a big holiday crowd, he officially opened the £2,500 remodelled ground.

In a bright and breezy speech declaring the ground open. Mr. Wilson skitted at the previous occasion on which he visited Kettering and commented in his newspaper column on the steeply sloping pitch.

"I am not sorry to come back again to the town because I once thought you were going to make me Mayor of Kettering," he said over the loud-speakers. amid laughter.

"I think at that time you might have given me anything I wanted, including a black eye! Really. I cannot believe I am back in Kettering. Arsenal, yes; Wembley, yes; but truly not Kettering?" (Laughter).

He continued that the last time he came it was for a match with Crystal Palace and they had had to burn that down!

The team that was originally to have played the Poppies in the opening match was Derby County, he understood.

"I NEEDED THE POLICE"

"But," Peter went on "I fixed that—I needed the Metropolitan Police!"

When he came down for the Crystal Palace match he sat next to George Allison, at that time Arsenal manager, who sometimes got players from Kettering one of whom was Eddie Hapgood.

Mr. Allison had come to get a second Hapgood, but he could not seem to find one that day.

"I said, 'Will the Poppies ever bloom again?' " he went on, "but they certainly have."

"GRAND JOB OF WORK"

The officials had done a grand job of work and he congratulated Mr. W. B. Wright, Mr. Frank Whitwell (chairman), and wished the club the very best of luck.

"I have the greatest pleasure in declaring this ground well and truly opened." Mr. Wilson concluded.

Soccer fans have long memories . . . many years ago I wrote a piece about Kettering Town (and its ground) which gave me the same popularity locally as Herod would have at a baby show. Tomorrow, Kettering's new ground is to be opened officially, and I've been asked to kick off. Just so long as there isn't an atom bomb in the ball.

CONGRATULATIONS to Kettering Town on their new ground. A few months ago they had one which sloped some 11ft. from goalmouth to goalmouth.

In fourteen weeks 11,500 tons of soil was bulldozed, material was "scrounged" from air raid shelters and from tank traps—with German prisoners of war moving the material which not so long ago had been erected against them—and everything was prepared for the grass seed to be sown.

Then came a snag. It just wouldn't stop raining. Finally it cleared up—at midnight one moonlight night. Mr. Bennie, a local contractor in charge of operations, rang up W. B. Wright. live-wire president of the club, and told him that a dry midnight was better than a wet daytime—and that was how the seed went in.

Kettering, with a centre forward who recently scored nine goals in a match, and with an enthusiastic chairman, Frank Whitwell, to back up Bill Wright, should go places.

PETER WILSON, well-known sports writer, who will formally declare Kettering Town F.C.'s renovated ground open on Monday. A match with the Metropolitan Police will follow to officially "christen" the pitch, on which several games have previously been played. His scathing criticism of the old ground after a Cup-tie draw with Crystal Palace some years ago will be recalled.

KETTERING SUPPORTERS APPROVE ALTERATIONS - from the new banking at the Rockingham Road end.

Kettering Town Football Club.

PRESIDENT : W. B. WRIGHT, ESQ.
CHAIRMAN : F. G. WHITWELL, ESQ.
TREASURER : H. MEAD, ESQ.

SOUVENIR PROGRAMME

OF THE

**OFFICIAL
OPENING OF GROUND**

Monday, September 16th, 1946

BY

PETER WILSON, ESQ.

(Sports Editor Sunday Pictorial)

Supported by

HIS WORSHIP THE MAYOR

Councillor A. E. MUNN, ESQ.

and

F. G. WHITWELL, ESQ.

Introduced by the President, W. B. WRIGHT, ESQ.

Followed by Football Match—

KETTERING TOWN v. METROPOLITAN POLICE

PROGRAMME SIXPENCE

(Entire proceeds to Ground Improvement Fund.)

Adverts supporting the Souvenir Programme of the opening.

I was of course, blissfully unaware of those momentous happenings. Fate somehow decreed that initiation should take place over twelve months later, on 1 November 1947, when I was taken to watch Kettering play Peterborough United in the FA Cup.

During the close season, the Poppies had signed the great Maurice Dunkley from Second Division champions, Manchester City. Dunkley, a former Kettering Park Road schoolboy, was a talented sportsman who played for both Kettering and Northampton before the war, also appearing on 37 occasions in the County Cricket side between 1937 and 1939.

Maurice Dunkley was born on 14 February 1914 and played football and cricket for Park Road School, Kettering. He joined Kettering Town FC at the age of 15 years and was playing regularly for the Poppies two years later. Five years later he joined Northampton Town FC and at the same time the Ground Staff of the County Cricket Club. Maurice signed for Manchester City in 1938 and stayed there until the end of the 1946-47 season. He made 201 first team appearances alongside famous names like Doherty, Brook, Bray, Swift, Herd and Toseland. In the 1946-47 season Dunkley played 36 League and FA Cup games and thus secured a Division II Championship Medal.

In a newspaper article of the time Dunkley expressed his reasons for leaving a glamorous league club for non-league football.

"I can see no future for myself in big football and am getting out while I still have the incentive to work for my living," he told our correspondent to-day at Northampton, where he lives with his wife and three-years-old daughter, at 47, Greenfield-road.

"I want some prospects of security and the terms under which I have signed to play for Kettering are that the club finds me a job."

SPOILS A MAN

Dunkley said that he is uncertain as to the nature of the work he would take up, but that arrangements to provide him with employment were being made by Mr. W. B. Wright, the Poppies' president.

"What I am doing," he continued, "is getting out of big football before I lose the urge to work. Football spoils a man. I have known many players who have been twelve, fourteen or more years with league clubs. Eventually there comes an end of the season that is the end of their professional careers. There is just a brief note from the directors. They are not retained. They are finished with football and have been too long in it to want to do anything else.

SECURITY OFFERED

"That is what I intend to avoid. I could have continued with Manchester City. I was on the retained list. It would have meant keeping two homes going, however, and I have spent long enough living away from my family at Northampton."

Dunkley, who was released by Manchester City at his own request, said that he knew nothing of reports that a Southern club had offered £6,000 for his transfer. "I have not been consulted about any such offer," he said, "but it could have made no difference because I had made up my mind to get out.

"I still want to play football, but I want security as well. Kettering have offered me this, and in return I shall play football for them."

6

In November 1947 Dunkley lined up in Kettering's FA Cup team against Peterborough, with another footballing cricketer, Leicestershire's Maurice Tompkin.

Cartoons originally published in KTFC supporters club booklet Who's Who? Drawn by George Boston.

Never Really Blended

Poppies' Exit from F.A. Cup

ELEVEN thousand five hundred and seventy-six people had their money's worth in the very keenly contested F.A. Cup tie between Kettering Town and Peterborough United, won by the latter 4—3.

Peterborough had a little better forward line, and were more open in their play, but the Poppies, if only for their "all in" efforts towards the close, fully deserved to draw. The chance came, but they failed to take advantage of a penalty kick. This was a glorious opportunity which settled the match.

A penalty kick in the first two minutes with another couple sandwiched between, was one indication of the fierceness of the struggle, in which the two respective half back lines stood out prominently. The Poppies' forwards never really blended. If they tried to they invariably fell to a ruthless defence. Both Campbell and Tear had a stiff afternoon, the former especially against the best player on the field, Ranshaw, the Peterborough winger.

The Poppies failed chiefly because of their inability to work up scoring positions, a marked contrast to the previous week's game.

Woolhead, well marked, was left too often to plough a lone furrow.

Woolhead (2) and R. Smith scored the Poppies' goals. Ground arrangements for the huge crowd were admirably carried out, and Mr. W. B. Wright and his colleagues are to be congratulated.

Result:—

KETTERING T. 3
PETERBORO' UTD. .. 4

The match had seven goals, four penalties, and was watched by an all time record crowd of 11526.

Sadly it ended in disappointment as Rex Smith, the Poppies right half, missed the final penalty in the last minute of the game giving the Posh a 4-3 victory.

There could have been no better introduction to football. A soccer-struck child, intoxicated by the smell of embrocation, I was forever smitten.

THE MEMORY LINGERS ON !

8

EARLY DAYS
1945-50

When normal footballing services resumed after the Second World War, Northampton Town remained the County's sole Football League club, under manager Tom Smith. The side competed in the Third Division South, (North Region) and, as a programme from 29 December 1945 indicates, included

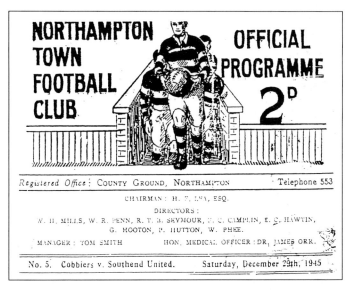

several players whose names would contest a place in the Cobblers' Hall of Fame. Chief amongst them is winger Tommy "Flash" Fowler, who would feature in 521 League games before leaving the club in 1962.

NORTHAMPTON TOWN FC. FIXTURES 1945-46

FIXTURES 1945-46

THIRD DIVISION — SOUTH
NORTH REGION

AUGUST

25. Walsall	...	A.	1	1
29. Watford	...	A.	2	4

SEPTEMBER

1. Walsall	...	H.	1	0
5. Southend United	...	A.	1	0
8. Port Vale	...	H.	1	0
15. Port Vale	...	A.	0	0
17. Watford	...	H.	3	0
22. Ipswich Town	...	A.	1	2
29. Ipswich Town	...	H.	3	3

OCTOBER

6. Notts County	...	H.	1	2
13. Notts County	...	A.	1	7
20. Queens Park R.	...	H.	0	2
27. Queens Park R.	...	A.	1	4

NOVEMBER

3. Clapton Orient	...	A.	0	1
10. Clapton Orient	...	H.	6	1

DECEMBER

1. Aldershot (*Friendly*)	...	A.	7	2
22. Norwich City	...	A.	1	2
25. Mansfield Town	...	A.	1	2
26. Mansfield Town	...	H.	4	0
29. Southend United	...	H.		

JANUARY, 1946

1 Norwich City	...	...	H.

FOOTBALL ASSOCIATION
ENGLISH CUP.

NOVEMBER

17. Chelmsford City	...	H.	5	1
24. Chelmsford City	...	A.	5	0

DECEMBER

8. Notts County	...	H.	3	1
15. Notts County	...	A.	0	1

JANUARY, 1946

5. Millwall	...	...	H.
7. Millwall	...	...	A.

CUP QUALIFYING COMPETITION.

JANUARY

12. Southend United	...	...	A.
19. Southend United	...	...	H.
26. Norwich City	...	...	A.

FEBRUARY

2. Norwich City	...	...	H.
9. Watford	...	...	A.
16. Watford	...	...	H.
23. Swindon Town	...	...	A.

MARCH

2. Swindon Town	...	...	H.
9. Notts County	...	...	A.
16. Notts County	...	...	H.
23. Mansfield Town	...	...	H.
30. Mansfield Town	...	...	A.

APRIL

6. Clapton Orient	...	...	H.
13. Clapton Orient	...	...	A.
20. Walsall	...	...	H.
22. Walsall	...		A.

9

In 1946-47, as the Football League reverted to its pre-war format, Northampton retained most of the previous season's side, adding new signings Archie Garrett and Jim Briscoe from Hearts. Garrett was a prolific striker who would score 50 goals in 94 league appearances for the Cobblers in his two brief spells with the club.

BRISCOE
NORTHAMPTON

Season 1946–7						48th Season
LEAGUE – DIVISION III (SOUTH)						
	Played	Won	Drawn	Lost	Goals	Points
1 Cardiff City	42	30	6	6	93–30	66
2 Queen's Park Rangers	42	23	11	8	74–40	57
3 Bristol City	42	20	11	11	94–56	51
4 Swindon Town	42	19	11	12	84–73	49
5 Walsall	42	17	12	13	74–59	46
6 Ipswich Town	42	16	14	12	61–53	46
7 Bournemouth and Boscombe Athletic	42	18	8	16	72–54	44
8 Southend United	42	17	10	15	71–60	44
9 Reading	42	16	11	15	83–74	43
10 Port Vale	42	17	9	16	68–63	43
11 Torquay United	42	15	12	15	52–61	42
12 Notts County	42	15	10	17	63–63	40
13 Northampton Town	42	15	10	17	72–75	40
14 Bristol Rovers	42	16	8	18	59–69	40
15 Exeter City	42	15	9	18	60–69	39
16 Watford	42	17	5	20	61–76	39
17 Brighton and Hove Albion	42	13	12	17	54–72	38
18 Crystal Palace	42	13	11	18	49–62	37
19 Leyton Orient	42	12	8	22	54–75	32
20 Aldershot	42	10	12	20	48–78	32
21 Norwich City	42	10	8	24	64–100	28
22 Mansfield Town	42	9	10	23	48–96	28

Cardiff City promoted to Division II. Mansfield Town transferred to Division III (North).

Second round FA Cup victory over Peterborough United by 8-1 in a second replay, after late equalisers had salvaged draws in the previous games, brought First Division Preston North End to Northampton. Although the Cobblers were beaten 2-1 it was a creditable performance - unlike the 8-0 Easter home defeat by Walsall. Despite this alarming setback the club achieved a satisfactory mid-table position of thirteenth.

Cobblers signings - Heaselgrave and Sankey. (The identity of the bespectacled little boy standing proudly between them will be revealed later).

Northampton Town 1946-47

Standing: Littlemore, Newman, Collings, Smalley, T Smith, Dennison, Steers, Jones, J Jennings, Scott, MacGregor, Dixon, Stanton, Pyle, Hilliard, Street. Centre: McKenna, Heaselgrave, Jenkins, Roberts, Sankey, Blunt, White, Baines, Morrall. Front: D Smith, Baucutt, Skelton, Strathie, W Jennings, Allen, Neal

Peterborough United continued in the Midland League, only seeking an alternative during the fifties when regularly applying for Football League membership.

Posh Put Paid to Poppies

THE Poppies are out of the Cup and Posh march on to the first round proper. With a second-half spurt in the divisional final at Peterborough to-day, Peterborough added three goals to the half-time score of one each.

PETERBOROUGH UTD. v. KETTERING TOWN

EARLY morning fog cleared by lunch time and the sun was shining when the teams went out for the F.A. Cup third round (divisional final) match at Peterborough between Peterborough United and Kettering Town. The pitch was very greasy on top, and still showed signs of morning dew.

Peterborough were not at full strength, Beardshaw, the centre-half, being unfit.

Barker was unfit and Kettering brought in Hawtin at inside-right. Barker failed to stand up to a test this morning.

Peterborough United: Silcocks; Bryan and Parrott; Rickards, Smith and Mitchell; Scobie, Brooksbank, Warnes, Padgett and Rudkin.

Kettering Town: Barton; Campbell and Smith; Drage, Sheen and Roberts; Henley, Hawtin, Woolhead, White and Burgess.

Referee: Mr. F. R. Archer (Northampton).

Loudspeakers were used to marshal the crowds, which were estimated at 8,000 at the start.

Scorers:

Peterborough:

    Brooksbank

    Mitchell

    Rudkin

    Scobie

Kettering:

    Hawtin

PETERBOROUGH	 4
KETTERING	 1

Despite modest performances in the league during the immediate post war years, Posh gave occasional notice of the cup fighting tradition for which the club would become renowned. In 1946/47 the side overcame Wellingborough and Kettering on the way to honourable second round, second replay defeat by Northampton.

11

Two years later the Doughboys and Poppies were again accounted for, en route to a first round meeting with Torquay United, which Peterborough lost by the only goal.

Peterborough United 1948-49

Back Row: Bryan, Rickards, Ferguson, 'Mr Posh', Blood (P/Man), Tapping, Smith (Trainer). Front: Parrott, Guest, Vaughan, Cockroft, Harkin, Fallon.

Kettering Town's first post-war campaign was in the Leicestershire Senior League, but admission to the Birmingham League was obtained for season 1946-47.

During that season the Poppies also retained a Senior League side and a reserve team in the United Counties League alongside locals Corby Stewarts and Lloyds, Rushden, Wellingborough, Peterborough Reserves and Desborough.

Kettering's final game seemed to have clinched the UCL title, centre forward Woolhead scoring 11 times in an incredible 18-0 victory over Holbeach. Rivals Wisbech Town, however, won their remaining match 5-0 to secure the championship on goal average.

United Counties League

Poppies Pile Up Their Greatest Score

KETTERING set their stall out to-day to compile a huge crop of goals against Holbeach to give them a chance of beating Wisbech for the United Counties League championship, which now depends on next Saturday's match between Wisbech and Eynesbury.

At the interval the Poppies had netted eight times, six of the goals coming from centre-forward Woolhead.

WOOLHEAD'S 11

THE Poppies' record win of 18 goals against Holbeach has altered the whole complexion of the United Counties League championship and has definitely placed the Poppies within the possibilities of the championship. Hitherto Wisbech have possessed by far the best goal average.

Kettering now go top of the league, the positions reading:—

	P.	W.	D.	L.	F.	A.	Pts
Goals							
Kettering T.	24	18	0	6	90	39	33
Wisbech	23	16	2	5	88	39	34

Wisbech now have to play Eynesbury Rovers at Wisbech on Saturday and to win the league they have to win the match by three clear goals. If Eynesbury score their task will be much harder and may mean a job for the mathematical decimal experts.

Every one of Woolhead's goals were unstoppable and his eleven is believed to be a club record. Holbeach were hopeless long before the finish. The United Counties League position is now interesting.

Incidentally, Chambers wired inability to come to keep goal. Alec Linnell obliged.

GOALS TIME-TABLE

This is how the goals came:—
(1) Woolhead, 2nd minute; (2) Sail, 4th; (3) Woolhead, 10th; (4) Woolhead, 25th; (5) Woolhead 29th; (6) Woolhead, 36th; (7) Sail, 40th; (8) Woolhead, 44th; (9) Woolhead, 49th; (10) Woolhead, 51st; (11) Henley, 60th; (12) Nearney, 66th; (13) Nearney, 72nd; (14) Woolhead, 79th; (15) Woolhead, 80th; (16) Roberts, 85th; (17) Woolhead, 87th; (18) Henley, 88th.

HOLBEACH LATE ARRIVING

Touch-line Critics Put on the Spot

MR. W. B. Wright, president of Kettering Town Football Club staged an effective reply to the critics of the club this afternoon. Holbeach were late in arriving and to fill in the time he invited the touch-line critics to come on the field and show the club officials how football should be played. The response was unexpected — quickly 24 volunteers stepped on the field, formed sides and provided plenty of amusement for the spectators, many of whom sat watching the game minus coats.

Humorous comments by Mr. Wright at the microphone added greatly to the fun.

W.B WRIGHT

Poppies Pipped on the Post

KETTERING Town were pipped on the post for the championship of the United Counties League which was decided on Saturday in favour of Wisbech, who defeated the wooden spoonists, Eynesbury Rovers, 5—0.

It was all a matter of goal average between Wisbech and Kettering, both of which clubs are known as the Poppies.

Kettering made a superhuman effort the previous Saturday to put their goal average in an unassailable position by defeating Holbeach 18—0. This wonderful win gave Kettering 90 goals for and 39 against.

Wisbech had 39 scored against them but prior to Saturday last had scored only 88 and they had to defeat Eynesbury by a minimum of 3—0 to lift the championship.

Their 5—0 victory gave it to them by three goals.

United Counties League

	P	W	D	L	F	A	Pts
Wisbech	24	17	2	5	93	39	36
Kettering Res	24	18	0	6	90	39	36
Rushden Town	24	14	3	7	63	41	31
Desboro' Town	24	12	3	9	73	61	27
Boston Reserves	24	11	4	9	74	58	26
Peterboro' Res	24	11	2	11	62	63	24
Wellingborough	24	9	5	10	75	70	23
Holbeach	24	8	8	10	59	109	22
Spalding	24	10	1	13	72	67	21
Kings Lynn	24	9	2	13	63	68	20
Stamford	24	8	2	14	60	85	18
S & L Corby	24	8	2	14	50	80	18
Eynesbury	24	4	2	18	53	108	10

RUSSIANS FIGHT A GALLANT ACTION

KETTERING v. RUSHDEN

ANIMATED scenes were witnessed on the Rockingham-road ground this afternoon when Kettering Town met Rushden in the first qualifying round of the English Cup.

The crowd was easily the largest of the season, the Rushden contingent being a large one. Rattles and bells were in strong demand and a number of people were wearing coloured favours.

TEAM CHANGES

Kettering made one change in their announced team to replace Sheen, who had been signed on during the week, his nececessary papers not having come through in time. In his place Drage deputised.

Rushden were unfortunate in not having the services of their outside-left, Bull, who had met with an accident yesterday at work. More played in his place. The teams were:

Kettering: Barton; Campbell and Smith; Tear, Drage and Roberts; Henley, Burt, Woolhead, White and Griffiths.

Rushden: Andrews; Mantle and Toms; Bland, Maycock and Peacock; Childs, Thorrington, Pipes, Nearney and More.

Mr. A. W. Jeffs (Peterborough) refereed.

KETTERING T. 2
RUSHDEN T. 0

The attendance was 7,434, and the gate £373.

500 Rattles Will Spur on the Poppies

NEXT Saturday Kettering F.C. supporters will be able to encourage their team in a worthy manner.

Before the English Cup game with Rushden at the Rockingham-road ground, members of the Supporters' Club will have 500 rattles and 20 0bells on sale at the entrance to the ground.

They are all ex-A.R.P. stock, and at all forthcoming games will help the spectators to wage "nerve war" on the Poppies opponents.

It is so certain that the din on Saturday will be indescribable that far-sighted supporters are thinking of buying another article of A.R.P. equipment —ear plugs!

Earlier in the season Rushden and Stewarts and Lloyds were both involved in exciting FA Cup matches against Kettering.

Cyril Freeman Secretary of Rushden Town from 1919 until his death in 1949.

The Russians eventual third place was somewhat disappointing after a pre-war dominance in which the club had won the UCL title on four successive occasions from 1934-38.

However, the side was well placed throughout the remainder of the forties, finishing runners up in 1949-50.

Rushden Town 1947

L-R Back Row: Inwood, Bland, Mantle, Clark, Andrews, Toms, Peacock, Robson
L-R Front Row: Childs, Thorington, Pipes, Thompson, Maddams

Stewarts and Lloyds attracted a record crowd to Occupation Road for their cup tie with the Poppies.

500 "Fans" on Train for Corby

KETTERING Station booking hall was jammed with crowds queueing for tickets as Poppies' supporters mingled with workers. Service men and week-end travellers just before the departure of the Corby Cup-tie special train at 1.30 to-day.

Before the Corby train drew into the platform 500 football fans were packed five deep in places in a crowd that extended for almost 100 yards along the platform.

The train of eight coaches quickly absorbed its passengers, except for knots of people who stood around some of the carriage doors that were locked. Before the station staff could open these doors, many of the younger fans, impatient to secure a seat, scrambled through the windows with an agility demonstrated by entrances made by both feet and head first.

There were few noise making instruments in evidence, and only one man used a rattle to give vent to his feelings, which like all his companions, were of confidence in the Poppies.

STEWARTS AND LLOYDS v. KETTERING TOWN

THE largest crowd ever seen on the Occupation-road ground, Corby, packed in for the eagerly anticipated F.A. Cup second qualifying round to-day.

The Stewarts and Lloyds side had four changes, which necessitated a reshuffle. Tommy Alexander, star outside-left, had travelled from his R.A.F. station in North Wales and his presence in the team, revealed over the loudspeaker system, was greeted with cheers.

Kettering team had a different left wing.

First arrivals at the ground was a Kettering couple, who were patiently waiting for the gates to open at 11.30. Some Corby supporters sported tiny "Steelman" mascots in their caps and lapels and many others had black and white favours. Extra police and ambulance men had been drafted in.

The pitch was in splendid condition and weather conditions were ideal, with a slight breeze blowing from the Occupation-road end.

Stewarts and Lloyds: Bellew; Haddon and Kerr; Burton, Bell and Probert; Kinnier, Paterson, Wright, Every and Alexander.

Kettering Town: Barton; Campbell and Smith; Drage, Sheen and Roberts; Henley, Burt, Woolhead, Hawtin and Burgess.

Referee: Mr. N. W. Hillier (Northampton). Linesmen: W. Loveday (Islip) and E. Small (Wellingborough).

STEWARTS AND
LLOYDS (CORBY .. 1
KETTERING TOWN .. 1
The gate was 5,714, and receipts £290 14s

The replay was lost 4-2.

Cup defeat at Desborough in 1947-48 would be the works side's last match in the competition for 45 years. Stewarts and Lloyds achieved a creditable fifth place in the UCL, but on 4 May 1948 played their final home fixture on the Occupation Road ground. As the programme notes explain, a new team was created - Corby Town Football Club.

STEWARTS & LLOYDS (Corby) FOOTBALL CLUB   279

(Social Section)

The

STEELMAN'S

Souvenir Programme

PRICE THREEPENCE

Block by courtesy of the "Evening Telegraph"

Club Chairman : W. MONTGOMERY, Esq.   Hon. Secy.: W. WISEMAN,
                                                              37, Occupation Rd.

Social Sect. Chairman : A. WATSON, Esq.   Hon. Secy.: J. DUNN, 98, Westfields Rd.

Tuesday, 4th May, 1948
DESBOROUGH NURSING CUP FINAL—REPLAY
VERSUS
DESBOROUGH TOWN
Kick off 6.45 p.m.

OUR ESTEEMED CHAIRMAN TALKS IT OVER WITH YOU.

The ringing down of the curtain on season 1947-48 has more significance in Corby than the normal end of a football season; it is in fact the final scene in a chapter of Corby football history.

Stewarts & Lloyds (Corby) F.C. was inaugurated during season 1935-36 and since that date has functioned as a section of the Company's Welfare and Recreation Club.

Like all Football Clubs it's fortunes have been of a fluctuating nature. Success, however, has not been entirely elusive or efforts unavailing, and it can be recorded that the County Senior Cup has twice in the Club's comparatively short life-time found a resting place at Corby. The County Junior Cup and numerous other trophies have also found temporary residence in " Steeltown," and, more important, despite what may be thought or said to the contrary, a high reputation has been attained for sportsmanship, courtesy and hospitality.

Space does not permit a detailed account of past struggles, achievements and failures to be recorded here, but opportunity must be taken to extend thanks to Messrs. Stewarts & Lloyds, Ltd., for the support given the club during it's connection with the Company, and for the ground provided by them which ranks second to none in the whole County.

The Company representatives have expressed the opinion that, with the growth of Corby in population and in status, and recognising that a football team is part and parcel of the life stream of a progressive town, the time is opportune for the club to cease as a unit of the Company's Recreational facilities and to become more representative of the Town. Steps are presently being taken to put this change-over into effect and details should be announced in the near future.

The large number of football enthusiasts in the Town will warmly appreciate the gesture of Messrs. Stewarts & Lloyds in offering to lease their splendid ground to the proposed Town F.C. over a period of years of sufficient duration to allow alternative accommodation to be secured, and for the assurance of the firm's representatives that the Company will continue to interest themselves in the club and give what assistance they can to assure success of the new venture.

A word of thanks to the Officials who over the years have given freely of their time to provide football entertainment; to the members and supporters who have encouraged the club in defeat as in victory.

THE PAST .. .. A MEMORY !
THE FUTURE .. .. GREAT EXPECTATIONS ! !

Stewarts and Lloyds side from May 1948 went on to play for the new senior club in its debut season. Back from left: Wilf Wiseman, Arthur Keep, Carvel White, Jimmy Baird, Ted Piskozub, Eddie Roe, Bill Littlejohn, trainer Charlie McCartney, Willie Montgomery. Front: Jackie Berry, Alex Mayes, Duncan McPherson, Gordon Collins, Jack Freebairn.

Charlie McCartney

Secretary Wiseman and Chairman Montgomery on the former's retirement from the position in 1959.

1947-48	P.	W.	D.	L.	F.	A.	Pts.
Wisbech Town	34	30	2	2	143	42	62
Brush Sports	34	22	6	6	133	60	50
Spalding United	34	22	5	7	92	50	49
Stamford Town	34	18	6	10	88	72	42
S & L Corby	34	16	6	12	77	72	38
Leicester City 'A'	34	17	3	14	87	77	37
Bourne Town	34	15	7	12	72	82	37
Kettering Res.	34	14	8	12	102	73	36
Desborough Town	34	14	7	13	60	62	35
Boston United Res.	34	12	5	17	92	99	29
Kings Lynn	34	10	8	16	63	78	28
Holbeach United	34	13	2	19	74	102	28
Wellingborough Town	34	9	9	16	53	88	27
Peterborough Utd Res.	34	10	6	18	62	98	26
Rushden Town	34	8	9	17	62	79	25
Abbey United	34	10	4	20	59	83	24
Symingtons	34	8	6	20	50	121	22
Eynesbury Rovers	34	7	3	24	50	121	17

It would be almost 10 years until the works side regained UCL status, and even longer before the town team secured "alternative accommodation" at the Rockingham Triangle.

The newly formed club gave immediate notice of its ambition by appointing Reg Smith, the former Millwall and England player, as full-time manager. Smith's stay was brief however, and he left the club in late August to return to his family in Dundee.

17

At the end of 1948-49, Corby Town's eleventh place was six positions lower than Stewarts and Lloyds the previous season.

CORBY TOWN 1948-49

Back Row: Davies (Trainer), Baird, Poole, Elder, Littlejohn, Roe, White, Garvey. Front Row: Copestake, Akers, Vint, Smith, McGuire.

In the event, Desborough Town, who had last won the UCL title in 1928, became champions, winning the league by a single point from Wisbech Town.

Commonly known as "Ar Tarn", due to the tendency for locals to take liberties with the King's English, Desborough's bucket carrying character from the Waterworks field revels in his side's success. (The droll, rather world weary wit of

1948-49	P.	W.	D.	L.	F.	A.	Pts
Desborough Town	38	25	5	8	118	55	55
Wisbech Town	38	25	4	9	148	70	54
Stamford Town	38	24	5	9	130	83	53
Rushden Town	38	22	7	9	114	62	51
Spalding United	38	21	4	13	112	89	46
Kettering Res.	38	20	5	13	84	60	45
Wellingborough Town	38	20	4	14	88	74	44
Rugby Town	38	20	2	16	91	76	42
Brush Sports Res.	38	15	10	13	95	88	40
Symingtons	38	15	6	17	99	93	36
Corby Town	38	16	4	18	89	101	36
Abbey United	38	14	7	17	101	100	35
Grantham Res.	38	15	5	18	86	110	35
Holbeach United	38	14	6	18	82	101	34
Peterborough Utd Res.	38	12	8	18	75	97	32
Eynesbury Rovers	38	14	4	20	98	119	32
March Town United	38	9	9	20	75	96	27
Boston United Res	38	11	4	23	80	141	26
Bourne Town	38	8	3	27	57	138	19
Northampton Town 'A'	38	8	2	28	61	139	18

ordinary Northamptonshire folk was beautifully captured in the regular Evening Telegraph cartoon feature, "Air Ada", created by Reg Norman).

AIR ADA - created by Reg Norman

" 'D'yeayer, Missiz,' I sez. 'I'yaw got any remarks t'mek bout me bein fat, sayum afawwa me fairce, not beine me back, cuz Ike near ya,' I sez."

18

Desborough Town

Back Row: Page, Crozier, Brown, Haynes, Pratt, Broome, Tear, Hewitt (Trainer)
Front Row: Sparkes, Clark, Mayes, Squires, Page, Wyldes, Jobson.

AR TARN'S BLAZE OF GLORY FINISH

DESBOROUGH finished their United Counties League games in a blaze of glory last night, when giving their best performance of the season by beating Stamford 6-0. This victory assures them of being at least runners-up.

After seven minutes Desborough were awarded a penalty for hands, TEAR converting the spot kick to give the home team the lead.

For a time Desborough penned Stamford in their half, the visitors being content to pack their goal to prevent the fast-moving Desborough forwards from scoring.

Stamford's goal bore a charmed life, but WYLDES found a gap to increase Desborough's lead just before the interval. Half-time: Desborough 2, Stamford 0.

Ar Tarn resumed in startling fashion, SQUIRES scoring the best goal of the match after the ball had only been touched three times from the kick-off.

Stamford re-arranged their half-back line in a nattempt to stop Desborough's onslaught. The home team, at top of their form, had the visitors' defence all at sea, and it was no surprise when they scored the fourth goal through WYLDES, the winger running in to head a perfect centre from Crozier past the goalkeeper.

To make certain of victory, SQUIRES scored a fifth goal, and to crown a good performance SQUIRES completed his "hat trick" when scoring the sixth goal.

Wellingborough Town's achievements in those early post-war years were modest, the highest UCL position attained being sixth in 1949-50.

The Doughboys were however, finalists with Kettering in the Northants Senior Cup in 1947, losing a hard fought replay 4-1..

Ex-soldier and 23 years old, this is George Sail, of 39, Crabb-street, Rushden. who has signed professional forms for Kettering Tn. F.C. He managed to get a free transfer from Notts County F.C. for whom he played as inside right. George played a good deal of football while he was in the Services, and last season Rushden Town F.C. had the benefit of his playing.

The following season Wellingborough lifted the trophy, beating Rushden Town in the final, and repeated their success in 1950 with a revenge victory over the Poppies.

TWELVE QUEUES, FIVE HOURS BEFORE KICK OFF
1947-51

In those early post war years, football facts could be gleaned from the pages of the Saturday Pink 'Un.

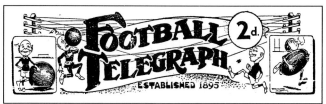

National results were reported, but pride of place was given to the performance of local teams and I quickly learned to follow their fortunes by interpreting the splendid cartoons liberally scattered throughout the pages.

Third Division South 'walkers' who marched across the centre pages of the 'Pink Un'.

Rushden v Kettering FA Cup

Many were the creation of artists Gus Fidler and Frank Bellamy. The latter was born in Kettering, educated at Stamford Road School and 'apprenticed' at the William Blamire advertising studio in the High Street, next to the Home and Colonial Stores.

Bellamy's drawings for the 'Sports Telegraph' provide many examples of a remarkable talent which, in 1950, found employment in Fleet Street. Work on the 'Boys Own Paper' and 'Micky Mouse Weekly' led to a contract with Hulton Publications, 'Swift' comic.

An early Frank Bellamy cartoon, circa 1946,

Inevitably, Frank was enticed to its more illustrious stablemate 'The Eagle', illustrating the legendary 'Dan Dare' page in 1957.

During the sixties he drew cult comic figures Thunderbirds, Doctor Who and Startrek, before achieving an ambition - the 'Daily Mirror's' Garth strip cartoon.

Frank Bellamy's work earned international recognition when, in 1972, he was presented with the Foreign Comics award by the American Academy of Comic Book Arts. Following his death four years later, aged 59, his drawings became highly collectable - the creation of a truly gifted artist.

Coincidentally, the Daily Mirror assignment had combined the talents of two Northamptonshire men. Writer Jim Edgar also hailed from Kettering and, during the forties, had lived just two doors away from our house in Holly Road. Late into the night he could be heard tapping away on a typewriter, after completing his day job as a clerk in the Fire Brigade Offices. Recognition eventually came when BBC Radio accepted a manuscript for its 'Morning Story'. All the neighbours celebrated his success, and I was allowed a morning off school to listen.

Occasionally a particular local football fixture caught the attention of the National press and I would be astonished to recognise familiar names in our morning copy of the 'Daily Herald'.

In November 1947 a headline proclaimed,
"Tommy Lawton to face Cobblers".

Then the most valuable player in British football, Lawton had joined Third Division Notts County from Chelsea for £20,000.

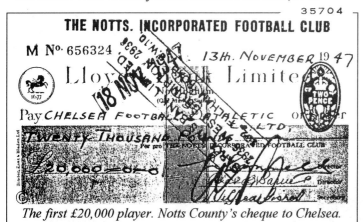

The first £20,000 player. Notts County's cheque to Chelsea.

He made his debut for his new club against Northampton on November 15th, the Saturday following his transfer. The level of interest in the match is clearly demonstrated in a contemporary newspaper report which informs us that;

"*.....crowds began forming four hours before kick off. Marshalled by police using 'portable radio equipment', they awaited in an orderly fashion attended by toffee apple vendors who did a roaring trade .... the home dressing room retained an air of calm and one Cobbler player whiled away time on a penny whistle ..... Back in Kenton, Middlesex, Mrs Lawton remained unaffected by the excitement surrounding her husband, saying*
"*I'm not at all worried about Tom. I shall just do my shopping as usual on Saturday afternoon ......*"

Tommy Lawton makes the acquaintance of Cobbler's centre half and captain Bob Dennison before his debut for Notts County, November 1947.

A MR. LAWTON BROUGHT HIS FOOTBALL BOOTS TO TOWN ON SATURDAY, AND THERE WAS ONLY ONE TOPIC OF CONVERSATION IN —

ONE AND A HALF TO TOMMY LAWTON PLEASE

—SCARCELY ENOUGH IN YOUR ACCOUNT TO BUY TOMMY LAWTON SIR.

IS THIS LAWTON THEY TALK ABOUT ON POINTS?

I RECKON IT'S ALL A LAWT O' NONSENSE

WHO IS THIS FELLER LAWTON?

'BUSES — BANKS — QUEUES — PUBS — AND CLUBS.

EVERY CORNER OF THE COUNTY GROUND WAS PACKED WITH —

PEOPLE

POLICE —

— PRESSMEN — AND PHOTOGRAPHERS. ALL WAITING TO SEE ONE MAN, AND HERE HE IS

TOMMY LAWTON, THE BIGGEST 'DRAW' IN SPORT SINCE TOM WEBSTER.

TO OUR SURPRISE. HE WORE NEITHER —

GOLDEN BOOTS. NOR

POUND NOTES IN HIS HAIR. BUT LOOKED

JUST LIKE AN ORDINARY FOOTBALLER

THERE WAS NOTHING ORDINARY, THOUGH, ABOUT THAT GOAL, WHICH LEFT JONES LOOKING LIKE

THAT'S LAWTON - THAT WAS!

THE OLD ADVERTISEMENT.

WE MUST NOT FORGET A GALLANT GAME BY DENNISON. WHO KEPT LAWTON —

WELL BOTTLED UP IN THE SECOND HALF.

ADAMS.

Northampton had its biggest football day on Saturday since 1936.

The visit of Tommy Lawton, making his first appearance for Notts County after the unparalleled publicity given to his transfer, attracted 18,300 supporters to the County Ground.

They saw the home team defeated by 2 goals to 1—Lawton headed an opportunist goal in the first five minutes—but the game was otherwise keenly contested, with Dennison keeping a firm hold on the visiting "star" performer.

The Cobblers' directors must have considered it very satisfactory to get

a gate of £1,525 for a match which, a week earlier, would have raised no more than £750.

Yet this gate included some thousands from Nottingham and great numbers from distant places like Dunstable, etc.

The game was a fair test of the Cobblers' potential support if Second Division status could be obtained.

The indications now are that 16,000 would be a top gate—possibly more against Leicester—but that would not be enough.

Notts County have spent over £17,000 on Lawton because they can reasonably expect regular gates of 35,000, with 45,000 for big attractions.

That raises a big problem for the Cobblers.

How can they hope for Second Division status when facing such a disadvantage?

Season 1947-8						49th Season
LEAGUE - DIVISION III (SOUTH)						
		Played	Won	Drawn	Lost	Goals Points
1	Queen's Park Rangers	42	26	9	7	74–37 61
2	Bournemouth and Boscombe Athletic	42	24	9	9	76–35 57
3	Walsall	42	21	9	12	70–40 51
4	Ipswich Town	42	23	3	16	67–61 49
5	Swansea Town	42	18	12	12	70–52 48
6	Notts County	42	19	8	15	68–59 46
7	Bristol City	42	18	7	17	77–65 43
8	Port Vale	42	16	11	15	63–54 43
9	Southend United	42	15	13	14	51–58 43
10	Reading	42	15	11	16	56–58 41
11	Exeter City	42	15	11	16	55–63 41
12	Newport County	42	14	13	15	61–73 41
13	Crystal Palace	42	13	13	16	49–49 39
14	Northampton Town	42	14	11	17	58–72 39
15	Watford	42	14	10	18	57–79 38
16	Swindon Town	42	10	16	16	41–46 36
17	Leyton Orient	42	13	10	19	51–73 36
18	Torquay United	42	11	13	18	63–62 35
19	Aldershot	42	10	15	17	45–67 35
20	Bristol Rovers	42	13	8	21	71–75 34
21	Norwich City	42	13	8	21	61–76 34
22	Brighton and Hove Albion	42	11	12	19	43–73 34
Queen's Park Rangers promoted to Division II.						

Such confidence was rewarded when, true to the script, Lawton headed an opening goal after only 5 minutes and, despite being tightly marked by the Cobblers centre half Bob Dennison, helped his side to their first away win of the season.

Poppies Win 2-1

Attendance at local matches during the late forties reflected the enormous popularity of the game at all levels, and ground records were established which have never been seriously challenged since. During 1948-49 a total of 41,271,414 watched the Football League Programme. In that same season Kettering's first team gate averaged 3,073, while the reserves attracted 1,699. It was rare for fans to travel to away games unless for a cup tie, when, as Frank Bellamy's splendid cartoon indicates, all means were employed to get to the match.

Some may even have regarded travelling as a breach of loyalty to the club's reserves. It is more likely, however, that most supporters simply lacked the wherewithal to follow their team away from home.

The days of 'universal' car ownership were some way off. The world was still a very big place and, unlike some of today's children who have jetted halfway around the globe several times before their tenth birthday, we had to make do with railway excursion trips to Skegness or annual summer evening 'mystery' bus tours on superannuated coaches. Only one family in our street owned a vehicle and that was a motorbike and sidecar. A short journey to Burton Latimer meant dressing up like Biggles with leather jacket, leggings, flying helmet, goggles and huge gauntlets.

Milk, bread, ('none of that new-fangled Adams cut stuff' in waxed paper wrapper), and coal were still delivered by horse drawn carts.

There was no weekly visit to out-of-town supermarkets to fill the car boot, and groceries were fetched as required from one of the dozens of corner shops. These were veritable treasure houses, the air pungent with paraffin, crammed with bundles of firewood, sacks of rice, bottles of Beetop sauce, cartons of Oxydol, but as the obligatory notice informed, 'no perishables on Sunday', (unless secreted in a brown paper bag). We usually used the Co-op, check number 20739, because as the legend printed on the cover of our order book reminded, 'A Roving Shopper gathers no Divi'.'

As anyone familiar with Northamptonshire's boot and shoe towns at that period will confirm, the established means of transport was the bike. Streets around the factories overflowed with hordes of cycling clickers, skivers, finishers and bottomstockers, sprig bags dangling from handlebars as they travelled to and from work.

Factory closing times were staggered to allow workers to disperse safely, and the air would reverberate to a chorus of hooters and sirens.

Today, following the decline of the industry, few of the hugely impressive Victorian edifices still preside over the production of boots and shoes. Surviving premises house anything from

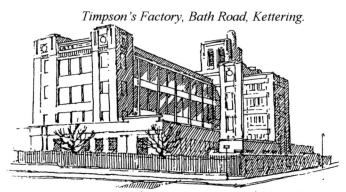

Timpson's Factory, Bath Road, Kettering.

printing presses to carpets, antique furniture to soft toys. Yet this is infinitely preferable to demolition, which inevitably brings in its wake another car park or patch of brickstrewn, nettle covered wasteground ideal for flytipping. Worse still are the vandalised shells targeted by youngsters bent on destruction, too young to recognise the ghostly strains of 'Workers Playtime' drifting through the shattered window panes.

Timpson's shoe factory, Bath Road, Kettering, was built in 1921 and, in its heyday during the late fifties, produced some 22,000 pairs a week. I always thought that on winter evenings, lights a-blazing, it resembled a huge luxury liner anchored out at sea. Now, empty and sadly derelict, it awaits the demolition men.

The traffic free streets made ideal all weather football pitches. At the bottom of our road, however, was a further blessing. A huge field, known locally as the Orchard, was the meeting place on Sunday mornings for

hordes of youths, who congregated for impromptu games with piles of coats for goal posts, on pitches that went on forever.

Raucous voices drifted across backgardens, shattering the tranquillity of the Sabbath, still widely observed in those times as a day of rest.

'Bloodys' and 'buggers' abounded, but none of the four lettered obscenities that pollute everyday public speech in our more enlightened age.

Just a little boy, I hovered on the fringes, desperate for a kick but somewhat in awe and trepidation, for these were men's games, fierce encounters between raw-boned players, many fresh from National Service, who tucked khaki trousers in socks and played in Army boots.

Every playtime at Avondale Infant School, my best friend John Lawman and I toed a soft leather ball across the small parcel of grass on the fringe of the playground acting out our footballing fantasies. Not for us the names from radio's 'Sports Report' or the back pages of the Sunday newspaper.

Kettering Chairman W B Wright, sadly pictured without his straw hat, introduces new signing Bert Henley to Rockingham Road in 1946.

Mannion, Doherty, Carter, or even Lawton. We preferred heroes closer to home. Like Poppies forwards Bert Henley and Arnold Woolhead.

It seems incredible today that, at the age of seven, I was allowed to go to football matches alone - my dad usually worked on Saturday afternoons - yet I'm quite certain that I did. It was a short journey to the ground and I suppose quite safe. I crossed the field at the bottom of our street, vaulted a five barred gate behind the North Park tennis courts and into Bath Road, on through one of the poets' streets, Wordsworth or Shelley - and was in Britannia Road in minutes. I doubt that I ever saw a car. The opposition sides had strange names - Cradley Heath, Oswestry - and Kettering usually won, our heroes invariably scoring.

Birmingham League

KetteringWin

28

Kettering Town 1949

Back Row: Summerly, Tart, Brown, Kettley, Woodward, Smith R, Campbell, Shelton, Mansfield. Front Row: Henley, Woolhead, Dean W, Tompkin, Connelly

In October 1949 Corby Town achieved a notable success defeating Peterborough 1-0 in the FA Cup at Occupation Road.

Corby Town FC prior to the first match of the 1949-50 season.
Left to Right (Standing): Keep, Baird, Poole, Elder, White, Middlemiss, Littlejohn, J Davies (Trainer). Seated: Burdett, Akers, Strathie, Copley, Allen.

Giant Killing Act Not a Fluke

CORBY DESERVED THEIR VICTORY

IT was five minutes from the end of Corby Town's gruelling cup-tie with Peterborough United and the score was 0—0. Then came the Ken Allen goal that sent Corby supporters wild with delight, plunged Peterborough into gloom, and the game was over. Corby had gained one of the best victories in their history.

Both sides were nervous at the start, and the players got rid of the ball as if it was red hot. But they settled down to fast, cup-tie football after the first quarter of an hour, and it was a ding-dong, dour struggle all the way, with the Steelmen holding a slight but increasing advantage.

There were narrow escapes for both sides during the game, and Copley had the ball in the net for the Steelmen during the first half, but was ruled offside.

Peterborough's nearest miss was when Martin, their star forward, hit the post with a fierce drive.

Outside partisan circles, it was thought before the game that if Corby could score early they would stand a chance, but that the longer the game went on without a goal the more Peterborough's seniority would tell.

It did not work out like that, and in the second half the Steelmen played the better football. There was no fluke about their win.

Peterborough were menacing with long, raking through passes from the halves to the forwards; which turned defence into dangerous attack in a few seconds. However, these thrusts were held by an unflurried Corby defence, and when they did break through Newball was there, in top form in goal.

The Corby forward line was in top form, and with speedy thrusts worried the Peterborough defence throughout the game.

If Corby continue to play as they did on Saturday, they might become this season's "giant killers" in the competition.

FA Cup

Corby v Peterborough October 29th 1949

Corby

Newball

Poole Matts

Keep Strathie Baird

Berry Akers Middlemiss Copley Allen.

Moulson

Vaux Wyle

Woods Wands Cockcroft

Houghton Widdowfield Robinson Martin Fallon

Peterborough.

In '40 Years on', the splendid history of Corby Town FC published in 1988, the game is remembered in the words of long-serving secretary Wilf Wiseman.

The draw for the Divisional Final gave Corby a home tie with Midland League neighbours Peterborough United and the Steelmen fought off a bid by Posh to have the game switched to their London Road ground to host the game on Saturday, October 29. A record crowd crammed into Occupation Road and the atmosphere of the occasion was recaptured in Wilf Wiseman's programme notes when Peterborough revisited Corby for a Senior Cup semi-final in 1964:

'No-one who was present that day will ever forget the spontaneous demonstration of a record crowd of 7,302 when the final whistle sounded with Corby triumphant', he wrote. *'Everyone present then will cherish their own particular memory of this great game in which 'Proud Posh' was humbled — the single goal in the 79th minute that gave Corby victory, the tremendous post hitting shot by Martin, the daring of Newball (a 22-year-old who grabbed his chance when Elder was struck down by a bout of flu in late August) in the Steelmen's goal or the speed of matchwinner Allen — but to me the outstanding incident was the split-second thinking of Ernie Middlemiss when he received the ball eleven minutes from time with Wands and Vaux in very close attendance. It looked as if Middlemiss would try to beat both defenders barring his path to goal but at the last moment he back-heeled the ball to where he knew Allen should be. Allen was there, and with a clear path to goal! Moulson touched but failed to stop the winger's shot and Corby were in the 4th Qualifying Round for the first time in their history!'.*

Corby's number nine that afternoon had recently joined the club from Lincoln City. If ever a centre forward was misnamed it was Ernie Middlemiss. He became a goal scorer of legendary status, scoring a remarkable 135 goals in 136 games during 3 seasons with the Steelmen.

Now in his seventies, Ernie recalls his days at Corby with great affection, grateful to move his family to a new house in Stephenson Way, complete with bathroom and a view over open countryside, a job in the tubeworks and a footballing wage of £5 a week.

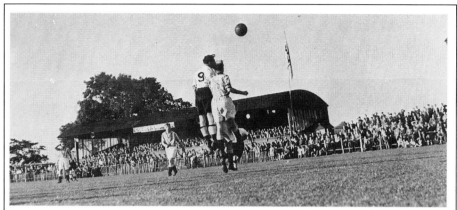

Ernie Middlemiss, scorer of a phenomenal 135 goals in 136 matches for Corby Town, in typical action at Occupation Road.

By a remarkable coincidence, Peterborough's centre-half that October afternoon was unexpectedly renewing an acquaintance with Middlemiss that had begun on Tyneside before the war. The Wands family had moved to Wallsend when young Alec's father, a coalcutter, was transferred from his workplace in Fife. Now, amazingly, the two boys, who had met playing football together for a Newcastle Schools side, found themselves in opposition at Occupation Road.

The situation was remedied the following season when Wands joined his old friend and signed for Corby Town.

Later that season, Northampton reached the fifth round of the FA Cup with a 2-1 victory over Bournemouth at the County Ground, before a crowd of 22,644. Derby County, with star players Bert Mozley, Leon Leuty, Johnny Morris, Jackie Stamps and Billy Steel, awaited. Thousands travelled to the Baseball Ground for the game, many by road, as indicated in the 'Chronicle and Echo' reporter's traffic survey.

31

As early as five hours before kick off there were already 12 queues outside the ground.

12 queues 5 hours before Cobblers' Cup-tie kick-off

THE cry "Up the Cobblers" was heard early in the morning at Derby, where Derby County were to meet Northampton in the fifth round Cup-tie at the Baseball Ground this afternoon.

Many hundreds of Northampton fans were unable to buy tickets for the Cup-tie in advance, and deciding to take no chances, arrived in Derby early by train or by bus.

One bus left Northampton at 7 a.m. and as soon as it arrived at Derby the passengers went on to the centre of the town for their breakfast.

MISSED NO MATCH

Among those who were on the bus were Mr. and Mrs. Leslie Munns, of 114, Boughton Green-road, Northampton, and Mr. and Mrs. Donald Forskitt, 10, Knightley-road, Northampton. They wore red and white hats, carried bell and rattles, and the two women wore scarves with the names of the Northampton players embroidered upon them.

"We have no tickets," Mr. Munn told a reporter, "so we decided to arrive early and take no chances."

"We have not missed a single match this season," said Mr. Forskitt, who was confident that Northampton would win. "This is quite a holiday for us, for when we went to Bournemouth we left at 5 a.m."

STREAM OF VEHICLES

A "Chronicle and Echo" reporter standing at the Welford-road—Harborough-road junction recorded the number of vehicles en route to Derby, via the Harborough road.

From 9.45 a.m. onwards his chart read: 9.45-10.0, 32 cars, five coaches and three motor-cycles; 10.0-10.15, 29 cars, seven coaches, two motor-cycles, one auto-cycle, and one taxi (with seven passengers); 10.15-10.30, 34 cars, 11 coaches and four motor-cycles; 10.30-10.45, 38 cars, 16 coaches including the Cobblers team coach) and three motor-cycles; 10.45-11.0, 41 cars, seven coaches, and two motor-cycles.

In addition to these, many coaches and cars went by the Welford road.

Many of the vehicles were decorated with claret and white and bore such slogans as "Look out Wembley, here we come," and "Cobblers for the Cup."

The game itself produced a brave performance by the Cobblers who, after being 3-0 down in seventeen minutes, might have salvaged a draw had not a controversial goal made a difficult task virtually impossible.

Not for the last time was a linesman's inability to influence the referee's decision critical for Northampton Town.

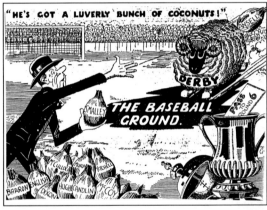

"HE'S GOT A LUVERLY BUNCH OF COCONUTS!"

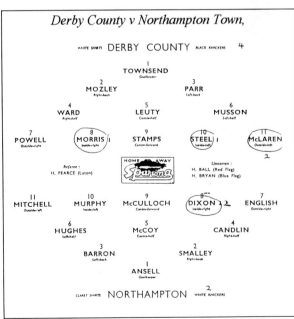

Derby County v Northampton Town,

Twenty years on—and still the fans argue

THE last time the Cobblers reached the fifth round of the FA Cup, 20 years ago, they were beaten 4-2 by Derby County, then lying ninth in the First Division.

The match, on February 11, 1950, drew a then record 38,063 crowd to Derby's Baseball Ground. Many of the thousands of Cobblers supporters who made the trip still argue to this day about several features of the match, including the state of the ground and Derby's disputed fourth goal.

The game was played on a pitch that was devoid of grass, save for small patches at each corner. The rest of the ground was a layer of mud which had been rolled down, and when the players ran out they found themselves almost ankle deep in it.

The goal that caused all the controversy came three minutes from the interval when the Derby left winger McLaren hit a shot which struck the inside of the post and bounced down onto the goal-line, where the Cobblers goalkeeper Ansell picked it up and cleared. The referee, however, awarded a goal, which was bitterly disputed. Cobblers players followed the official upfield, appealing to him but he let the goal stand and refused to consult his linesman.

Full-back Bill Barron, now 52 and a clerk at British Timken, lives today at 185, Headlands, Northampton.

About the fourth goal, he says: "The shot hit the upright and before it had even come off the upright the referee had given a goal. I was standing on the goal-line with Ansell and it was a good four to six inches away from the line. It was never a goal and I still say to this day that if they hadn't got that one we'd have drawn."

Mr. Maurice Candlin, the Cobblers skipper at the time, and now at 48 licensee of the Old Swan, Earls Barton, recalls the game and especially the controversial fourth goal. "As far as I was concerned it definitely wasn't a goal." The ball, he said, was not over the line and the referee should have consulted his linesman, who was in a very good position to see the incident, and who, Mr. Candlin, feels, also thought it was no goal.

Extracts from the report, 1970

Maurice Candlin, Northampton skipper, leads out his side for the second half of their FA Cup tie against Derby County at the Baseball ground, 1950. Arthur Dixon, scorer of both Cobblers' goals, is third in line.

The Cobblers league form had improved and the previous season's twentieth place was forgotten as the club achieved its highest league position since finishing runners up in 1927-28.

"Lankies" Told Curb Hooligans

Get More Support if They Did

COUN. R. Frisby, a member of Higham Ferrers Town Council Parks Committee and a vice-president of the Football Club, referred to "hooliganism" at the "Lankies" annual dinner on Friday.

He appealed: "If you can possibly curb some of the hooliganism and rowdyism on the stand, you will get more people to watch you and also encourage such people as us to spend the town's money on you."

In himself and Ald. J. W. Barker, the Club had two good friends on the Council Parks Committee, and they were doing what they could for the Club. They were hoping to get something done to the stand during the summer—something to make the crowd more comfortable and the place look better.

UP TO THEM

In their own interests it was up to them to try and control the children. They knew what was happening to the stand. There were children running all over it and doing damage, he said.

	Season 1949-50					51st Season	
	LEAGUE – DIVISION III (SOUTH)						
		Played	Won	Drawn	Lost	Goals	Points
1	Notts County	42	25	8	9	95-50	58
2	Northampton Town	42	20	11	11	72-50	51
3	Southend United	42	19	13	10	66-48	51
4	Nottingham Forest	42	20	9	13	67-39	49
5	Torquay United	42	19	10	13	66-63	48
6	Watford	42	16	13	13	45-35	45
7	Crystal Palace	42	15	14	13	55-54	44
8	Brighton and Hove Albion	42	16	12	14	57-69	44
9	Bristol Rovers	42	19	5	18	51-51	43
10	Reading	42	17	8	17	70-64	42
11	Norwich City	42	16	10	16	65-63	42
12	Bournemouth and Boscombe Athletic	42	16	10	16	57-56	42
13	Port Vale	42	15	11	16	47-42	41
14	Swindon Town	42	15	11	16	59-62	41
15	Bristol City	42	15	10	17	60-61	40
16	Exeter City	42	14	11	17	63-75	39
17	Ipswich Town	42	12	11	19	57-86	35
18	Leyton Orient	42	12	11	19	53-85	35
19	Walsall	42	9	16	17	61-62	34
20	Aldershot	42	13	8	21	48-60	34
21	Newport County	42	13	8	21	67-98	34
22	Millwall	42	14	4	24	55-63	32

Notts County promoted to Division II. Each Third Division extended to 24 clubs, Colchester United and Gillingham being elected to Southern Section.

Crowd behaviour in those days was generally exemplary, but exceptions occurred. Warning notices were posted around the ground at Kettering after the 2-1 Birmingham League Challenge Cup Final victory over Kidderminster Harriers, because of demonstrations by home supporters against the referee and visiting players.

A more surprising account appears in an "Evening Telegraph" report from April 1949 referring to the persistent misbehaviour of youngsters in the grandstand at Higham Ferrers.

I was now becoming more aware that football was an international game.

In the early summer of 1950 England were widely regarded as favourites for the World Cup due to be staged in Rio de Janeiro. On 29 June, the day before their opening game against the USA at Belo Horizonte, despite confidence in the England camp, omens were not good. The pages of the Evening Telegraph inform that our cricketers lost the second test against the West Indies by 325 runs, ('Those two little pals of mine, Ramadhin and Valentine'), and the United States Government had announced its intention to attack North Korea. Bertrand Russell predicted that Russia would become involved and the ensuing World War 3 would last for 10 years. Little wonder that England's subsequent 1-0 defeat barely made the back pages, dismissed by experts as a 'freak result'.

County football interest centred upon Ted Duckhouse, (later player-manager of Rushden Town), joining Northampton from Birmingham City, and Kettering's election to the Southern League.

The Poppies new chairman, F J Pascoe, managing director at British Timken, had succeeded W B Wright (the man with the straw hat), and the club had become a limited company. Mr Pascoe brought a new manager, Bob Calder, the former Queen's Park player

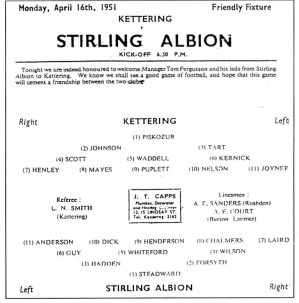

Monday, April 16th, 1951   Friendly Fixture

KETTERING

STIRLING ALBION

KICK-OFF 6.30 P.M.

Tonight we are indeed honoured to welcome Manager Tom Fergusson and his lads from Stirling Albion to Kettering. We know we shall see a good game of football, and hope that this game will cement a friendship between the two clubs.

Right   KETTERING   Left

(1) PISKOZUB

(2) JOHNSON   (3) TART

(4) SCOTT   (5) WADDELL   (6) KERNICK

(7) HENLEY   (8) MAYES   (9) PUPLETT   (10) NELSON   (11) JOYNER

Referee: J. T. CAPPS   Linesmen:
L. N. SMITH   Plumber, Decorator   A. E. SANDERS (Rushden)
(Kettering)   and Heating Engineer   A. E. COURT
        13, 15 LINDSAY ST.   (Burton Latimer)
        Tel. Kettering 2162

(11) ANDERSON   (10) DICK   (9) HENDERSON   (8) CHALMERS   (7) LAIRD

(6) GUY   (5) WHITEFORD   (4) WILSON

(3) HADDEN   (2) FORSYTH

(1) STEADWARD

Left   STIRLING ALBION   Right

who renewed the pre-war practice of attracting good class Scottish players to Rockingham Road. In April 1951, following the England v Scotland international at Wembley, Stirling Albion visited Kettering for a friendly fixture.

This, and an exciting 'revenge' FA Cup victory over Peterborough, were rare highlights of a disappointing first Southern League season.

In February, after a 3-1 victory over Barnsley, in Round 3, Northampton visited Highbury for a 4th Round tie against Arsenal. A

massive crowd of 72,408, including 15.000 from Northampton, witnessed a memorable game.

Although Northampton lost 3-2, Jack English scoring both Cobblers' goals, it was a valiant fight and, as at Derby, fortune deserted the underdog. Injury to centre-half Duckhouse a few minutes into the game reduced the side to 10 men - no substitutes of course - but he returned, almost scoring an equaliser with a shot that cannoned off the crossbar in the final minutes of the game.

DUCKHOUSE

CANDLIN

WILL THE HIGHBURY 15,000 BE AT THE COUNTY GROUND?

(TO THE EDITOR OF THE "CHRONICLE & ECHO")

F.A. CUP—FOURTH ROUND

Arsenal v. Northampton Town

SATURDAY, 27th JANUARY, 1951

KICK-OFF 2.45 p.m.

ARSENAL

COLOURS—SHIRTS: RED, WHITE SLEEVES AND COLLARS. KNICKERS: WHITE. STOCKINGS: BLUE, WHITE RINGS, WHITE TOPS.

Goal
Platt

2		3
Right Back		Left Back
Barnes		**Smith, L.**

4	5	6
Right Half	Centre Half	Left Half
Shaw	**Compton, L.**	**Forbes**

7	8	9	10	11
Outside Right	Inside Right	Centre Forward	Inside Left	Outside Left
Cox	**Logie**	**Goring**	**Lewis**	**Roper**

Referee	Linesmen
Mr. G. Tedds (Nottinghamshire)	Mr. S. Pankhurst (Warwick) Red Flag
	Mr. W. M. Pritchard (Hailsham) Yellow Flag

Owing to the clash of Colours, both Clubs are required to change—
Arsenal will wear White, Northampton, Blue.

11	10	9	8	7
Outside Left	Inside Left	Centre Forward	Inside Right	Outside Right
Mitchell	**Hughes**	**McCulloch**	**Dixon**	**English**

6	5	4
Left Half	Centre Half	Right Half
Davie	**Duckhouse**	**Candlin**

3		2
Left Back		Right Back
Southam		**Smalley**

Goal
Ansell

NORTHAMPTON TOWN

COLOURS—SHIRTS: CLARET, WHITE FACINGS. KNICKERS: WHITE. STOCKINGS: CLARET AND WHITE HOOPS

CONGRATULATIONS to the Cobblers for their grand display and never-say-die spirit at Highbury. They were no doubt helped on by the enthusiastic vocal support of the 15,000 supporters who are said to have been present. Financially the Cobblers' share of the £8,728 will be more than welcome. What the Cobblers need, however, is at least 15,000 supporters at every home match, and what is more the team is good enough to deserve at least that amount of support and without it cash may have to be raised by other means.

I was not able to be at Highbury on Saturday, but I am on Spion Cop every home match, wet or fine when my work permits, and at the next home match against Swindon hope to join the 15,000 who travelled to London and ensure a gate of at least 15,001.—J. W. Thorpe, 59, Randall-road Northampton.

ENGLISH

MITCHELL

McCULLOCH

Perhaps the disappointment affected league form as the team slid from the heights of the previous year to finish in twenty first place.

BARRON

HUGHES

Season 1950–1					52nd Season	
LEAGUE – DIVISION III (SOUTH)						
	Played	Won	Drawn	Lost	Goals	Points
1 Nottingham Forest	46	30	10	6	110–40	70
2 Norwich City	46	25	14	7	82–45	64
3 Reading	46	21	15	10	88–53	57
4 Plymouth Argyle	46	24	9	13	85–55	57
5 Millwall	46	23	10	13	80–57	56
6 Bristol Rovers	46	20	15	11	64–42	55
7 Southend United	46	21	10	15	92–69	52
8 Ipswich Town	46	23	6	17	69–58	52
9 Bournemouth and Boscombe Athletic	46	22	7	17	65–57	51
10 Bristol City	46	20	11	15	64–59	51
11 Newport County	46	19	9	18	77–70	47
12 Port Vale	46	16	13	17	60–65	45
13 Brighton and Hove Albion	46	13	17	16	71–79	43
14 Exeter City	46	18	6	22	62–85	42
15 Walsall	46	15	10	21	52–62	40
16 Colchester United	46	14	12	20	63–76	40
17 Swindon Town	46	18	4	24	55–67	40
18 Aldershot	46	15	10	21	56–88	40
19 Leyton Orient	46	15	8	23	53–75	38
20 Torquay United	46	14	9	23	64–81	37
21 Northampton Town	46	10	16	20	55–67	36
22 Gillingham	46	13	9	24	69–101	35
23 Watford	46	9	11	26	54–88	29
24 Crystal Palace	46	8	11	27	33–84	27
Nottingham Forest promoted to Division II.						

At Occupation Road, Corby achieved the first of successive UCL championships beating Spalding for the title by a single point. For a vital away fixture against the Tulipmen on 21 April the Steelmen were supported by 30 coaches, and a special chartered train full of fans, swelling the crowd at the Sir Halley Stewart Ground to a record 5,317.

NIGHTMARES!

Corby won 4-1, Ernie Middlemiss scoring twice, and three wins from their final four league fixtures procured the title. Corby's side included the veteran Maurice Dunkley. Middlemiss describes the little winger as "the finest crosser of the ball I ever played with. He was so accurate, he always made sure the lace was on the other side of the ball when you jumped to head it."

1950-51 Division 1	P.	W.	D.	L.	F.	A.	Pts
Corby Town .	34	26	4	4	123	34	56
Spalding United	34	25	5	4	101	48	55
Kettering Res.	34	19	7	8	85	73	45
Rushden Town	34	17	7	10	87	55	41
Abbey United	34	15	11	8	88	61	41
Stamford	34	17	7	10	77	71	41
Eynesbury Rovers	34	15	6	13	74	51	36
Holbeach United	34	16	3	15	71	70	35
Wellingborough Town	34	16	2	16	49	75	34
Peterborough Utd Res.	34	13	7	14	75	75	33
March Town United	34	15	2	17	72	68	32
Coventry City 'A'	34	12	6	16	62	65	30
Desborough Town	34	14	2	18	60	72	30
Boston United Res.	34	10	5	19	59	77	25
Symingtons	34	10	2	22	57	88	22
Bourne Town	34	8	6	20	55	92	22
Grantham Res.	34	6	5	23	57	98	17
Northampton Town 'A'	34	5	7	22	34	93	17

Corby Town UCL Champions 1950-51

Back Row: Wiseman, Cummings, Dunkley, Poole, James Garvey, Elder, Smith, Wands, Akers, Middlemiss, Montgomery.
Front Row: John Garvey, Horne, Strathie Copley, Allen.

Peterborough's manager, former Sunderland and England player, Bob Gurney continued the rebuilding policy began on his appointment in February 1950. New faces included ex-league players Frank Bee (Blackburn Rovers) and Johnny Dawson (Manchester City).

Early season optimism, reflected in attendances of over 6,500, evaporated as the side struggled and gates had fallen by half at the end of an undistinguished season.

STRATOCRUISING
1951-52

During the summer of 1951 Bob Gurney secured the services of three men destined to play major roles in Peterborough's 'glory years'; Ken Moody, Norman Rigby and George Hair.

UNITED'S 'BIG THREE' ON VIEW TODAY

Rigby, Moody and Hair, two full-backs and a left-winger, are Peterborough United's "big three" in the signing stakes this season. Ken Moody, burly right-back from Grimsby Town, joined his ex-club-mate George Hair, when he signed for "Posh" last Saturday.

Hair was the first big signing of the close-season, while big Norman Rigby, from Notts County, came to the club's first trial on August 4 and put pen to paper there and then. Here are pen - pictures of these three ex-League players in view in to-day's first match of the season at London Road against Notts County.

Ken Moody has played regularly for the Mariners, making 114 League appearances. He is 5ft. 8½in. tall and weighs 12st. 5lb. He learned his football with Humber Utd., crack side of Grimsby junior soccer until it folded up early in the war. He went South to work and played a good deal for Arsenal and Fulham. With the Gunners he reached the semi-final of a war-time cup competition.

When called up, Moody joined the Army and spent a good deal of his time in Palestine during the days of the Stern gang trouble.

Norman Rigby, star full-back of Notts County's promotion - winning team, was the subject of £10,000 bids by other League clubs two seasons ago. He was born at Newark and played in local football before joining Notts. County in 1944. He was then centre-half, but County developed him as a full-back.

Last year he did not play so well and lost his regular first-team place. Bob Gurney

tried to sign him the Thursday before the first trial match, but he explained that he still had a slight doubt then because he had been promised by County that he would receive the benefit due to him. He felt his chances of getting the cash might diminish if he joined a non-League club.

George Hair, from whose "precision" centres Tommy Briggs scored many of his 36 League goals in 1949-50, is 26 years old. He has been found a job at Mitchells and will live in Peterborough. He was placed on Grimsby's transfer list in May, having asked for a move during last season.

George joined Grimsby from Newcastle United on February 3, 1949, at a cost of £6,000. He cost Newcastle £10—his signing-on fee. One of the few players to wear contact lenses, George carries them in his pocket and slips them "on" under his eye-lids just before a game. Normally he wears spectacles.

In 1948-49, Hair made 14 Second Division appearances, played 37 times in 1949-50 and appeared 14 times last season.

TO-DAY'S TEAM

United's selected team to-day was: Moulson; Moody, Rigby; Walker, Machin, Cliff Woods; Dowson, Swinscoe, Brown, Bee, Hair.

OUTSIDE LEFT. the "ELECTRIC" HAIR

Much was made in the press of George Hair's detective eyesight in his Newcastle United days and later, considerable interest was expressed when he experimented with an early version of contact lenses.

Newcastle United players held a practice match this morning and in a corner of the field there was an experiment that was as interesting a way as the practice march itself. George Hair brought his contact glasses back from London and tried them out in ball play.

"They are grand, in a few minutes I forgot I had them on and was seeing the ball better than I had in months."

A further addition to the playing staff was made shortly after the start of the season when centre forward Andy Donaldson, a former team mate of Hair at St James' Park joined the Posh.

A contemporary report in a Newcastle newspaper noted Donaldson's move to Peterborough, reminding readers that he had once commanded a huge transfer fee when moving to Middlesborough some years previously.

The club attained a creditable 5th place at the end of the season but lost manager Gurney to Darlington. His successor was former Newcastle United goalkeeper Jack Fairbrother.

MIDLAND LEAGUE FINAL CHART 1951-52						
	P.	W.	D.	L.	F.	A.	P.
Notts. F.	42	33	6	3	105	29	72
Notts C.	42	30	3	9	108	54	63
Bradford C.	42	25	4	13	96	71	54
Hull City	42	21	8	13	80	54	50
Peterboro. U	42	20	10	12	90	71	50
Scarboro	42	19	10	13	92	76	48
Scunthorpe	42	21	6	15	69	61	48
Gainsboro.T	42	16	16	10	81	74	48
Boston U.	42	18	7	17	89	72	43
Worksop T	42	15	12	15	72	82	42
Goole	42	15	10	17	66	76	40
Rotherham	42	16	7	19	80	78	39
Frickley C.	42	14	11	17	65	73	39
Grimsby T	42	15	7	20	73	73	37
Mansfield T	42	12	13	17	63	65	37
Bradf'd P.A.	42	14	9	19	66	76	37
Doncaster R	42	11	10	21	72	96	32
Halifax T	42	12	8	22	71	96	32
Lincoln C	42	12	7	23	78	118	31
Grantham	42	13	3	26	65	95	29
Denaby U	42	11	7	24	51	90	29
York City	42	8	8	26	63	120	24

Peterborough United Football Club 1951-52

Mr M R Gurney, Hall, Walker, Moulson, Rigby, Woods C, Moody, Preston
(Manager)   Dowson, Swinscoe, Donaldson, Martin, Hair   (Trainer)

On a wider stage British football had suffered something akin to a shock during May 1951, when a number of matches were held against continental sides as part of the Festival of Britain celebrations. English champions Tottenham (Arthur Rowe's team of 'push and run' fame, whose players adorned every square inch of my bedroom walls), and Scottish leaders

Arthur Rowe

Hibernian, lost to Austrian clubs, whilst First Division West Bromwich Albion, Charlton Athletic and Middlesbrough were all convincingly beaten by European opposition.

The Sporting Record Annual of 1951, however, had the answer to the 'Continentals' style. It refers to, *football "ambassadors touring Europe spreading good will and playing football in the traditional fashion of English gentlemen. Against European soccer players who are tough and frequently excitable, however, this approach does not bring success. The English footballer must learn to be aggressive, which should not be alien to the British Bulldog".*

For the lads from the Avondale estate and, as I now realise, almost everywhere else across the British Isles, life began to conform to a regular pattern. School followed by weekends.

'We come along, on Saturday morning
Greeting everybody with a smile
We come along, on Saturday morning
Knowing its well worth while.
As members of the Odeon Club
We all intend to be,
Good citizens when we grow up
And champions of the free,
We come along, on Saturday morning
Greeting everybody with a smile, smile, smile.
Greeting everybody with a smile.

Saturday morning pictures - Hopalong Cassidy, Flash Gordon and a piece of cake on your birthday - was the first part of a ritual. Afternoons would find us at the Poppies - rain or shine, first team or reserves. Threepence secured admission by the entrance at the bottom of Britannia Road - 'Come this way boy, not through the turnstile'. At least money changed hands. Less generous lads stood on bicycle saddles and watched from over the tin fence at the Cowper Street end, or waited until half time to get in for nothing.

In the long wait to kick off, time was filled in fiercely fought tennis - ball contests on the slopes behind the top goal. Once the match began, however, there were other fascinations besides the game. The prototype for popular radio comedian Al Read's football supporter who, after continually deriding the efforts of a particular, unfortunate player, greets his match winning goal with the accolade, 'There, I always said he was a good'un', might well have originated on the Kettering terraces.

The home supporters' droll, often caustic wit, was highly amusing when directed at players, officials or, as often was the case, in sympathy with the spectators' lot. The typical half-time comment, 'You think that was bad? Wait till the second half. It'll be a bloody sight wuss!'

Yet there they were, week in, week out, queuing behind a corrugated tin wall, enveloped in steam, to urinate into an asphalt gully. As for other lavatorial needs, suffice it to say that hundreds of elderly men can now attribute their acute constipation to the privations endured on football grounds during that era.

My own football career had graduated from street, playground and park to real pitches with goalposts, referee and corner flags. When first selected to play for the school team I was so proud I went to bed in my tangerine jersey every night for a week. Some years earlier I had acquired my first football shirt from an unknown benefactor. It had a lace up collar and bore a series of red, amber and black hoops. After scouring the pages of my Boys Book of Soccer I identified its colours as those of Bradford Park Avenue!

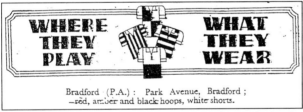

Bradford (P.A.) : Park Avenue, Bradford ; —red, amber and black hoops, white shorts.

Their most famous player had been the enigmatic Len Shackleton, 'The Clown Prince of Soccer', who, before lining up with George Hair and Andy Donaldson at Newcastle United, had worn the self-same multicoloured jersey. From that moment he became my idol, retaining the dubious privilege until 1958, when toppled from his pedestal by Albert Quixall's superior hairstyle!

Albert Quixall(Sheffield Wednesday and England)

On the local scene, Corby Town repeated their UCL triumph, this time by a more comfortable margin of 5 points.

Ernie Middlemiss scored a phenomenal 53 goals in 49 matches, but failed to agree terms for the new season, the Steelmen's first in the Midland League, and moved to Kettering Town together with Alec Wands.

1951-52 Division 1	P.	W.	D.	L.	F.	A.	Pts
Corby Town	38	28	3	7	126	60	59
Spalding United	38	25	4	9	103	46	54
Holbeach United	38	24	6	8	108	63	54
Bedford Reserves	38	23	3	12	104	56	49
Rushden Town	38	20	5	13	95	86	45
Symingtons	38	16	11	11	91	84	43
Bourne Town	38	19	4	15	92	85	42
Stamford	38	17	6	15	79	81	40
Desborough Town	38	17	5	16	80	73	39
Kettering Reserves	38	17	4	17	89	33	38
Eynesbury Rovers	38	15	5	18	78	87	35
Peterborough Utd. Res	38	13	7	18	63	72	33
Northampton Town 'A'	38	14	5	19	69	90	33
Biggleswade Town	38	12	7	19	62	81	31
March Town United	38	11	9	18	62	97	31
Boston United Reserves	38	12	6	20	82	91	30
Coventry City 'A'	39	12	6	20	53	68	30
St Neots Town	38	11	7	20	67	89	29
Wellingborough Town	38	13	3	22	61	102	29
Grantham Reserves	38	6	4	28	53	119	16

The Poppies completed a memorable year in splendid fashion. Their Southern League position improved to seventh, and an FA Cup run ended in an honourable 3-0 defeat by Bristol Rovers on a quagmire of a pitch at Eastville.

Kettering Town prior to their trip to Bristol Rovers, 1951.

From the back: Calder, Waddell, Summerly, Joyner, Scott, Gallacher, Whent, Mansfield, Manager of Granada Cinema, Alderman Goode, Pickering, Potts, Reynolds, Stenhouse, Johnson, Barron

But it was the final of the Maunsell Cup against Northampton that provided a fitting climax.

Before 8,082 spectators, including an excited ten year old, the Poppies defeated the league side 4-0. A somewhat prosaic account of the famous victory, reproduced from the 'Chronicle and Echo', appeared in a commemorative brochure specially commissioned by F J Pascoe - the final paragraph containing a truly remarkable explanation of the Chairman's enforced absence from the match.

MAUNSELL CUP FINAL
KETTERING 4 NORTHAMPTON 0

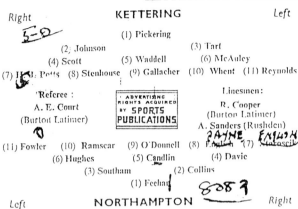

Right   **KETTERING**   Left

5-0

(1) Pickering

(2) Johnson   (3) Tart

(4) Scott   (5) Waddell   (6) McAuley

(7) J. Potts   (8) Stenhouse   (9) Gallacher   (10) Whent   (11) Reynolds

Referee :	ADVERTISING RIGHTS ACQUIRED BY SPORTS PUBLICATIONS	Linesmen:
A. E. Court (Burton Latimer)		R. Cooper (Burton Latimer) A. Sanders (Rushden)

PAYNE ENGLISH

(11) Fowler   (10) Ramscar   (9) O'Donnell   (8) English   (7) Motoscill

(6) Hughes   (5) Candlin   (4) Davie

(3) Southam   (2) Collins

(1) Feehan

8083

Left   **NORTHAMPTON**   Right

Programme shows incorrect score. An over excited Kettering fan credited the Poppies with an extra goal.

The shadows were lengthening as eleven tired but happy players of Kettering Town struggled through swarms of delirious supporters at Rockingham-road, Kettering, after beating Northampton Town in the final of the Maunsell Cup on May 1st.

It was a great triumph for the supporters ... it was even greater for the players of this Southern League club. Here, indeed, was a team emerging from the shadows.

Forced into the obscurity of non-League football by the near slavery of present-day commercialised soccer, the men of Kettering—most of them with big transfer fees on their heads—went all out from the start to show that they were just as good as their Third Division rivals from nearby Northampton.

This was the moment for which these soccer exiles had long waited.

And the cheers which developed into a victory roar must have brought back memories of bigger successes—but none would have been more pleasing.

It did not take long for Kettering to surge into their winning stride, Jimmy Stenhouse, whose skill earned him a Scottish international cap at Wembley in 1947, putting them ahead with a neatly flicked goal from the six-yard line.

Alas, poor Jimmy suffered a severe knock on the head ten minutes later when he collided in mid-air with his own wing-half, Bobby Scott, and was considerably weakened for the rest of the match. In between, Stenhouse had headed against the bar with goalkeeper Feehan groping the air.

Had Stenhouse scored it would have been number three—Canadian Jackie Whent had added a second after some grand work by centre-forward Jackie Gallacher and amateur outside-right Jimmy Potts.

Northampton had no answer to this power play. Kettering played Scottish-style football and their opponents did the reeling.

Three minutes before the interval, Brian Reynolds, who is by way of being a Northamptonshire county cricketer, scored a third goal when he made a glorious dive to head past Feehan.

It was the same in the second half. For a while it looked as if the full time training of Northampton would tell, but an excellent Kettering defence stood firm. Goalkeeper Pickering was the big man and on one occasion he showed all the stop-form which has raised his value to £7,000—the fee which Chelsea want for him—when he turned a hostile drive from Davie round the post at full stretch.

Pickering, claimed by knowledgeable ones to be the longest goal-kicker in the game, frequently turned defence into attack with his effortless annihilation of distance. At times he was throwing the ball farther than Feehan was kicking it.

It was from a typical Pickering clearance that Gallacher added lustre to a fine display by scoring the last goal of the match. Picking up a Pickering space-eater near the penalty area, the centre-forward rounded Candlin and beat Feehan with a drive into the roof of the net.

Amid all the joy, however, the players had one disappointment—their chairman, Mr. F. J. Pascoe, managing director of British Timken, was not present for his team's greatest hour. As his side was soaring, so, too, was Mr. Pascoe. He was strato-cruising back from a business trip in the United States.

44

Despite this rather surprising result Northampton had achieved an improved eighth place in the Third Division South. Their regular side included Joe Payne, Freddie Ramscar, Felix Staroscik and Kislingbury born defender Ben Collins

Season 1951-2						53rd Season
LEAGUE – DIVISION III (SOUTH)						
	Played	Won	Drawn	Lost	Goals	Points
1 Plymouth Argyle	46	29	8	9	107–53	66
2 Reading	46	29	3	14	112–60	61
3 Norwich City	46	26	9	11	89–50	61
4 Millwall	46	23	12	11	74–53	58
5 Brighton and Hove Albion	46	24	10	12	87–63	58
6 Newport County	46	21	12	13	77–76	54
7 Bristol Rovers	46	20	12	14	89–53	52
8 Northampton Town	46	22	5	19	93–74	49
9 Southend United	46	19	10	17	75–66	48
10 Colchester United	46	17	12	17	56–77	46
11 Torquay United	46	17	10	19	86–98	44
12 Aldershot	46	18	8	20	78–89	44
13 Port Vale	46	14	15	17	50–66	43
14 Bournemouth and Boscombe Athletic	46	16	10	20	69–75	42
15 Bristol City	46	15	12	19	58–69	42
16 Swindon Town	46	14	14	18	51–68	42
17 Ipswich Town	46	16	9	21	63–74	41
18 Leyton Orient	46	16	9	21	55–68	41
19 Crystal Palace	46	15	9	22	61–80	39
20 Shrewsbury Town	46	13	10	23	62–86	36
21 Watford	46	13	10	23	57–81	36
22 Gillingham	46	11	13	22	71–81	35
23 Exeter City	46	13	9	24	65–86	35
24 Walsall	46	13	5	28	55–94	31
Plymouth Argyle promoted to Division II. Port Vale transferred to Division III (North).						

Northampton Town 1952

Back Row: Collins, Candlin, Feehan, Duckhouse, Wilson, Hughes.
Front Row: English, Payne, McCulloch, Ramscar, Fowler.

45

Kettering v Rushden October 1952

Jackie Gallacher, goalscoring hero in the Poppies Maunsell cup triumph, challenges Coleman the Rushden keeper during a 1952 FA Cup tie..

This evocative photograph, which captures the spirit of the fifties, portrays a section of the crowd at the Cowper Street end during the same Kettering v Rushden FA Cup match.

PETERBOROUGH ARE THE POSH
1952-53

A truly golden season.

Peterborough began the FA giant killing tradition that was to make the Posh the most feared of non-league opposition by defeating Third Division Torquay. But first they needed to dispose of Corby Town in the 3rd Qualifying Round. Corby had already beaten Kettering 2-0 in a replayed match at Rockingham Road, after drawing the original game 1-1.

"HAE YE NO HEER'D O' BANNOCKBURN ?"

F.A. CUP. CORBY vs. KETTERING.

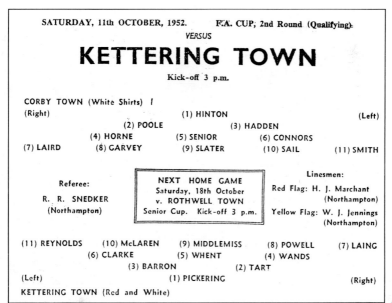

SATURDAY, 11th OCTOBER, 1952.   F.A. CUP, 2nd Round (Qualifying).

VERSUS

KETTERING TOWN

Kick-off 3 p.m.

CORBY TOWN (White Shirts)

(Right)   (1) HINTON   (Left)
            (2) POOLE   (3) HADDEN
        (4) HORNE   (5) SENIOR   (6) CONNORS
(7) LAIRD   (8) GARVEY   (9) SLATER   (10) SAIL   (11) SMITH

Referee:	NEXT HOME GAME	Linesmen:
R. R. SNEDKER	Saturday, 18th October	Red Flag: H. J. Marchant
(Northampton)	v. ROTHWELL TOWN	(Northampton)
	Senior Cup. Kick-off 3 p.m.	Yellow Flag: W. J. Jennings
		(Northampton)

(11) REYNOLDS   (10) McLAREN   (9) MIDDLEMISS   (8) POWELL   (7) LAING
        (6) CLARKE   (5) WHENT   (4) WANDS
            (3) BARRON   (2) TART
(Left)   (1) PICKERING   (Right)
KETTERING TOWN (Red and White)

The first Corby v Peterborough game at Occupation Road attracted a record 10,239 attendance and ended all square with no goals. There were certainly plenty in the replay, Posh emerging victors 5-3.

47

TWO TOUGH CUP-TIE HOURS TAKE TOLL OF CORBY
Peterborough 5   Corby 3

AFTER two hours of some of the toughest Cup-tie football I have ever seen, Peterborough qualified to entertain Southern League Bedford Town in the fourth qualifying round of the FA Cup tomorrow week.

Jack Fairbrother, Peterborough player-manager and formerly with Newcastle, told me "the Midland League is the toughest in the country."

Judging from this display between two of its leading lights—Corby are at the top of the table at present—I can believe it.

Tackling was so fierce and so many risks were taken that it is a wonder there were no serious injuries.

But the 9,843 crowd got a feast of thrills, and no-quarter effort with a fair proportion of skill. One excited spectator had a brief argument with the referee and was escorted from the field by a policeman.

Uphill fight

Peterborough, I thought, just deserved to win but Corby took the honours for a grand uphill fight.

Two goals down in 18 minutes—Martin and Hair scored for United—they battled on bravely.

Garvey failed with a penalty kick in the first minute of the second half but with right-back Poole limping on the right wing, they equalised in a glorious five-minute spell through goals by Slater and Laird.

Rigby, Peterborough captain, who bravely decided to take a penalty kick himself put his side ahead with only two minutes to go. Then Corby hit back again. Garvey equalised with almost the last kick.

They wilted slightly in extra time and I was not surprised. Donaldson and Campbell got the winning goals for the persistent Peterborough.

Great defence

Corby, a big side who would not disgrace the Third Division had great defensive workers in centre-half Senior and Connors and first-class wing-forwards in Smith and Laird.

A Sheffield Wednesday director watched Senior, a big strapping stopper who was formerly with Huddersfield.

I liked best the outside-left Smith, a go-ahead raider from Crewe. He should not remain long with the steel-workers.

Though the former Grimsby players, Moody, the best back afield, Wood, Campbell and Hair, did good service for Peterborough, the stars were Woollard, Rigby, Paddy Sloan, Irish international of Arsenal and Italy fame, and Anderson, who gained a winner's medal with Manchester United.

Woollard gave a stylish display. He has already attracted the attention of several League clubs, including the Spurs. Rigby, once with Notts County, steadied the side when in difficulties and Sloan provided the ball artistry.

Donaldson, transferred from Newcastle to Middlesbrough for £17,000 a few seasons back, was a mixture of the brilliant and mediocre.

<table>
<tr><td colspan="5" align="center">PETERBOROUGH</td></tr>
<tr><td colspan="5" align="center">Fairbrother</td></tr>
<tr><td></td><td>Moody</td><td></td><td colspan="2">Woollard</td></tr>
<tr><td></td><td>Anderson</td><td>Rigby</td><td></td><td>Wood</td></tr>
<tr><td>Campbell</td><td>Sloan</td><td>Donaldson</td><td>Martin</td><td>Hair</td></tr>
<tr><td colspan="5" align="center">------------</td></tr>
<tr><td>Matthews</td><td>Smith</td><td>Slater</td><td>Garvey</td><td>Laird</td></tr>
<tr><td></td><td>Connors</td><td>Senior</td><td>Sail</td><td></td></tr>
<tr><td></td><td>Smith</td><td></td><td>Poole</td><td></td></tr>
<tr><td colspan="5" align="center">Hinton</td></tr>
<tr><td colspan="5" align="center">CORBY TOWN</td></tr>
</table>

Alex Laird

Colin Senior

Bedford Town were accounted for by 2-1 and then, for the first time in the club's history, came victory over Football League opponents - incidentally Torquay had provided the opposition back in 1948 when the Devon club had managed a 1-0 success.

'No club feared here,' says Fairbrother

It was only a little giant, but Peterborough killed it well and truly to reach the Second Round of the F.A. Cup for the first time since 1928. What a surprise for Torquay, and what a disaster in its way for the Devon club.

United's was the second best performance in the Cup of the whole day; and their 2—1 victory was a reward earned entirely without luck's aid.

There were moves which the Torquay defence was just incapable of holding; one in the first half covered half the length of the field in a style reminiscent of the First Division.

"We fear no club left in the draw if we are on our home ground," said the player-manager after the match. His confidence is well founded.

The crowd of 12,948 paid close on £1,000 to see an exhibition of football that has only been topped this season in the Corby encounter.

A great encouragement to the home club was that these spectators came almost entirely from the city and near-district, as Torquay brought only a handful of supporters with them. If Peterborough had been drawn against a nearby team there is no doubt whatsoever that the record 15,300 "gate" would have been smashed.

As it was, only five other ties had more spectators: Bath (14,000), Coventry (17,000), Crystal Palace (21,340), Port Vale (14,586) and Bradford (13,524).

Peterborough United 1952-53

Back Row: Anderson, Moody, Fairbrother, Butler, Wood, Woollard,
Front Row: Sloan, Bardy, McCulloch, Donaldson, Hair.

THOUSANDS of words in scores of newspapers have already described the great and lesser moments of Peterborough's memorable F.A. Cup first round tie with Torquay United. All have hailed it as a victory well deserved, and this summary, written in the light of studied reflection, must inevitably begin by endorsing that opinion.

To win at all was an achievement. To win so well, and so definitely on merit, put the victory in the "great" class. And, if United had been allowed the "goal" Donaldson "scored" 40 seconds after Martin's first, I believe United's fame would have known no bounds.

For this was truly Peterborough's "purple passage" of the game. They had the Torquay defence in a tangle, and might well have built up a big score had , the inspiration of that second quick goal not been denied them.

About the disallowed point was almost as much mystery as the scorer of Torquay's equaliser. When Donaldson calmly pushed the ball into the Torquay net from Martin's across - the - goalline pass, referee Clapton appeared to signal a goal. Then, catching sight of a flagging linesman, he consulted his colleague, and the wild cheering stilled as he placed the ball for a free-kick. From the position of the kick Donaldson was made the offside offender.

This let off gave Torquay heart and they beat down on the home defence with the fierceness of waves battering their Devon coast. Then it was that we saw the greatness of Jack Fairbrother. We have long acknowledged his personality, his command and his competence as a manager, but now we can praise without reservation his ability as a goalkeeper.

In that nerve - racking spell which preceded Torquay's goal, Fairbrother reigned supreme. As the ball bobbed too and fro in front of the goalmouth, with determined Torquay straining every sinew to drive it home, he made a succession of saves which can be described only as brilliant. The

| Torquay | 1 |
| United | 2 |

SCORERS mins.
Martin (United) 55
—— (Torquay) 80
Sloan (United) 87

TEAMS
United: Fairbrother; Moody, Woollard; Anderson, Rigby, Wood; Campbell, Sloan, Donaldson, Martin, Hair.
Torquay: Webber, G.; Drinkwater, Stitfall; Lewis, D., Webber, E., Norman; Muir, Shaw, Collins, Marchant, Edds.

ATTENDANCE.
12,938 (£963)

hammer-drive from Shaw he stopped right on the line was a masterly piece of work, and so was the full-length dive which punched away a ball Edds had sent bobbing towards the far post.

* * *

IN the end the Peterborough goal fell, and it is still a matter for conjecture who scored. White shirts and blue were all mixed up together on the goal-line, and more than one foot touched the ball before Fairbrother scooped it up and came out of the "scrum." But all in vain — the whistle had blown.

No one seemed to know who applied the finishing touch. There were strong claims for Collins and little Edds, claims for Collins and little Edds.

Anyhow, a goal it was, and with only ten minutes left for play United looked like facing the long journey to Torquay in mid-week.

But, as at Spalding (so long ago, it seems), now at London-road, the game was saved, and this time won, in the dying minutes.

And the goal made a hero of Paddy Sloan, who had been singularly subdued for most of the match. Donaldson, it was, who began the triumphant movement. His shrewd pass sent Fred Martin tearing away down the left-wing. Martin swung the ball into the centre and Sloan's curly head bobbed up to nudge the ball into the net, well beyond George Webber's reach.

SO Peterborough won through. It was a victory in which every member of the side played a worthy part, with the half-backs emerging as the men of the match. Seldom have Anderson, Rigby and Wood given such a consistently sound and intelligent display. It was Anderson's best game since joining United. Time after time he came through with the ball and rarely wasted a pass.

Terrier-like Fred Martin, playing better than ever, was in many respects Peterborough's match winner. He scored the first goal — a real opportunist effort, nipping between off-balance Drinkwater and the advancing goalkeeper to hook the ball into the net — made the second, and generally harrassed the Torquay defence from all quarters.

Donaldson's calm and accurate distribution was another pleasing feature, while Campbell was the fastest player in either side.

In the goalless first half there was a spell when Peterborough's play became scrappy, quite out of character with the form shown after the interval. The forwards seemed out of touch with one another, wasting chances by sending the ball straight to the foot of a Torquay man.

* * *

At the end of it all it was nice to see Torquay centre-half manager Eric Webber run half the length of the field to shake hands with Jack Fairbrother. It put the seal on a splendid occasion.

And Jack Fairbrother's after-match comment was typically modest. "I don't think anyone can say it was a fluke," he said to me. They can't. — F.J.J.

The second round brought Bristol Rovers, current leaders of the Third Division South to London Road. Only one goal separated the sides, scored by Rovers' Vic Lambden, but the Posh were now established on the football map.

50

YES, PETERBOROUGH ARE THE 'POSH'

PETERBORO' 0, BRISTOL R. 1

THEY call Midland Leaguers Peterborough United " The Posh." How they came by the name I don't know. Nor apparently does anyone else. But I'm thinking it could be something to do with the quality of their football.

For believe me, there is class in this team of ex-League stars who are now playing in the so-called backwoods of Soccer. There was class enough yesterday to baffle these strong promotion-challenging Bristol Rovers, flummox them and have them floundering.

If only they'd had one really strong thruster like Rovers' Vic Lambden or Geoff Bradford, they —and not the Third Division leaders—could have been in the hat for the Third Round draw tomorrow.

'Posh' Knocking at Door

Canvassing for League Admission

FOOTBALL League club representatives met in London today to thrash out problems of finance and other aspects of the game, — and Peterborough United officials outside the conference room for an opportunity to canvass support for their claim for League admittance.

The League representatives were to discuss points of policy preparatory to the annual meeting in London on June 13 and prominent on the agenda was a discussion on finance following the Budget decision to give no relief to professional soccer, but to exempt the amateur game.

Some clubs intend to press for an increase in the minimum admission price, which is now 1s. 9d.

Among other matters to be discussed were the continuance of the ban on televising League games; the playing of some League games by floodlight; substitutes in League games; a revision of the League to four divisions, with two-up and two-down promotion and relegation in all sections.

Peterborough's application will be decided at the annual meeting.

The Peterborough representatives were Messrs. F. Stimson (chairman) C. L. Palmer (vice-chairman) and Jack Fairbrother (player-manager).

Peterborough's confidence was demonstrated by application for admission to the Football League. It proved to be unsuccessful. Posh supporters were to become accustomed to such disappointment, as the 'closed shop' policy of league clubs consistently barred the door to new members.

Park Road Junior School's matches invariably took place in the late afternoon or on Saturday mornings. Away games at Corby were real adventures. We caught a service bus from a stop about half a mile from school to the old bus station in Corby village, and walked to the 'Wessie', (The West Glebe). The teachers were usually there to meet us. Primary School games masters were a special breed in those days. None favoured tracksuits adorned with an abundance of FA coaching badges. Pipes, leather patched elbows and bicycle clips were de rigeur. Team selection and tactics were basic in the extreme. Big boys defended, little 'uns attacked. Words of advice proffered from touchlines usually urged us to 'boot it'.

It was all a million years away from the chauffeured, multikitted, computerised lifestyle enjoyed by today's youngsters. But so was newting up the pits, playing 'catty' in the street, listening to 'Dick Barton, Special Agent', reading Dan Dare in the 'Eagle', collecting blue and white cigarette cards from discarded 'Turf' packets, scraping names in the ice on the inside of bedroom window panes and squatting in the darkness of the outside lavatory.

51

On the morning of the Taylor Cup semi-final against Our Lady's RC School at Corby, we departed from normal practice and travelled to the game by hired coach. I sat next to right half Ginger Rogers as the bus left the school gate crammed with excited players and supporters.

It was all too much for Ginger. We had travelled barely a hundred yards down Park Avenue when he was spectacularly ill, mostly over me. The coach dropped him off at the next corner and continued to Corby without him. I can still picture the boy, chalk white face beneath a mop of marmalade hair, football boots in hand, watching forlornly from the kerb. And thinking, "If we lose, it'll be your fault." We did. The gallant ten man team fought hard, but went down 2-1.

Can Corby Cut Down Forest?

NOTTINGHAM Forest Midland League champions for three successive seasons, beat Scarborough 4—1 last night and are now equal on points with the Steelmen.

Each club has 68 points from 45 games and the stage is set for the match of the season at Corby tomorrow evening.

The winning side will become undisputed champions: what will happen if there is a draw has not yet been decided.

Centre-forward Slater is still on the "doubtful" list for Corby and if he is unable to turn out it is likely that Mitchell will play.

Just a short distance away across the West Glebe in Occupation Road, manager Wally Akers' side was also enjoying a successful season. That epic FA Cup campaign in the Autumn had indicated that Corby Town was a side to watch, and so it proved.

The final league match of the season brought Nottingham Forest Reserves to Occupation Road for a game that would decide the championship. The importance of the fixture can be seen by the position at the top of the table prior to the match.

Corby Town's Midland League Side 1952-53

Back Row: Poole, Horne, Hinton, Hadden, Garvey, Connors.
Front Row: Laird, Smith, Senior, Matthews, Slater.

52

A 2-1 defeat consigned the Steelmen to runners-up but, as the match report indicates, it was a close run thing.

Resolute Corby Just Failed

CORBY TOWN 1, NOTTINGHAM FOREST RES. 2

PLAYING polished football, Nottingham Forest Reserves captured the Midland League title for the fourth successive year, on Friday — but they were made to fight for it every inch of the way by a resolute Corby side that would not admit defeat.

In those days a favourite game on the way home from school was to spot the appearance of the latest, distinctive H-shaped aerials on chimney stacks down our street. Ours didn't arrive until January 1953, and until then I'd had to scrounge a space on the lino in front of a neighbour's nine-inch Peto Scott, with a glass 'enlarger' for magnification. At last in early anticipation of the forthcoming Coronation, we had our own magnificent twelve inch Ultra.

Soon we were watching 'Whirligig' and Mr Turnip, real life drama featuring Captain Carlson and the 'Flying Enterprise', and 'What's My Line' with that 'stroppy' Gilbert Harding.

Two broadcasts later that year remain etched in my memory. And neither was the Coronation.

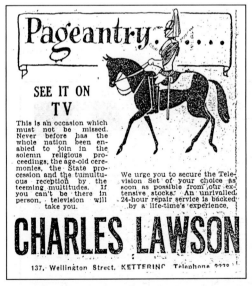

On 2 May, the day after Corby's brave attempt to win the Midland League, I watched the legendary Stanley Matthews' virtuoso performance secure the FA Cup for Blackpool at Wembley Stadium.

Wembley Stadium! Just a few weeks earlier, together with hundreds of others from the area, I travelled to London for the Schoolboy International.

A veritable convoy of buses left Kettering early on Saturday morning. Once on board our York's coach, 'HMS Ark Royal', we opened our cases. Bottles of spruce, penny packets of broken crisps, 'mullocks' galore for the stomach, Charles Buchan's Football Monthlies for the soul. There was a toilet stop at Luton, followed by the obligatory two hour lunch stop at St Albans. While fathers and teachers found 'watering holes', hordes of boys climbed the steep hill to the market. There we spent precious shillings on water pistols with

53

leaking rubber handles, penknives guaranteed to shed fifteen blades, picksticker and corkscrew within a couple of days, and, best of all, those marvellous metal bombs with ribbons of highly explosive pink caps.

The next stop was Wembley, twin towers and all. Inside the ground, hours before kick off, a white suited Arthur Caiger mounted the rostrum in the centre circle, waved a baton, and thousands of untrained voices dutifully bawled, 'keep right on to the end of the road', from Daily Express song sheets emblazoned with Union Jacks.

As for the football, 80,000 spectators were privileged to witness the precocious talents of a young inside forward who crowned a marvellous performance by scoring two of England's goals - Bobby Charlton.

Bobby Charlton slamming in a hard shot.

After fish and chips and processed peas at the Empire Cafe, Hendon, we finally arrived back in Kettering, to trudge home swathed in rosettes, happy and hoarse from the umpteenth chorus of 'Lulu had a baby', and clutching those jealously guarded but fatally flawed presents from St Albans Market.

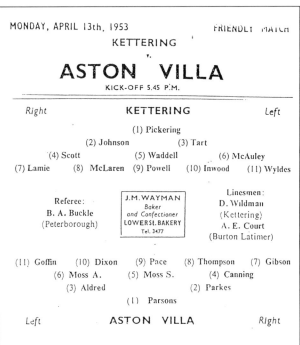

MONDAY, APRIL 13th, 1953   FRIENDLY MATCH

KETTERING

v.

ASTON VILLA

KICK-OFF 5.45 P.M.

Right		KETTERING		Left
		(1) Pickering		
	(2) Johnson		(3) Tart	
	(4) Scott	(5) Waddell	(6) McAuley	
(7) Lamie	(8) McLaren	(9) Powell	(10) Inwood	(11) Wyldes

Referee:
B. A. Buckle
(Peterborough)

J.M. WAYMAN
Baker
and Confectioner
LOWER St. BAKERY
Tel. 3477

Linesmen:
D. Wildman
(Kettering)
A. E. Court
(Burton Latimer)

(11) Goffin	(10) Dixon	(9) Pace	(8) Thompson	(7) Gibson
(6) Moss A.		(5) Moss S.	(4) Canning	
	(3) Aldred		(2) Parkes	
		(1) Parsons		

Left		ASTON VILLA		Right

On 12 April, I had seen my first 'Premier' division side when Aston Villa visited Rockingham Road for a benefit game in recognition of 21 years meritorious service given to the Poppies by secretary Frank Summerly and treasurer Harry Mead.

54

Kettering led the Southern League table until early March but finished a creditable fourth, Headington (now Oxford United) lifting the title.

Northampton so nearly clinched promotion to the Second Division finishing third behind Bristol Rovers and Millwall. In a match at Norwich, wing half Tommy McClain had a memorable game of mixed fortune. He was first booked, then carried off, returned to score and was then sent off!
Bob Dennison, centre half hero back in 1947, was now manager and widely tipped to move on to 'greater things'.

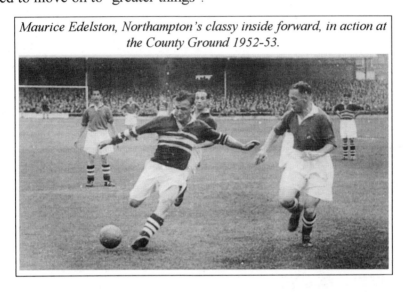

Maurice Edelston, Northampton's classy inside forward, in action at the County Ground 1952-53.

There was no FA Cup run to cheer, but the league record of 26 wins and 109 goals was the Cobblers best to date, with Jack English, Willie O'Donnell and Freddie Ramscar each scoring over 20 goals.

In the United Counties League, fourth placed Rushden Town, hosted a benefit match for the former Cobbler Bobby King on April 20th.

Season 1952–3   54th Season

LEAGUE – DIVISION III (SOUTH)

		Played	Won	Drawn	Lost	Goals	Points
1	Bristol Rovers	46	26	12	8	92–46	64
2	Millwall	46	24	14	8	82–44	62
3	Northampton Town	46	26	10	10	109–70	62
4	Norwich City	46	25	10	11	99–55	60
5	Bristol City	46	22	15	9	95–61	59
6	Coventry City	46	19	12	15	77–62	50
7	Brighton and Hove Albion	46	19	12	15	81–75	50
8	Southend United	46	18	13	15	69–74	49
9	Bournemouth and Boscombe Athletic	46	19	9	18	74–69	47
10	Watford	46	15	17	14	62–63	47
11	Reading	46	19	8	19	69–64	46
12	Torquay United	46	18	9	19	87–88	45
13	Crystal Palace	46	15	13	18	66–82	43
14	Leyton Orient	46	16	10	20	68–73	42
15	Newport County	46	16	10	20	70–82	42
16	Ipswich Town	46	13	15	18	60–69	41
17	Exeter City	46	13	14	19	61–71	40
18	Swindon Town	46	14	12	20	64–79	40
19	Aldershot	46	12	15	19	61–77	39
20	Queen's Park Rangers	46	12	15	19	61–82	39
21	Gillingham	46	12	15	19	55–74	39
22	Colchester United	46	12	14	20	59–76	38
23	Shrewsbury Town	46	12	12	22	68–91	36
24	Walsall	46	7	10	29	56–118	24

Bristol Rovers promoted to Division II.

Stars assembled for Bobby King's Testimonial game at Rushden April 20th 1953

Back Row: B Inwood, Croy, G Inwood, Bowen, Adams, French, Williams, Wilson, Evans, Duckhouse (partly hidden).
Front Row: Dennison, King, Staroscik, Hancocks, Mitchell.

Bobby King's Benefit

England Winger Got Three Goals

THREE goals by England winger, Hancocks, and three that Rushden men put past Williams, the English international goalkeeper, were part of the fine entertainment at Rushden on Monday, when, in his benefit match, King led the Russians against a powerful guest eleven.

There were many changes in the visiting side, which won by 6—3. Not one of the five invited Northampton Town men turned out, and the Arsenal batch included Evans and Dodgin in place of Lionel Smith and Cox. Smith was present but decided not to play owing to an ankle injury received against Scotland on Saturday. Dodgin took the place of Croy in the second half.

Rushden: Coleman; Gibbs, Toms; Martin, Maddams, Gell; Holmes, King, Lawrence, Campbell, Pipes.

Guest XI: Williams (Wolves); Wilson (Northampton), Evans (Arsenal); Bowen (Arsenal), Croy (Northampton), French (Northampton); Hancocks (Wolves); Staroscik (Northampton), Adams (Northampton), Inwood (Kettering), Mitchell (Luton).

Meanwhile mid-table Desborough (listed here for a Maunsell Cup tie at Peterborough)

Steed	Draper	Garvie	Denton	Garfield G
	Garfield P	Keep	Crozier	
	Wyldes		Patrick	
		Nimmo		
Colours-Red & White		Linesmen-Lambert, Leigh		

and lowly Wellingborough - represented against Kettering Reserves on March 23.

McInnes	Maggs	Bugby	Rochester	Wollacott
	Dixon	Watson	Parker S	
	Byles		Parker R	
		Freeman		

complete a review of the fortunes of the County's senior clubs during 1952-53.

Rushden Town had achieved a major coup during the summer of 1952 by signing centre half Ted Duckhouse from Northampton Town.

Ted Duckhouse signs for Rushden Town in 1952.

Brittain, Ambridge (Sec), Duckhouse, Robinson (former ref), Langley (Sec Supporters Club), Walker, Harris.

Ken Ambridge, a long serving official at Rushden Town well recalls the signing of Duckhouse. At an annual general meeting, attended by over 400 supporters, a disgruntled fan suggested that the club sign Duckhouse, then residing in a Cobblers' clubhouse, as he understood that the player had not been retained by Northampton.. Ambridge, newly appointed secretary, duly made contact, offering as inducements accommodation in a house in the Wellingborough Road, (purchased by the Supporters Club at a price of £900), and employment with Swindalls, local coal merchants.

Duckhouse signed, and remained at Hayden Road for four seasons, before returning to live in the West Midlands. On his departure, the re-sale of the house realised only £500. Not surprisingly it proved to be the club's only venture into the property market.

1952-53 Division 2	P.	W.	D.	L.	F.	A.	Pts
Rothwell Town	28	23	4	1	123	29	50
Symingtons Res.	28	16	5	7	71	50	37
Rushden Res.	28	14	5	9	77	60	33
Raunds Town	28	13	7	8	71	61	33
Huntingdon United	28	13	5	10	95	62	31
Higham Town	28	14	3	11	63	52	31
Eynesbury Reserves	28	13	3	12	64	60	29
Desborough Res.	28	11	7	10	76	63	29
Warboys Town	28	11	6	11	71	71	28
Finedon Town	28	11	4	13	72	72	26
B. Timken Duston Res.	28	11	2	15	57	95	24
St Neots Res.	28	7	7	14	67	83	21
Wellingborough Res.	28	6	7	15	52	93	19
Bedford Avenue	28	5	6	17	48	86	16
Irthlingborough Town	28	5	3	20	38	101	13

Rothwell Town were Second Division champions, a huge 13 point margin separating 'The Bones' from nearest rivals Symingtons Reserves. Pink 'Un cartoons appear to have neglected to represent 'The Bones' but Market Harborough based Symingtons were depicted as the 'Corsetmen'.

Rothwell Town UCL Division 2 Champions 1952-53

Back Row: Tebbutt, Strathie, Severn, Gordon, Underwood, Childs.
Front Row: Robson, Longhurst, Linnett, Henley, Cleaver, Robertson.

Included in the Rothwell team was Jim Strathie, a former Cobbler, Kettering's centre half against Peterborough in 1947 and a commanding figure in Corby's UCL successes in the early fifties.

Opponents respected his uncompromising but highly effective style of play, which is more than can be said for the visiting supporter who, during one game, hurled abuse at Strathie from the comparative safety of Rothwell's stand.

"You Fenian bastard!" he shouted repeatedly at the giant centre half, who remained apparently unaffected by the barrage of insults. He was, however, merely biding his time.. Eventually, awarded a free kick some five yards from the touchline in front of the grandstand, he turned his back on the play, and aimed a ferocious shot at his foul-mouthed abuser. The heavy leather ball struck the spectator full in the face, knocking him senseless. Recognising natural justice, the referee awarded the opposition a throw in, and the game continued.

Other notable team members were Bert Henley, the much travelled prolific goalscorer, Joe Childs, a youthful member of Rushden's all conquering post-war side, former Poppy Dougie Cleaver, Broughton born schoolboy international Malcolm Underwood and flying winger Vic Longhurst, whose son David died tragically while playing for York City.

58

MAGICAL MAGYARS,
FAIRBROTHER AND FORD
1953-54

The second memorable television broadcast of 1953 took place on a fittingly grey November afternoon when a country, previously buried deep in the pages of my stamp album - Maygar Posta: Hungary - played England at Wembley.

My formal education received a further setback when I took time from school to watch Billy Wright's team put those foreigners in their place. My father made a particularly perceptive observation as the two sides took the field, comparing the English players rather stiff, determined, gentlemanly appearance with that of their opponents who were, in his words, 'flash sods'.

Billy Wright leading out the England Team against Hungary, 1953.

When Hungary scored an early goal it was 'just a fluke' - shades of Belo Horizonte. They went on to score six against England's three, playing exquisitely. Puskas, Koscis, Hideguti.

'Freak result', my dad said. "Wait till we play them again."

I'd seen enough. Frantically I cycled into town to buy a sachet of cherry red dye. Back home, I soaked my football shirt until it bore a passing resemblance, in a bad light, to those famous Hungarian jerseys. How I longed to be a flash sod too!

In December 1953, we left the adventure playground of a council estate where I'd grown up. It was an end to the anarchic street games - 'Knock down Ginger', 'Spotlight on Sally', and 'Release'. Goodbye to the backgarden menageries, teeming with racing pigeons, ferrets and Rhode Island Reds. Farewell to the processions, tramping past our gate. Truckpushers, garden field bound; bucket wielding neighbours scooping precious manure from under the very hooves of delivery horses; thirsty workers clutching jugs heading for the outdoor beer house, or the plethora of working men's clubs.

Our new house, in a Victorian terrace opposite a factory, represented my parents' investment against an uncertain future. Such prudence was beyond my comprehension. I deeply resented the move, coming so soon after entry to Grammar School, where the only code of football played used a strangely shaped ball. For two years my great passion suffered almost total abstinence, restricted to crowded playground games within the narrow confines of a basketball court.

On Saturdays I was again cast into the role of frustrated spectator.

The season of 1953-54 saw Peterborough maintain progress, both in the Midland League, where they achieved their highest position to date finishing runners up to the seemingly invincible Nottingham

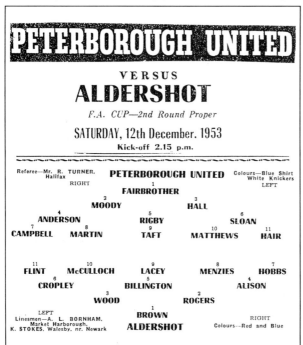

MIDLAND COUNTIES LEAGUE Final Table—1953-4							
	P	W	D	L	F	A	P
Nottm. F.	46	33	6	7	139	44	72
Peter'ro'	46	27	8	11	111	73	62
Doncaster	46	26	8	12	93	56	60
Corby T.	46	26	8	12	115	76	60
Roth'ham	46	24	9	13	118	74	57
Hull C.	46	23	8	15	103	71	54
Notts. C.	46	23	7	16	104	74	53
Granth'm	46	23	6	17	100	85	52
Wisbech	46	20	11	15	92	79	51
Grimsby	46	20	8	18	74	62	48
Worksop	46	19	10	16	73	61	48
Lincoln	46	18	7	21	94	88	43
Scunth'pe	46	16	11	19	75	80	43
Boston	46	18	7	21	93	112	43
Brad'd PA	46	16	10	20	105	103	42
Gainsb'ro'	46	17	8	21	82	98	42
Denaby	46	16	10	20	68	90	42
Frickley	46	14	13	19	70	81	41
Scarboro'	46	14	10	22	80	97	38
Mansfield	46	17	3	26	80	120	37
Goole	46	13	8	25	84	134	34
Brad'd C.	46	12	7	27	79	123	31
York C.	46	13	5	29	72	125	29
Halifax	46	8	6	32	56	154	22

Forest Reserves, and by recording another successful FA Cup run. Victories over Grays Athletic and Hitchin Town brought Aldershot to London Road.

Record crowd sees United make history

PETERBOROUGH 2, ALDERSHOT 1.

So this was the most important match in Peterborough United's history. It was worthy of the title; it was the best cup-tie seen at London Rd. since the epic replay with Corby Town last season. Better than the match with Torquay; better than the match with Bristol Rovers. And for the praise—a team, eleven men; as good a football machine as any non-league club would ever want or need to possess.

And so to Third Division Cardiff City in the 3rd Round.

As this newspaper report indicates, hopes were high for yet another Peterborough success. For player manager Jack Fairbrother, about to take up office at Coventry City, Ninian Park would prove to be an appropriate stage upon which to make a final appearance.

First a word about the losers. Surely, unless it is because of their weak finishing, they cannot languish much longer at the foot of the Third Division South if they can produce this form. It was freely suggested after the match that their football was little behind that of Bristol Rovers when they visited London Road last season (writes the sports editor).

Together with United, they produced a first-half which would have been a credit to any of the leading teams in the Third Divisions. Ken Moody, who has watched a good deal of Third North football this season, told me after the match that he was sure Aldershot would finish in the top half of the northern league table if they played in that competition instead of the Third Division South.

OPTIMISM WAS THE KEY-NOTE

At 9.12 this morning, cheered by a small but enthusiastic band of supporters, the hope and pride of the City set out from Peterborough North Station on the long journey to Cardiff—a journey which will make football history.

Perhaps some of those supporters remembered that day in 1928, when Peterborough and Fletton United set off for Birmingham in just the same way, with just the same hopes and fears—and gave Birmingham City the fright of their lives!

Be that as it may, optimism was the keynote expressed by the joking, cheerful team, and th beaming, jovial "Mr. Posh" — whos top hat, monocle and silver-knobbed stick looked somewhat incongruous against his light brown overcoat.

Before the kick off Mr Posh, sporting as always top hat, monocle, silver knobbed cane and spats, circumvented the ground no doubt causing great amusement and disbelief among Cardiff supporters. We locals, of course, were used to the antics of such unlikely mascots. Kettering had a bell waving friar - resplendent in red habit and grotesque tonsured wig; Corby favoured a kilted highlander with black and white sporran and Bedford, a huge Eagle.

The game was lost 3-1, but Peterborough had performed with courage and no little skill. With only nine minutes remaining and scores level at one each, pre-match worries over the threat posed by Cardiff international centre forward Trevor Ford were fully justified. His finely taken goal put the Welshmen ahead and a third, scored on the break as Peterborough pushed forward seeking an equaliser, put the result beyond doubt.

Mr Posh (Tom Keeble) introduces himself to the Ninian Park crowd.

Trevor Ford, Cardiff City

BUT FOR FORD PETERBORO' WOULD HAVE HAD A REPLAY

A subdued Jack Fairbrother summed it all up after THE match. He said, on hearing of the F.A. Cup-feats of other minor clubs: "Not one of these teams could have played better than we did today in defeat."

And but for one man, in my opinion, Peterborough United would be meeting Cardiff City at London Road next Thursday in the replay. International centre-forward Trevor Ford—in the same way as Joe Bradford at Birmingham 26 years ago—pulled the game out of the fire for Cardiff when it seemed that a football sensation was to be created.

THINK OF IT: Peterborough were never given a chance by any of the experts. "A different class" they said in assessing the chances. Thousands of supporters had cheerfully made the 380-mile return journey simply for the privilege of seeing "The Posh" take the field against a First Division side at Ninian Park—nothing more.

Yet there it was—nine minutes from the end with the scores level. How Cardiff had failed to take the lead early in the second half no one quite knew. But all that mattered was that a team of part-time professionals from the unfashionable Midland League were holding a side worth over £100,000 by today's transfer standards; a side led by one of the greatest centre-forwards in the world.

Trevor showed his class

Trevor Ford showed his class in shattering the hopes of the Northants. contingent just as they had begun to examine their watches every few seconds to discover how far from glory was their battling eleven.

Many claim he was off-side as at exactly 3.46 p.m. he waited a few yards from the foot of the far post to collect a high, hard Thomas centre. If he was off-side, it must only have been by a matter of feet.

Ford hit that Thomas centre on the half-volley, and the slippery ball rocketed into the near-side of the net, grazing the post as it went in.

It all looked so simple after Cardiff's feeble attempts in the previous 80 minutes, but the angle at which the shot was taken made it the goal of a master. And a master's touch was what was needed at that moment to pierce a heroic defence and end the stalemate.

The third goal was unfortunate, for it came as a result of Peterborough's all-out efforts to equalise in the closing stages.

It was a remarkable tribute to the United's efforts that the Cardiff defence was actually kicking-out after gaining the lead for the first time. As the ball sailed several times into the touchline stand, there were jeers from many of the Welsh supporters, who, admiring Peterborough's pluck, were eager to see the non-League side earn a replay.

Fairbrother was succeeded by yet another goalkeeper, Arsenal's George Swindin. The event was duly recorded in Charles Buchan's Football Monthly 'Transfer Trail' feature.

Fairbrother to Coventry City - Swindin to Peterborough

SWINDIN

February 3: John Walton, Bury inside forward to Burnley. George Swindin, Arsenal goalkeeper to Peterborough Utd as player manager - no fee.

John Walton would eventually play for the Poppies, while fans of television's 'Lovejoy' programme might be surprised to learn that the actor Ian McShane's father was the same Harry McShane, transferred nine days later from Manchester United to Oldham Athletic.

February 12:Harry McShane, Manchester Utd. winger, to Oldham Ath.

Centre forward Taft scored 42 league goals and 3 in the cup to become Peterborough's most prolific scorer to date.

The Peterborough side that met Cardiff City at Ninian Park

Back Row: Hall, Matthews, Fairbrother, Rigby, Moody, Anderson.
Front Row: Campbell, Martin, Taft, Sloan, Hair.

Corby Town meanwhile were unable to repeat their league success of the previous year but managed a commendable 4th place, Fred Slater scoring 41 goals.

The Corby side included the two Harrisons, Walter and Jim, who although unrelated, had played together in Leicester's cup final team against Wolves in 1949.

Jim Harrison

Walter Harrison - a grand attacking half back who won a Cup Final medal with Leicester City in 1949 and won England 'B' caps against Holland and Finland.

Northampton winger Jack English topped the 3rd Division South goalscorers with 21 goals but, finishing in 5th place, the club lost ambitious manager Dennison to Second Division Middlesbrough.

There was little to cheer elsewhere. Kettering earned an FA Cup trip to Leyton Orient.

Season 1953-4					55th Season	
LEAGUE-DIVISION III (SOUTH)						
	Played	Won	Drawn	Lost	Goals	Points
1 Ipswich Town	46	27	10	9	82-51	64
2 Brighton and Hove Albion	46	26	9	11	86-61	61
3 Bristol City	46	25	6	15	88-66	56
4 Watford	46	21	10	15	85-69	52
5 Northampton Town	46	20	11	15	82-55	51
6 Southampton	46	22	7	17	76-63	51
7 Norwich City	46	20	11	15	73-66	51
8 Reading	46	20	9	17	86-73	49
9 Exeter City	46	20	8	18	68-58	48
10 Gillingham	46	19	10	17	61-66	48
11 Leyton Orient	46	18	11	17	79-73	47
12 Millwall	46	19	9	18	74-77	47
13 Torquay United	46	17	12	17	81-88	46
14 Coventry City	46	18	9	19	61-56	45
15 Newport County	46	19	6	21	61-81	44
16 Southend United	46	18	7	21	69-71	43
17 Aldershot	46	17	9	20	74-86	43
18 Queen's Park Rangers	46	16	10	20	60-68	42
19 {Bournemouth and Boscombe Athletic	46	16	8	22	67-70	40
{Swindon Town	46	15	10	21	67-70	40
21 Shrewsbury Town	46	14	12	20	65-76	40
22 Crystal Palace	46	14	12	20	60-86	40
23 Colchester United	46	10	10	26	50-78	30
24 Walsall	46	9	8	29	40-87	26
Ipswich Town promoted to Division II.						

losing 3-0 before a crowd of 15,000. Centre forward Ernie Middlemiss has vivid memories of the game. Having collided painfully with the Orient goalkeeper shortly before half time he climbed, fully dressed, into an empty bath at the interval, obviously suffering from concussion. Trainer Alf Mansfield lifted him out, dowsed his head with a cold, wet sponge, and sent him out for the second half. Still no substitutes in those days!

A fortnight later, plagued by blinding headaches and double vision, Ernie finally took himself to the doctors for treatment.

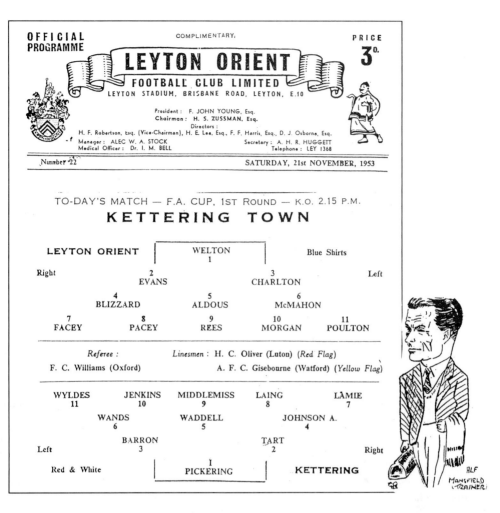

OFFICIAL PROGRAMME

COMPLIMENTARY,

PRICE 3ᴰ.

LEYTON ORIENT
FOOTBALL CLUB LIMITED
LEYTON STADIUM, BRISBANE ROAD, LEYTON, E.10

President : F. JOHN YOUNG, Esq.
Chairman : H. S. ZUSSMAN, Esq.
Directors :
H. F. Robertson, Esq. (Vice-Chairman), H. E. Lea, Esq., F. F. Harris, Esq., D. J. Osborne, Esq.
Manager : ALEC W. A. STOCK   Secretary : A. H. R. HUGGETT
Medical Officer : Dr. I. M. BELL   Telephone : LEY 1368

Number 22   SATURDAY, 21st NOVEMBER, 1953

TO-DAY'S MATCH — F.A. CUP, 1ST ROUND — K.O. 2.15 P.M.

KETTERING TOWN

LEYTON ORIENT

WELTON
1

Blue Shirts

Right

2
EVANS

3
CHARLTON

Left

4
BLIZZARD

5
ALDOUS

6
McMAHON

7
FACEY

8
PACEY

9
REES

10
MORGAN

11
POULTON

Referee :
F. C. Williams (Oxford)

Linesmen : H. C. Oliver (Luton) (Red Flag)
A. F. C. Gisebourne (Watford) (Yellow Flag)

WYLDES
11

JENKINS
10

MIDDLEMISS
9

LAING
8

LAMIE
7

WANDS
6

WADDELL
5

JOHNSON A.
4

Left

BARRON
3

TART
2

Right

Red & White

PICKERING
I

KETTERING

ALF
MANSFIELD
(TRAINER)

In the United Counties League British Timken emerged as the County's most successful side. Peterborough Reserves were the best of the rest while Rothwell Town lifted the second Division Title for the second successive season.

1953-54 Division 1	P.	W.	D.	L.	F.	A.	Pts
March Town United	38	26	6	6	108	35	58
Holbeach United	38	25	5	8	100	39	55
Spalding United	38	21	8	9	92	55	50
B. Timken Duston	38	20	8	10	72	46	48
Peterborough Utd. Res	38	20	8	10	85	63	48
Symingtons	38	19	9	10	96	78	47
Kettering Res.	38	16	10	12	106	83	42
Corby Res.	38	15	10	13	65	59	40
Rushden Town	38	17	5	16	75	78	39
Wisbech Res.	38	16	6	16	61	84	38
Coventry City 'A'	38	14	8	16	72	67	36
Stamford	38	14	8	16	84	89	36
St Neots Town	38	14	7	17	74	94	35
Bedford Res.	38	13	5	20	72	63	31
Desborough Town	38	11	9	18	65	85	31
Boston United Res.	38	13	4	21	82	105	30
Biggleswade Town	38	11	7	20	56	83	29
Northampton Town 'A'	38	8	10	20	57	80	26
Wellingborough Town	38	10	4	24	48	109	24
Bourne Town	38	6	5	27	59	127	17

65

1953-54 Division 2	P.	W.	D.	L.	F.	A.	Pts
Rothwell Town	28	18	5	5	96	46	41
B. Timken Duston Res.	28	18	3	7	83	41	39
Rushden Res.	28	15	5	8	70	48	35
Finedon Town	28	15	4	9	76	50	34
St Neots Res.	28	12	7	9	67	68	31
Wellingborough Res.	28	11	8	9	68	56	30
Eynesbury Res.	28	14	2	12	57	72	30
Warboys Town	28	11	4	13	50	57	26
Kempston Rovers	28	10	6	12	67	92	26
Desborough Res.	28	11	3	14	52	64	25
Bedford Avenue	28	9	7	12	49	63	25
Raunds Town	28	9	4	15	63	75	22
Symingtons Res.	28	7	5	16	67	86	19
Huntingdon United	28	6	7	15	59	78	19
Higham Town	28	8	2	18	69	104	18

Rothwell Proud Champions

IT was a proud day for Rothwell Town when they made certain of the U.C.L. Div. 2 championship after a resounding victory over their visitors, Huntingdon.

The "Bones" fielded the team which has kept them top of the league since October 11 but the visitors had seven changes due to injuries.

The visitors put up a stubborn defence but their attack finished badly.

Rothwell kept up their attack to make the final score 8—0.

Strathle, who played with a sprained ankle, found it hard going, but he never once let the side down.

Amongst the Northampton A team listed for their UCL game against Desborough on 17 November 1953 are several players due to feature more prominently later. Ray Yeoman, John Draper, Joe Payne, Gordon Burn and young Welsh forward, Ken Leek.

> Desborough Town
> Nimmo
> Patrick   Wyldes
> Keep   McStay   Steed
> Garefield Draper Deane Parker Wollacott
>
> Jones B   Burn   Doherty   Leek   Kilgannon
> Jones J   Eaves   Yeoman
> Wilson   Payne
> Draper
> Northampton A

During the summer the World Cup Championships were held in Switzerland.

The WORLD Cup
1954 CHAMPIONS 1954
—GERMANY
RUNNERS UP - HUNGARY

Although Hungary had defeated England 7-1 in that eagerly awaited return fixture in Budapest, they failed to win the World Cup, losing 3-2 to West Germany in the final. England were eliminated in the quarter finals by former champions Uruguay, 7-0 victors over Scotland in the qualifying section.

THAT MAN LAWTON AGAIN
1954-56

There are tangled threads that weave inexorably through our lives, constantly linking people, places and events. So it was that our new entry-sharing neighbour was the same Cec Campbell who had played right back for Kettering in that far off, fateful cup tie against Peterborough in 1947. Apart from the occasional defection to Filbert Street, Leicester, many Saturday afternoons in the fifties were spent on the terrace at Rockingham Road. There were worse places to be.

Jesse Pye

On leaving league football, many former stars continued to ply their trade in the lower divisions. There were no lucrative contracts as pundits on Sky television, no £2,000 cheques for opening Tesco supermarkets. They played on, giving delighted non-league crowds a belated opportunity to witness famous, albeit somewhat superannuated, performers.

Opposing sides at Kettering occasionally included former internationals such as Jimmy Logie and Lionel Smith (Gravesend October 8th 1955), Paddy Sloan (Bath City September 1st 1956), Jessie Pye and Bobby Langton (Wisbech April 19th 1958), Roy Paul (Worcester September 27th 1958), Stan Mortenson and Charlie Fleming (Bath City March 7th 1959).

Most players, however, combined their football with the rigours of full-time employment. It is difficult to appreciate the demands made upon the typical part-timer during this period. Ernie Middlemiss recalls the problems of accommodating night shift work at Corby Steelworks with, 'the more important business' of playing football for Kettering Town in the Southern League. After completing an eight hour stint in the tubeworks he was collected by Chairman Pascoe's limousine from the checkout at seven o'clock on Saturday morning and rushed to join the team coach at Rockingham Road for the arduous trip to Weymouth. A fitful sleep was then snatched under blankets on the backseat during the long journey. Arriving home after the match in the early hours, stiff and exhausted, there was no prospect of a lie-in that morning. The Sunday shift meant doubletime, and anyway, 'you couldn't let the rest of the gang down by not turning up'. At half past six, he mounted his bike and urged aching legs to pedal the mile or so to work.

During the summer of 1954 concrete terracing behind the Cowper Street goal brought a sad end to our tennis ball matches on the asphalt.

Disappointment was shared by Poppies supporters as the team could only achieve a lowly fifteenth league position and suffered FA Cup elimination, 5-1 by celebrated Northern amateurs, Bishop Auckland.

Corby's fortunes slumped too, and only a first ever meeting with Football League opposition in the FA Cup salvaged a poor campaign.

A brave performance before a home crowd of 6,763 could not prevent Watford recording a 2-0 success.

At Northampton, new manager Dave Smith suffered a frustrating season, his side finishing appropriately in thirteenth place. Two fixtures, highlighted by Frank Grande, in his 'History of the Cobblers', vividly demonstrate the different problems guaranteed to have managers reaching for the Valium. In an FA Cup match at home to Coventry, Cobbler's goalkeeper Alf Wood raced out to collect a 70 yard clearance, slipped, and allowed the ball to trickle over the line for the only goal of the game. To add further injustice, Staroscik missed a penalty, squandering the chance of an equaliser.

Season 1954-5						56th Season
LEAGUE – DIVISION III (SOUTH)						
	Played	Won	Drawn	Lost	Goals	Points
1 Bristol City	46	30	10	6	101–47	70
2 Leyton Orient	46	26	9	11	89–47	61
3 Southampton	46	24	11	11	75–51	59
4 Gillingham	46	20	15	11	77–66	55
5 Millwall	46	20	11	15	72–68	51
6 Brighton and Hove Albion	46	20	10	16	76–63	50
7 Watford	46	18	14	14	71–62	50
8 Torquay United	46	18	12	16	82–82	48
9 Coventry City	46	18	!1	17	67–59	47
10 Southend United	46	17	12	17	83–80	46
11 Brentford	46	16	14	16	82–82	46
11 Norwich City	46	18	10	18	60–60	46
13 Northampton Town	46	19	8	19	73–81	46
14 Aldershot	46	16	10	20	75–71	45
15 Queen's Park Rangers	46	15	14	17	69–75	44
16 Shrewsbury Town	46	16	10	20	70–78	42
17 Bournemouth and Boscombe Athletic	46	12	18	16	57–65	42
18 Reading	46	13	15	18	65–73	41
19 Newport County	46	11	16	19	60–73	38
20 Crystal Palace	46	11	16	19	52–80	38
21 Swindon Town	46	11	15	20	46–64	37
22 Exeter City	46	11	15	20	47–73	37
23 Walsall	46	10	14	22	75–86	34
24 Colchester United	46	9	13	24	53–91	31
Bristol City promoted to Division II.						

The second game was against Leyton Orient on January 29th 1955. At half-time, after being booked for kicking the ball away from between the legs of East London idol Vic Groves, full back Ron Patterson was attacked by a home supporter. His injuries prevented him resuming in the second half joining Don Adams (eye wound) and Jack English (broken collar bone) on the casualty list.

Northampton asked the FA to replay the match, but the London club escaped with a warning.

Individual honours were achieved by Gwyn Hughes, chosen to represent the Third Division South against the North, and Tommy McClain picked for the Football Combination XI against a Dutch side.

On March 21st 1955, AJ Darnell, a founder member and the club's first president died at the age of 90.

Continuing loss of revenue rendered the financial situation so serious it prompted the decision to revert the entire playing staff, except Tommy Fowler, to part-time for the new season.

In the United Counties League, British Timken again achieved the County's leading position, finishing runners up to Spalding United.

1954-55 Division 1	P.	W.	D.	L.	F.	A.	Pts.
Spalding United	27	21	2	4	78	28	44
B. Timken Duston	27	16	3	8	82	40	35
Holbeach United	28	13	8	7	69	43	34
Rushden Town	28	15	1	12	61	67	31
Kettering Res.	28	13	3	12	73	67	29
Biggleswade Town	28	14	1	13	64	68	29
Stamford	28	13	3	12	74	83	29
Wellingborough Town	28	11	6	11	62	64	28
Kings Lynn Res.	28	10	7	11	70	67	27
Wisbech Res.	28	11	5	12	66	81	27
St Neots Town	28	10	5	13	56	64	25
Corby Res.	28	9	6	13	50	66	24
Bedford Res.	28	9	4	15	55	53	22
Bourne Town	28	8	6	14	54	69	22
Desborough Town	28	4	3	20	38	52	12
Programme not completed							

The Timken side, listed below for their successful Senior Cup Final against Peterborough United, contained several familiar names, including the Corby duo Wands and Middlemiss.

Northants Sen. Cup—FINAL

Saturday, 12th March at 3.15

Referee—D. HACKERS. Northampton.

PETERBOROUGH UNITED
Colours—Blue Shirts. White Knickers

RIGHT

LEFT

1
BICKERSTAFFE

2
SENIOR

3
STAFFORD, G.

4
WILLIAMS

5
T. G. BASS

6
BUTLER

7
MARTIN

8
McNAMEE

9
BULL

10
EMERY

11
REYNOLDS

11
DONALDSON

10
HUGHES

9
MIDDLEMISS

8
McKAY

7
SQUIRES

6
WANDS

5
CLARKE

4
SCOTT

3
BARRON

2
CRAIG

1
ROWLEY

LEFT

RIGHT

BRITISH TIMKEN
Colours—Yellow and Black Black Knickers

Linesmen—W. G. Soames. W. Morris

On the same summer's day in 1954, two of Swindin's close season signings joined the club. Ellis Stafford from Sheffield Junior football and Denis Emery of lowly Eynesbury Rovers. Ellis was to serve the club in various capacities for over 30 years, while many regard Denis Emery as the finest player ever to wear a Peterborough shirt. Although they were to enjoy remarkable success over the next half dozen years the 1954-55 season was comparitively lean.

Peterborough had suffered a rare cup calamity, losing 2-1 at home to Boston United in the qualifying round. Application for league status was once again submitted and, as the programme notes of March 12th indicate, hopes were high.

The lavish preparations were in vain, however and the club continued in the Midland League.

In 1955-56, unprecedented success came to George Swindin's team which won the Midland League for the first time and defeated Alf Ramsey's Ipswich Town in the FA Cup.

Peterborough United 1955-56 - Champions of the Midland League for the first time.

(Back) Anderson (Trainer), Shaw, Clarke, Lowery, Rigby, Killin, Farrow, Swindin (Manager)
(Front) Hails, Emery, Donaldson, Gibson, Hair.

Although defeat followed in the next round at home to Swindon, the game against Ipswich helped reinforce the new Midland League champions perennial application for League status.

UNITED'S GREAT DAY

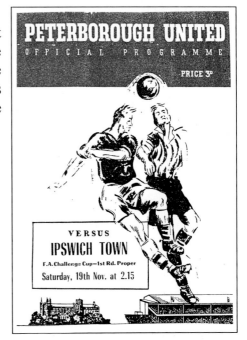

PETERBOROUGH UNITED
OFFICIAL PROGRAMME
PRICE 3ᴰ

VERSUS
IPSWICH TOWN
F.A. Challenge Cup—1st Rd. Proper
Saturday, 19th Nov. at 2.15

IT WAS A GREAT DAY FOR PETERBOROUGH—THEY ARE NOT MY WORDS, THEY BELONG TO MANAGER GEORGE SWINDIN, WHO SPOKE THEM JUBILANTLY AFTER SATURDAY'S MATCH.

And it was a great day. For most of the game Peterborough ran Ipswich Town, one of the glamour teams of the Third Division, off their feet . . . and the whole country knew of their great triumph.

On radio, Charlie Buchan, one of the all time greats of football, said: "A great performance . . . pick of the day's wins. Surely this must be a great argument in favour of them getting into the League."

On TV, Cliff Michelmore said: "A fine win and a great day for Peterborough."

Commenting after the TV film, Kenneth Wolstenholme said: "It must strengthen their claims for League football."

And so it went on, all over the country the great deed of little Peterborough was acclaimed . . . except maybe in Ipswich. But even there no one could say that the best team did not win.

Even a disheartened Alf Ramsey, manager of Ipswich, said: "Peterborough played the better football, there was no luck in it. My boys did not get moving and on the day's showing the best team win."

RESULT

PETERBORO'   3
(Emery 2, Hair 1)

IPSWICH TN.   1
(Parker)

Attendance: 20,671
Receipts: £2,127

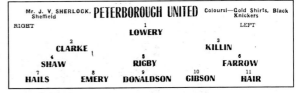

Mr. J. V. SHERLOCK, Sheffield   PETERBOROUGH UNITED   Coloursi—Gold Shirts, Black Knickers

RIGHT
1
LOWERY
LEFT

2
CLARKE
3
KILLIN

4
SHAW
5
RIGBY
6
FARROW

7
HAILS
8
EMERY
9
DONALDSON
10
GIBSON
11
HAIR

McLUCKIE   PARKER   GARNEYS'BLACKMAN   GRANT   REED
11   10   9   8   7

ELSWORTHY   REES   MYLES
6   5   4

MALCOLM   ACRES
3   2

McMILLAN
1

LEFT   RIGHT

Linesmen—Mr. C. H. Pegg,   IPSWICH TOWN   Colours—Black and White
Mr. R. G. Rudd   Hoops. White Knickers

71

However, Football League clubs closed ranks and the Posh were once again denied.

Northampton reached the FA Cup Third round after beating first Millwall and then non-league Hastings United. 'Special preparations' were the only departure from the usual pre-match build up for the visit of Second Division Blackburn in January 1956.

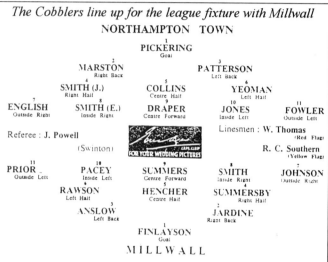

The Cobblers line up for the league fixture with Millwall

NORTHAMPTON TOWN

1
PICKERING
Goal

2   3
MARSTON   PATTERSON
Right Back   Left Back

4   5   6
SMITH (J.)   COLLINS   YEOMAN
Right Half   Centre Half   Left Half

7   8   9   10   11
ENGLISH   SMITH (E.)   DRAPER   JONES   FOWLER
Outside Right   Inside Right   Centre Forward   Inside Left   Outside Left

Referee : J. Powell   Linesmen : W. Thomas
(Swinton)   (Red Flag)

R. C. Southern
(Yellow Flag)

11   10   9   8   7
PRIOR   PACEY   SUMMERS   SMITH   JOHNSON
Outside Left   Inside Left   Centre Forward   Inside Right   Outside Right

6   5   4
RAWSON   HENCHER   SUMMERSBY
Left Half   Centre Half   Right Half

3   2
ANSLOW   JARDINE
Left Back   Right Back

1
FINLAYSON
Goal

MILLWALL

Brine baths were only special preparation

Northampton Town's only special training for Saturday's Cup-tie with Blackburn Rovers was done last night when the players visited the Northampton public baths to have brine baths.

Otherwise the ten part-timers will carry on as usual with training sessions tonight and Thursday night and the regular weekly practice match tomorrow morning.

As manager David Smith says, "If there was any extra way I could make the team win, I would do it in league matches. We always go out to do our best and so far that has not been too bad."

Peter Pickering

Northampton lost 2-1, although few of the crowd could enjoy a game played throughout in swirling fog. The Cobblers goalkeeper was the same Peter Pickering, who had performed with such distinction for Kettering in that memorable 1952 Maunsell Cup Final.

Northampton Town's league position of 11th was a slight improvement on the previous season.

Corby Town's youth policy began to bear fruit with the elevation to the senior side of several young players, including full back Len Chalmers and winger Andy McCabe. Both were signed by league clubs during the season. McCabe joined Chesterfield and Chalmers Leicester City, for whom he later appeared in a tragic role during the Cup Final against Tottenham in 1961.

The Steelmen's league position, however, disappointed once again.

Kettering, too, were in the Southern League doldrums until the famous Tommy Lawton joined the club from Arsenal in February 1956. Although no longer England's most valuable player, Lawton was still a household name.

The signing achieved national prominence, taking place on BBC television's popular 'Sportsview' programme.

Season 1955-6					57th Season	
LEAGUE – DIVISION III (SOUTH)						
	Played	Won	Drawn	Lost	Goals	Points
1 Leyton Orient	46	29	8	9	106–49	66
2 Brighton and Hove Albion	46	29	7	10	112–50	65
3 Ipswich Town	46	25	14	7	106–60	64
4 Southend United	46	21	11	14	88–80	53
5 Torquay United	46	20	12	14	86–63	52
6 Brentford	46	19	14	13	69–66	52
7 Norwich City	46	19	13	14	86–82	51
8 Coventry City	46	20	9	17	73–60	49
9 Bournemouth and Boscombe Athletic	46	19	10	17	63–51	48
10 Gillingham	46	19	10	17	69–71	48
11 Northampton Town	46	20	7	19	67–71	47
12 Colchester United	46	18	11	17	76–81	47
13 Shrewsbury Town	46	17	12	17	69–66	46
14 Southampton	46	18	8	20	91–81	44
15 Aldershot	46	12	16	18	70–90	40
16 Exeter City	46	15	10	21	58–77	40
17 Reading	46	15	9	22	70–79	39
18 Queen's Park Rangers	46	14	11	21	64–86	39
19 Newport County	46	15	9	22	58–79	39
20 Walsall	46	15	8	23	68–84	38
21 Watford	46	13	11	22	52–85	37
22 Millwall	46	15	6	25	83–100	36
23 Crystal Palace	46	12	10	24	54–83	34
24 Swindon Town	46	8	14	24	34–78	30
Leyton Orient promoted to Division II.						

RUSHDEN ASSOCIATION FOOTBALL
=====SUPPORTERS' CLUB=====

RUSHDEN TOWN v.

Corby Town Res.

RUSHDEN TOWN

Right Wing   Left Wing

1
Garner

2   3
Gibbs   Stanway

4   5   6
De Banke   Meakin   Summers

7   8   9   10   11
Solowiew   Roberts   Henley   Laxton   Head

11   10   9   8   7
McCabe or Kirk   Garvey   Dicken   Fulton   Clark

6   5   4
McLachlan   Chalmers   Baird

3   2
Young   Poole

1
McGraw

Left Wing   Right Wing

CORBY TOWN RES.

Referee: Mr. D. R. Wildman, Kettering

Player-manager offer is made

TOMMY LAWTON, the 36-year-old Arsenal and former England centre-forward, had a talk with Poppies' directors "behind closed doors" in a Kettering hotel today, when he was offered the player-manager's job.

The ex-international is considering the offer.

The Kettering directors announced this morning that Arsenal had given them permission to approach Lawton.

TV MILLIONS WILL WATCH LAWTON SIGN FOR POPPIES

Kettering vice - chairman, Ald. R. W. Tailby, and secretary Mr. Frank Summerly travel up to London on the 4.20 train this afternoon to complete the deal.

TOMMY LAWTON will become Kettering Town's player-manager between 8.0 and 8.30 this evening. He is expected to sign in the B.B.C. television programme "Sportsview"

Tommy Lawton signs for the Poppies - February 2nd 1956. This picture taken from a TV screen in Kettering shows Frank Summerly (KT Secretary), Reg Tailby (Director), Tommy Lawton and David Coleman (BBC Sportsview).

As contemporary reports indicate however, the decision to purchase the great man was not without controversy, leading to the resignation of both director W Miller and manager Bob Calder.

Poppies' director resigns

KNEW NOTHING OF LAWTON MEETING

LATEST development at Kettering following yesterday's meeting of the club directors with Tommy Lawton to offer him the job of Poppies' player-manager, has been the resignation of director Mr. W. Miller.

Mr. Miller, a director club since it became a lim company in 1950, told the "Friar" today: "You can say my resignation is in the post.

"I knew nothing of yesterday's meeting with Lawton until I read about it in the newspapers.

"I am alarmed that such a serious step should have been taken without the full board being in attendance. Absolutely no regard has been paid to manager Bob Calder's feelings and I object very strongly to the fact that the manager should have learnt from the Press about the offer made to Lawton."

Lawton's debut was against Yeovil and, as the supporters' club programme notes wisely anticipate, improvement would require both time and patience.

Yeovil returned to Somerset 2-1 winners, but by the time another West Country side, Exeter City Reserves, visited Rockingham Road in late April, the tide had begun to turn and supporters could look forward to the new season with justifiable optimism.

The side against Exeter included the nucleus of the team that would begin the 1956-57 season. Young Jim Standen, on loan from Arsenal, was to find

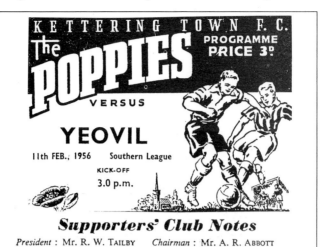

KETTERING TOWN F.C.

The **POPPIES**

PROGRAMME PRICE 3ᴰ

VERSUS

YEOVIL

11th FEB., 1956   Southern League

KICK-OFF

3.0 p.m.

Supporters' Club Notes

President : Mr. R. W. TAILBY   Chairman : Mr. A. R. ABBOTT
Treasurer : Mr. H. AMEY,   Secretary : Mr. G. SMITH,
24 Albert Street, Kettering   42 Naseby Road, Kettering

First of all a short letter to Mr. Tommy Lawton.

"On behalf of all supporters and the members of my committee, I would like to welcome you to Kettering Town F.C. as player-manager. May I wish you luck and a very successful term of office.—Signed, A. R. ABBOTT (chairman)."

What a terrific last fortnight it has been. I think everyone in England knows that there is a football club in Kettering. It surely is the greatest publicity the club has ever received in its history. More tonight when we see part of this game on television. All this publicity goes to show what a great player and well-liked personality we have in our player-manager. He has a great task in front of him, of putting Kettering back on the football map. It will be a hard one, but with your wholehearted support his task will be considerably lightened. We cannot, and must not, expect complete success straightaway : we must be patient and give Tommy a chance to "settle in." I am sure that his great knowledge of the game, and his splendid personality, will bear fruit in the near future.

fame in later years as goalkeeper in West Ham's European Cup Winners Cup team and a useful seam bowler for Worcestershire.

SOUTHERN LEAGUE.

POPPIES DRAW

WITH eleven wins out of twelve to their credit since March 10, the Poppies got a shock today. Without Lawton they were losing 4—1 to Exeter Res. at the interval.

Kettering—minus player-manager Tommy Lawton with damaged foot—were hoping to gain their twelfth win in their last 13 games.

Exeter made a number of changes before the start.

Kettering: Standen; McDonald, Jackson; Canning, Shearer, Taft; Goodwin, Prosser, Toseland, Thomas, Robinson.

A Goodwin corner fell beautifully and CANNING bustled Lobbett over the line to equalise.

Result: Kettering 4, Exeter Res. 4.

Attendance 2,918.

The reserve side also enjoyed end of season success by winning a sadly devalued UCL First Division, comprising just nine teams, from runners up Rushden Town.

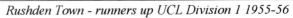

1955-56 Division 1	P.	W.	D.	L.	F.	A.	Pts
Kettering Res.	16	13	1	2	44	20	27
Rushden Town	16	9	2	5	50	29	20
B. Timken Duston	16	8	4	4	39	23	20
Wellingborough Town	16	6	5	5	37	33	17
Corby Res.	16	6	5	5	29	29	17
St Neots Town	16	8	1	7	29	30	17
Rothwell Town	16	6	4	6	36	38	16
Bourne Town	16	2	4	10	25	34	8
Desborough Town	16	1	0	15	18	73	2

Rushden Town - runners up UCL Division 1 1955-56

Back Row: Laxton, Stanway, Holmes, Summers, DeBanke, Mabelson
Front Row: Solowiew, Gibbs, Henley, Duckhouse, England.

CHAMPIONS
AND
GIANT KILLERS
1956-57

After two years of enforced inaction, scrounging occasional games for such unlikely sides as Little Bowden Albion and Kettering Scouts United, I joined a group of enthusiasts, chiefly fellow dissident Grammar school boys and old Junior school friends, to form a new team. Aided by the obligatory adult secretary, genial and compliant Bill Draper, we entered Kettering Youth United in the local under 16 league for the 1956-57 season.

The first year coincided with Kettering Town's most successful post-war campaign to date. Fortunately the Youth League had comparatively few fixtures and we were able to follow Lawton's team in many of its more memorable matches.

The season opened with an away draw at Merthyr.

In the manager's programme notes for the first home match of the season against Hereford, Lawton introduced his new signings, both on and off the field, and spelled out his managerial philosophy.

Star new signing Amos Moss had played at Kettering for Aston Villa in the 1953 Frank Summerly testimonial game,

First of all a big welcome to our new players who will, once you get to know them, be popular with you. John Wheeler from Huddersfield Town, Amos Moss from Aston Villa, Len Geard from Brentford,John Baxter from Desborough, John Storey from Corby, Tom Savage from Enfield and local boys Steve Squires and Brian Reynolds, who will report the first week in September from cricket duty. Not forgetting too, all our young amateurs who will, I hope one day, be some of the big names in football.

We have had a bit of a sort out since last we met. Alf Mansfield will take over duties of first team trainer, Ken Burton, second team trainer with Dave Cairns second team manager and Jock Watson in charge of our lads in the third team...... we shall have conferences each week and study reports on the whys and wherefores of matches and what we can do to improve our club. This team will work together and they will not be just 'yes' men. Only by a great team spirit right through the club can we hope for success and that means the Chairman and Directors right down to the youngest amateur. Our Supporters Club which has done such a magnificent job for so many years, will I hope, continue on the lines they have set themselves.

Well the stage is set. All the players are fit. What we need now are good results. but don't expect miracles, football is a funny game.

Tommy Lawton

while new goalkeeper Jack Wheeler was understudy to the great Harry Hibbs at Birmingham City before joining Huddersfield Town in 1948.

Less auspicious names amongst the team were local players, inside forward Geoff Toseland, full back John Storey and wing half Harry Johnson. (The latter would enjoy a remarkable run of 42 Southern League games before inexplicably disappearing from the first team scene early the following season).

Geoff Toseland

Jack Wheeler

Geoff Toseland
Kettering born Geoff started football with Avondale Colts. He moved on to play for Geddington and Rothwell, where he was spotted and signed on as a professional with Sunderland. He spent four seasons at Roker Park, making six first team appearances.

Jack Wheeler, Kettering's goalkeeper 1956-57, who left with Lawton for Notts County at the end of the season. He did not miss a game as trainer between 1957-83.

Shortly after the start of the season Norman Plummer, a cup finalist with Leicester City in 1949, became the side's regular centre half.

By September 22nd Kettering were sitting on top of the league and hopes were high for a prestigious FA Cup run as we travelled to Spalding for a First Qualifying Round match.

Tulips gamble against the Poppies

TOMMY LAWTON will be opposed by a 19-year-old centre half, Ralph Robinson, when the Poppies travel to Spalding on Saturday for an F.A. Cup match.

I had been to Spalding before. A perennial 'treat' during my Holly Road days was the Sunday evening mystery coach trip. For one ever prone to incipient travel sickness the whole experience was purgatory. Once Stamford, with its narrow streets and sharp bends, was negotiated not even the promise of a pub stop for American Cream Soda and

SPALDING U.F.C.
OFFICIAL PROGRAMME

Season 1956-57   No. 6
Sat. Sept. 22nd, 1956
(F.A. CUP)
SPALDING
UNITED
v
KETTERING
TOWN

3D

crisps could compensate for the inevitability of our ultimate destination. The ever receding horizon confirmed expectations. Market Deeping, a widening sky, drainage ditches, the occasional windmill, the rich dark soil. Then, to almost universal excitement, the first tulip field, and then the second, and the eighth, and the seventeenth .... Yes I'd been to Spalding before!

Disappointment at the 3-2 defeat was short-lived as league results continued to impress.

Spalding crush Poppies' hopes

Spalding United 3, Kettering Town 2

Victory at Bedford was followed on October 13th by a remarkable 6-4 win over Chelmsford. Lawton scored four times, three with his head.

BEST summing up of this shock defeat that saw Kettering's F.A. Cup hopes crash at the first fence at Spalding on Saturday, came from Amos Moss, skipper of the beaten side. He told reporters after the match: "Spalding deserved to win. We played below standard."

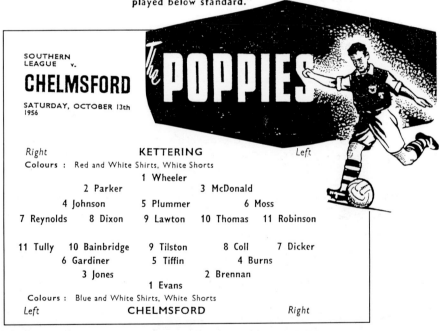

SOUTHERN LEAGUE v.

CHELMSFORD

SATURDAY, OCTOBER 13th 1956

Right   **KETTERING**   *Left*

Colours : Red and White Shirts, White Shorts

1 Wheeler

2 Parker   3 McDonald

4 Johnson   5 Plummer   6 Moss

7 Reynolds   8 Dixon   9 Lawton   10 Thomas   11 Robinson

11 Tully   10 Bainbridge   9 Tilston   8 Coll   7 Dicker

6 Gardiner   5 Tiffin   4 Burns

3 Jones   2 Brennan

1 Evans

Colours : Blue and White Shirts, White Shorts

Left   **CHELMSFORD**   *Right*

Poppies' victory was entirely due to Lawton

KETTERING TOWN 6   CHELMSFORD 4

PHEW! That was one's first reaction at the end of this truly extraordinary Southern League match at Rockingham Road on Saturday, in which the scoring see-sawed. Tommy Lawton, in front of a special group of friends, up for his son's christening yesterday, can claim the credit for the win.

Several of the Kettering team happened to strike a patch of bad form together. The defence, who the previous week had saved the day at Bedford, seemed doomed to fritter away the lead whenever it was in Kettering hands. Something had to be done, and Lawton chose the right match to pull something out of the bag, in the way that only the few really great footballers can.

Four goals was his reward, the last three with his head, and he laid on the fifth, and prompted one spectator who had not seen him for seven years to say he was still as good in the air as ever.

79

The Style and Success of Tommy Lawton

Extracts reprinted from an article in the 'Empire News and Chronicle', October 1956

CONFIDENT LAWTON LOOKS AHEAD

By DOUGLAS IBBOTSON

SUCCESS has come suddenly to Kettering Town. Just six months ago player-manager Tommy Lawton came and planted his ideas at Rockingham Road. Today the club are virtually at the top of the Southern League beanstalk.

THE season that was to take Tommy Lawton to the top rung of the ladder began inconspicuously with a 1—1 draw. At once Kettering Town's manager found himself facing a critical problem.

John Shearer, his Scottish centre-half, inadvertently caused it. Because of family commitments the competent Shearer had not done a full stint of pre-season training.

"I tackled him about it and he told me the story," said Lawton. "I sympathised with him, but I had no alternative but to drop John, who had been one of the key men in last season's revival.

"I signed Norman Plummer, the old Leicester City centre-half, whom I knew from my playing days. He, I was confident, would play the type of game I wanted." Note that Lawton, even in a crisis, still insisted on finding the man to fit the style.

"I put Shearer in the third team. He didn't like this. I told him that it would be most unfair to drop out of the reserves an 18-year-old lad who was doing extremely well.

"*Finally Shearer agreed that I had been fair to everybody. He did a magnificent job looking after the youngsters in the 'A' side.*"

The incident illustrates the second principle in Lawton's creed as a manager. One follows from the other: Sign only the players who fit into your established style, and insist that you have a staff who will drill home that style at all levels in the club.

STERN but FAIR

NOW the old England centre-forward showed his players that he is both stern and fair as a manager. Lawton lays great stress on the combination of these two qualities, which are not found in every manager.

"Discipline is the only weapon which a manager can use," he explains. "One disgruntled or unhappy player is like a bad apple in a barrel. In no time at all the rest will be contaminated.

"That's why it's so important to be fair as well as stern. Through no fault of his own, John Shearer might have become an unhappy player. But he didn't—and he is doing magnificently."

Tommy Lawton
Centre-forward

Bob Thomas
Inside-left

—the plan which brought success to struggling Kettering Town, which took them from the bottom of the Southern League to a nine-point lead at the top. The plan which has brought success—with three capital S's.

—AND IT ALL ADDS UP TO SUCCESS

Norman Plummer
He plays the right type of game

Jack Wheeler
He keeps the right sort of goal!

Ray Parker
Right-back

Harry McDonald
Left-back

Harry Johnson
Right-half

He picks good men who fit his style

Amos Moss
Left-half

Brian Reynolds
Outside-right

Arthur Dixon
Inside-right

Maurice Robinson
Outside-left

Alf Mansfield
Trainer

80

I had witnessed Tommy's phenomenal heading ability in less public circumstances.

An innovation during Lawton's era was the formation of an 'A' team comprised almost entirely of young, local players, who competed in Division 1 of the UCL.

Although only fourteen, fellow Youth United player Barry Stanley and I, boys amongst men, were welcomed into midweek training sessions. We changed in the dressing room with our Saturday heroes, then trooped out onto the hallowed turf, or more frequently to the asphalt carpark.

Hanging from a metal pole, fixed high on the changing room wall, was a short length of rope from which dangled a large, leather football. Everyone had to take it in turn to jump and head the ball. Few succeeded in doing much better than to brush the ball with the top of the head, until Lawton. Timing his jump to perfection, he leapt high above the ball, appeared to hang there for seconds, before crashing his forehead down with such force the entire stanchion rocked with the power of the header.

Lawton seemed to inhabit Olympian heights far removed from mere mortals. He bestrode the football field like a colossus.

Tommy Lawton holds court in the Kettering dressing room - 1956. Geoff Toseland, Ray Powell and Bobby Wyldes are in attendance.

It was a considerable surprise therefore to see the great man in Woolworths one Saturday morning carrying a brown shopping bag, and very much in tow of his wife. (She, of course, always did her shopping on Saturdays). I did a double take, skirting round the counter trying hard not to stare. Could this somewhat shrunken figure leaning forlornly over the Pick 'n Mix be the same giant that had terrorised defences from Hampden Park to Berlin's Olympic Stadium?

Reg Abbott, long time secretary of the Poppies Supporters Club had many dealings with the player manager. He remembers, like many others, the groan of disappointment echoing around the ground when late team changes informed the crowd that the star wasn't playing .... again. (He actually made 26 appearances scoring 17 goals during the season).

The league was won by eight points and Lawton, fulfilling his declared intention, moved on to become the new manager of his former club Notts County. He later confided to Mr Abbott that leaving Kettering was 'the worst day's work of my life'.

Significantly, only five regular first team players remained with the club to begin the new season.

SOUTHERN LEAGUE TABLE					Goals		
	P.	W.	L.	D.	F.	A.	P.
Kettering T.	42	28	4	10	106	47	66
Bedford T.	42	25	9	8	89	52	58
Weymouth	42	22	10	10	92	71	54
Cheltenham T.	42	19	8	15	73	46	53
Gravesend and Northfleet	42	21	10	11	74	58	53
Lovells A.	42	21	14	7	99	84	49
Guildford C.	42	18	13	11	68	49	47
Hereford U.	42	19	15	8	96	60	46
Headington U.	42	19	16	7	64	61	45
Gloucester C.	42	18	16	8	74	72	44
Hastings U.	42	17	16	9	70	58	43
Worcester C.	42	16	16	10	81	80	42
Dartford	42	16	16	10	79	88	42
Chelmsford C.	42	16	17	9	73	85	41
Tonbridge	42	14	16	12	74	65	40
Yeovil T.	42	14	17	11	83	85	39
Bath C.	42	15	19	8	56	78	38
Exeter C.	42	10	22	10	52	89	30
Merthyr T.	42	9	22	11	72	95	29
Barry T	42	6	25	11	39	84	23
Kidderminster H.	42	7	25	10	60	83	*20
Llanelly	42	5	29	8	39	123	18

* Four points deducted for playing ineligible players.

Kettering Town Football Club.   Southern League Champions 1956/7

Standing L. to R. Prosser, Plummer, Lawton, Wheeler, Johnson, McDonald, Storey
Sitting L. to R. Toseland, Thomas, Goodwin, Moss, Robinson, Parker.

Poppies'

Championship Dinner

Central Hall,

Tuesday, 7th May, 1957

OXTAIL SOUP

ROAST TURKEY

Chipolata Sausages   Stuffing

Roast and Creamed Potatoes

Garden Peas

Sliced Beans

FRUIT SALAD

AND

DE LUXE ICE CREAM

BISCUITS AND CHEESE

COFFEE

TOAST LIST

H.M. THE QUEEN

The Chairman

CHAMPIONS OF THE SOUTHERN LEAGUE
KETTERING TOWN FOOTBALL CLUB

To Propose — Mr. A. C. Norris-Telling,
Chairman of the Southern League

To Reply — Mr. J. F. Nash,
Chairman of Kettering Town Football Club

Presentation of
Southern Football League Championship Shield
and personal mementoes to players

THE VISITORS

To Propose — Mr. R. W. Tailby,
President of the Kettering Town
Supporters' Club and Vice-Chairman
of Kettering Town Football Club

To Reply — Mr. F. C. A. Dunmore,
President of the Northamptonshire
Football Association

ARTISTES

JEAN   SPENCER
Vocalist

FRED   LEWIS
Character Impressionist
and Entertainer

Peterborough, too, enjoyed a successful year lifting the Midland League title for the second successive time and embarking upon yet another FA Cup run. In Round 3 Second Division Lincoln City salvaged a 2-2 draw at London Road with a controversial last minute penalty.

The replay was one of the most exciting games imaginable. With Posh leading 2-1, a similar late Lincoln goal took the tie into extra time, when a further 5 goals contributed to an incredible 5-4 Peterborough victory.

Peterborough Utd. 2;
Lincoln City 2.

LUCKY Lincoln ! It took a hotly-disputed penalty in the last minute to give them a second bite at the F.A. Cup cherry when they m-e-t Peterborough United at London Road on Saturday.

For much of the game Lincoln had been a very definite second best and they were fortunate to be only 2—1 down as we reached that fatal last minute.

LINCOLN CITY 4   PETERBOROUGH 5

30 AMAZING MINUTES AT
SINCIL BANK

FEW half-hours of football could be crammed with more incidents and excitement than the extra-time which Lincoln's last-minute goal compelled in yesterday's Cup-tie. It would have been only understandable if reaction had set in among United's valiant eleven. Victory was almost accomplished when Neal's fine header from a free kick by Munro pulled Lincoln's chestnuts out of the fire.

The parallel with Saturday's events was obvious, but United hid their dismay with an outburst of new activity which showed up once more the fallibility of City's defence. These holes so apparent in the first half, had been mended after the interval. Now United opened them again, and in the 14th MINUTE came the first of three goals in an amazing nine-minute spell.

By it, Lincoln were thoroughly shattered and looked well worth a 5-2 defeat. Yet they showed again the class of football they can play—and therein emphasised the quality of United's victory —by fighting back to score twice in the closing minutes.

Posh went through to meet Second Division Huddersfield Town in the 4th Round. By now Peterborough's giant killing reputation was widely known and even Bill Shankly's team knew a tough game was in prospect.

As this newspaper report indicates, the scene was set for an epic contest.

PETERBOROUGH—or a large part of it—descended on Huddersfield this morning. For several hours before the Huddersfield - United game at Leeds Road there were scenes comparable with those seen at a Cup semi-final.

The conga was a speciality put on by one group of Posh supporters in the middle of a main street, and the Yorkshire town seemed dominated by people wearing red and white rosettes, striped top hats and bowlers, in fact anything that made them stand out.

84

Within two minutes of the start, however, a promising young inside forward named Denis Law had given Huddersfield the lead and, despite a fierce revival led by wing halves Henry Cockburn and Bernard Shaw, Town scored again through Dave Hickson to make the game safe. Neutral observers were all agreed that the final 3-1 scoreline flattered the league club.

Denis Law

Local feeling, illustrated poetically in this topical cartoon, was strongly of the opinion that League football was the only just reward for Peterborough's success.

Sadly 'try, try again' proved to be prophetic words once more.

Peterborough United 1956-57

Back Row: Shaw, Douglas, Rigby, Walls, Barr, Cockburn.
Front Row: Hails, Emery, Donaldson, Smith, Hogg.

Northampton's season included a 2-0 1st Round cup defeat against Southampton, for whom former player Tommy Mulgrew scored the second goal, and ended with the club in 14th place in the Third Division South. Goalkeeper Pickering earned League representative honours and testimonials were awarded to full back Ron Patterson and winger Tommy 'Flash' Fowler - Fowler had played in that post-war Maunsell Cup Final at

LEAGUE – DIVISION III (SOUTH)	Played	Won	Drawn	Lost	Goals	Poin
1 Ipswich Town	46	25	9	12	101–54	?
2 Torquay United	46	24	11	11	89–64	?
3 Colchester United	46	22	14	10	84–56	?
4 Southampton	46	22	10	14	76–52	?
5 Bournemouth and Boscombe Athletic	46	19	14	13	88–62	?
6 Brighton and Hove Albion	46	19	14	13	86–65	5
7 Southend United	46	18	12	16	73–65	4
8 Brentford	46	16	16	14	78–76	4
9 Shrewsbury Town	46	15	18	13	72–79	4
10 Queen's Park Rangers	46	18	11	17	61–60	4
11 Watford	46	18	10	18	72–75	4
12 Newport County	46	16	13	17	65–62	c
13 Reading	46	18	9	19	80–81	4
14 Northampton Town	46	18	9	19	66–73	4
15 Walsall	46	16	12	18	80–74	4
16 Coventry City	46	16	12	18	74–84	4
17 Millwall	46	16	12	18	64–84	4
18 Plymouth Argyle	46	16	11	19	68–73	4
19 Aldershot	46	15	12	19	79–92	4
20 Crystal Palace	46	11	18	17	62–75	4
21 Exeter City	46	12	13	21	61–79	3
22 Gillingham	46	12	13	21	54–85	?
23 Swindon Town	46	15	6	25	66–96	?
24 Norwich City	46	8	15	23	61–94	?

Ipswich Town promoted to Division II.

Kettering eleven years earlier and had recently ended a run of 227 consecutive games.

Wellingborough, Rothwell, Rushden and both Kettering and Corby's reserve sides had transferred allegiance from the ailing UCL to the Central Alliance. Forays into the industrial Midlands made a distinct change from familiar excursions to such charming rural venues as Fenland Park, Wisbech, although County sides achieved little success during that first season.

CENTRAL ALLIANCE Division I South				Goals		
	P.	W.	D.	L.	F. A.	P.
Skegness T.	30	24	2	4	100 39	50
Long Eaton U.	30	19	6	5	78 57	44
Ilkeston T.	30	19	4	7	71 30	42
Stamford	30	18	3	9	93 54	39
Grantham Res.	30	15	8	7	73 55	38
Rushden T.	30	14	6	10	64 64	34
St. Neots	30	13	5	12	60 58	31
Wellingborough T.	30	13	5	12	65 66	31
Kettering Res.	30	12	6	12	74 61	30
Anstey R.	30	9	7	14	62 77	25
Derby Co. A.	30	10	4	16	45 48	24
Notts Co. A	30	9	4	17	64 98	22
Brush	30	9	2	19	59 93	20
Rothwell T.	30	7	4	19	49 67	18
Corby Res.	30	7	2	21	52 79	16
Potton U.	30	7	2	21	55 114	16

Desborough remained faithful to the old league but, despite the absence of familiar local rivals, could only manage eighth place.

UNITED COUNTIES LEAGUE Division I				Goals		
	P.	W.	D.	L.	F. A.	P.
St. Neots Res.	30	25	4	1	106 33	54
Kempston R.	30	21	2	7	94 39	44
Kettering A.	30	19	2	9	110 43	40
Northampton A.	30	16	7	7	113 45	39
British Timken	30	17	5	8	83 42	39
Higham Tn.	30	16	7	7	94 76	39
Wootton B.C.	30	14	5	11	73 61	33
Desborough T.	30	13	4	13	79 76	30
Finedon Tn.	30	15	0	15	64 76	30
Biggleswade Res.	30	12	4	14	69 68	28
Rushden Res.	30	10	4	15	58 100	24
Wellingborough Res.	30	10	3	17	45 71	23
Eynesbury Res.	30	7	8	15	54 72	22
Bedford Ave.	30	9	3	18	55 79	21
Raunds Tn.	30	3	3	24	43 150	9
Huntingdon U.	30	2	1	27	33 148	5

THE STUFF OF
DREAMS .... AND NIGHTMARES
1957-58

After the euphoria of the Lawton era, Kettering came down to earth in 1957-58. New manager, ex-Burnley full back Harold Mather, had needed to rebuild the side, bringing in the former Cobblers, Draper, Marston and Morrow. Time would prove the wisdom of these signings.

Bill Draper

The season started badly however, worsened with F.A. Cup defeat at Corby and by October, with only 3 wins

Jack Froggatt signs for the Poppies

from thirteen games and in twentieth place in the league, had reached desperation point. But with November came a saviour. Jack Froggatt, former England, Portsmouth and Leicester City skipper accepted the post of player coach. His transfer fee of £6000 was then a record for a non-league club.

The unlikely Mather-Froggatt partnership was doomed however, and the former resigned in January 1958. His record read...

P	W	D	L	F	A	P
23	8	3	12	47	52	19

Not surprisingly he was succeeded as player-manager by Froggatt, who was to justify his reputation to such an extent that many regard him as Kettering's finest ever player.

Unlike Lawton, who tended to be selective about where and when he played, Froggatt never turned a game down, displaying commitment and skill far beyond the call of duty. My abiding memory of Jack Froggatt is of a Senior Cup match against Desborough one cold, wet night in December 1961. Only a few minutes of the game remained when, mudstained, shirt clinging with rain and sweat, sleeves rolled to the elbow, he urged his side forward for one last effort. Kettering were winning 5-0 at the time.

Well Supporters, by the time you read this I shall be Player Manager of the Club. I do hope that our relationship will be a long and happy one and that we can carry on giving you the pleasure on the football field that you are accustomed to.

The match last Saturday did not go too well although the result belies our brand of Football. We had two good goals disallowed, one before Hastings had scored and it knocked the stuffing out of the lads.

With three home matches coming along I hope you will come along and cheer the team along for it is that kind of support that helps the boys along to victory.

Yours in Sport,

J. Froggatt.

From programme notes January 18th 1958. Kettering beat Yeovil 6-0.

Those who played with him remember his brand of humour. 'Never have sex on the Friday night before a match', he used to say. 'Wait until Saturday lunchtime'.

Kettering Town 1957-58

Back Row: Froggatt, Marston, Roberts, Plummer, Smith T, Wyldes, Burton.
Front Row: Morrow H, Walton, Draper, Toseland, Savage T.

Froggatt immediately set about restoring Kettering's fortunes. Only 3 more games were lost as the side rose to a final eighth place and respectability.

While recovering from an appendix operation in December 1957 I was compensated by a Saturday afternoon trip to the County Ground for the Cobblers F.A. Cup match with Bournemouth. I had been many times before as a little boy, usually travelling by double decker bus on its tortuous route via Walgrave, Moulton and the intriguingly named Buttocks Booth - to watch the cricket.

Apart from the names of better known players; Frank Tyson, Jock Livingstone, George Tribe, Dennis Brookes, and of course, the cricketing-footballers Bill Barron and Brian Reynolds, I remember little about the games.

Brian Reynolds, known to the locals as 'Bronc' is a Kettering born lad. Perhaps best known for his cricketing feats, which started with Kettering Town, before he successfully gained his County Gap. He started his football career with Avondale. 'Bronc' played for the Poppies for two years before signing and playing for Peterborough for three years. He then re-signed for the Poppies.

Afterwards, as a treat, dad bought fish and chips from 'Hugh Triem's' near the bus stop in the Kettering Road. Eventually he accepted that such extravagance was wasted on a football fanatic and, realising that he was unlikely ever to convert his elder son to his own first sporting love, the visits ceased.

So this was my first football match at Northampton. It was strange to see the normally sedate arena, where only polite clapping disturbed the silence, transformed by mildly raucous, excited football supporters. I wandered around seeking a suitable place to stand, finally settling for a spot on the duckboards spread across the cricketing outfield. A Bournemouth fan stepped aside in deference to my newly purchased claret and white rosette - those were the days!

The Cobblers won 4-1. One goal was gifted by Bournemouth's Ollie Norris, who in the previous season had contrived to help defeat my beloved Spurs by adopting the infuriating ploy at throw-ins of leaping up and down in front of the frustrated thrower. Only a tiny revenge, but satisfying.

The Third Round tie against Arsenal captured everyone's imagination, reviving memories of the Highbury epic of 1951. As Frank Grande recalls, 'it was still the pantomime season in Northampton - Cyril Fletcher in 'Sleeping Beauty' at the New Theatre, 'Cinderella' at the Rep.'
But Hans Christian Andersen could never have written the fairy tale about to unfold at the County Ground.

On December 14th, the Saturday following victory over Bournemouth, young Irchester born inside forward Bobby Tebbutt played for Northampton's second team in a Football Combination match at the County Ground against Arsenal Reserves. A crowd of over 9,000, swelled by many seeking tickets for the cup tie in prospect, watched the Cobblers win 2-1.

Queing for cup tickets outside the County Ground, December 1957.

It proved to be an omen. Just 48 hours before kick off, Tebbutt learned that he would be facing the First Division giants when regular first team player Alan Woan became stricken with food poisoning.

Many thought he might have had his chance before, following a series of promising performances in the reserves alongside other local youngsters, Tony Claypole, Bob Peacock and Tony Haskins.

On the morning of the game Bobby received a telegram from the representatives of the local Schools' Football Association wishing him and his side well.

WELLINGBOROUGH, RUSHDEN AND DISTRICT SCHOOLS' FOOTBALL ASSOCIATION.

To. Bob. Tebbutt

PRESIDENT:
(R, Dudley Pendered, Esq., J.P.

HON. SECRETARY/TREASURER:
Mr. C. H. Lowe,
18 Elm Street,
WELLINGBOROUGH.
PHONE WELLINGBOROUGH 3775.

4d January

Best wishes for your success today and in future, from us, and all boys and teachers of above Association. Also best wishes for success of whole team

C H Lowe Hon Sec.
B. Kirby Committee

Just six minutes into the game, his headed goal gave the Cobblers the lead and inspired the team to a famous 3-1 victory.

Teammate Barry Hawkings cartoon of Bobby Tebbutt

FOOTBALL ASSOCIATION CHALLENGE CUP

Third Round **"COBBLERS"**

v.

SATURDAY, JANUARY 4th, 1958

Kick-off 2.15 p.m.

ARSENAL

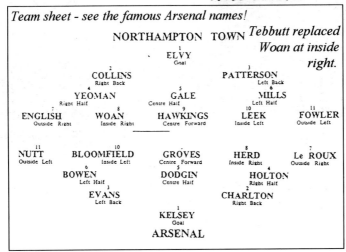

Team sheet - see the famous Arsenal names!

NORTHAMPTON TOWN

Tebbutt replaced Woan at inside right.

ELVY
Goal

COLLINS
Right Back

PATTERSON
Left Back

YEOMAN
Right Half

GALE
Centre Half

MILLS
Left Half

ENGLISH
Outside Right

WOAN
Inside Right

HAWKINGS
Centre Forward

LEEK
Inside Left

FOWLER
Outside Left

NUTT
Outside Left

BLOOMFIELD
Inside Left

GROVES
Centre Forward

HERD
Inside Right

Le ROUX
Outside Right

BOWEN
Left Half

DODGIN
Centre Half

HOLTON
Right Half

EVANS
Left Back

CHARLTON
Right Back

KELSEY
Goal

ARSENAL

The following morning newspaper reports paid tribute to the Cobblers' performance and particularly, to 'village-lad' Tebbutt.

Look what the lad from the village did . .

The goal that began the rout of Arsenal. Dave Bowen fails to stop Bobby Tebbutt's header - success for the lad from Irchester.

CHAMPAGNE TOUCH TUMBLES ARSENAL

Arsenal Humbled By Northampton

BARGAIN BOYS

ARSENAL BASHED

Northampton just run rings round 'em

THESE are the bargain-basement men of Northampton who humbled Arsenal and gave manager Dave Smith the happiest day of his life.

REG ELVY, goalkeeper, £350 give-away from Blackburn Rovers.

BEN COLLINS, right-back, 29-year-old local, signed for £10.

RON PATTERSON, left-back and captain, transferred five years ago from Middlesbrough for a small fee.

RAY YEOMAN, right-half, 22-year-old Scot who came to the ground and asked for a trial when stationed near Northampton during his National Service.

COLIN GALE, 23-year-old centre-half, cost a £1,500 fee from Cardiff two seasons ago.

ROLEY MILLS, left-half, 23-year-old local, cost £10.

JACK ENGLISH, veteran outside-right, has been with the club for 10 years. Scored two goals against Arsenal in the Cup in 1951.

BOBBY TEBBUTT, 21-year-old local boy who gave up his job as an apprentice printer to play football. Signed for £10.

BARRY HAWKINGS, centre-forward, cost £1,000 from Lincoln City at the beginning of the season. Former with Coventry.

KEN LEEK, inside-left, signed as a junior after winning a Welsh Boys Club International Cap.

TOMMY FOWLER, 31-year-old veteran outside-left, has been with the club 11 seasons.

92

ARSENAL? JUST POP-GUNNERS!

Northampton Town 3, Arsenal 1.

NORTHAMPTON TOWN, bottom of the Third Division South six weeks ago, are on top of the world now.

Heady with success after sweeping Arsenal out of the Cup, they fear none of the teams in today's Fourth Round draw.

They will learn who their next opponents are while enjoying one of the sweets of success—a day's golf and lunch, paid for by the club directors.

Champagne

They celebrated with champagne in the dressing room after the match, but turned down the chance of a champagne and caviar dinner at a swank hotel.

It was offered by wealthy supporters, overjoyed at the way the little club had humbled the once powerful and glorious Gunners.

Heartbreaking

Then they asked Dave Bowen, Arsenal's left half, and captain of Wales, to share the champagne.

It was a heartbreaking moment for Bowen.

He was once a Northampton player, and still lives in the town.

Raising his glass he wished his old club further success in the Cup.

Chairman Mr. Phillip Hutton told me that another reward he has promised them, the summer tour of Sweden, is definitely on.

Vice-chairman Wally Penn said:

"I've been connected with football for more than forty years and this is the greatest moment of all."

He and the Mayor of Northampton, Councillor Fred Saunders, toured the dressing room to shake

This defeat could be the BEST thing in the world for them if it produces team-building action.

Arsenal's day of despair was a day of dreams for Bobby Tebbutt, 23, who was playing for his Irchester (Northants) village team eighteen months ago.

He got his place because inside-right Alan Woan had food poisoning—and stepped into stardom by scoring the first goal in the sixth minute of his first Cup-tie.

"It was marvellous," he said later. "Dad, Mum, my brother and everybody from the village came to see me.

"My goal was the first I've ever headed in for the senior team."

Off to Dance

"I shan't have any special celebration tonight. I shall go to the local dance as usual."

Danny Clapton put Arsenal level fifteen minutes before half-time but when Northampton turned on the heat in the second half Arsenal melted away.

The ever-present suggestion of a Northampton success became reality when centre forward Barrie Hawkings lobbed in a goal, and then inside left Ken Leek cracked in another.

Arsenal were whipped. Northampton weren't giant-killers—THEY WERE THE GIANTS!

The Cobblers side that defeated Arsenal 3-1 on January 4th 1958.

Back Row: Smith, Yeoman, Collins, Elvy, Gale, Patterson, Mills, Jennings
Front Row: English, Tebbutt, Hawkings, Leek, Fowler.

Ray Yeoman and Ken Leek had both played in Northampton A's side at Desborough back in 1953. Leek was now on the verge of International honours and was attracting the attention of First Division clubs.

Ironically, although they were no doubt pleased to escape from Northampton after the defeat, the entire Arsenal half back line of Holton, Dodgin and Bowen were later to return to the County Ground in rather different roles.

A quick reward for the cup hero was provided by Wellingborough outfitter HD Holloway who had promised Tebbutt a free suit if the Cobblers won.

A victor's spoils. Bobby Tebbutt, goalscoring hero against Arsenal, is pictured being measured for a new suit by Wellingborough tailor, and Cobblers fan, HD Holloway. The new suit had been promised if the Cobblers won.

Cobblers' Cup win suited Bobby —at tailors expense

ALTHOUGH Wellingborough outfitter Mr. H. D. Holloway is an Arsenal supporter, he is presenting a £15 suit to Bobby Tebbutt, the Cobblers' Irchester-born inside right, who shattered Arsenal's Cup dreams on Saturday.

The day before the big game, Bobby called at Mr. Holloway's shop in the Market Square, Wellingborough, to see about a new suit.

"If the Cobblers win you can have one free," said Mr. Holloway with a smile.

A group of players gathered around the radio at lunchtime on Monday January 6th to listen to the 4th round draw, but were denied another home tie..

Hoping for a good draw. Patterson, Tebbutt, Leek. Mills.

Off to Anfield. Cobblers players Tebbutt, Smith, Hawkings and Fowler leaving for Southport to prepare for the Fourth Round tie against Liverpool.

The opposition proved to be Liverpool, winners after a replay with Southend. Northampton prepared for the match at the seaside at Southport but serious training was hampered by the weather.

Heavy snowfalls had put the match in doubt until the very morning of the game, which eventually went ahead after snow was cleared from the pitch and heaped around the touchlines.

Training on the beach Jennings, English, Smith, Leek, Fowler, Tebbutt, Hawkings..

Snowballing. Smith, Elvy, Gale, Leek, Mills, Yeoman, Hawkings.

Thousand of fans travelled to Liverpool for the game and made their presence felt in the forbidding atmosphere at Anfield.

Cobblers' supporters arriving at Lime Street Station, Liverpool.

When the gates to the ground were opened at one o'clock, more than a score of mounted policemen helped marshal the crowd.

* * *

During the night and this morning, dozens of workmen— some of them members of Liverpool Supporters' Club — had toiled to take the top layer of snow from the pitch. The ground still bore a wintry mantle, however, when play began.

NORTHAMPTON HAD KOP "ROAR" OF ITS OWN

As excitement mounted before the start, a young Cobblers' cheer-leader was sent off the pitch by a large police-sergeant, who was loudly booed by visiting fans. Later the same Northampton supporter returned to the field with a Liverpool counterpart for a "tour."

* * *

The Cobblers' supporters divided allegiance over colours. Half of them sported claret and white favours and the other half were clad in the blue and white colours which the team played in today.

* * *

One Cobblers' cheer-leader was snowballed by the crowd on the terraces but nothing daunted he carried on waving a monster rattle.

		LIVERPOOL		
		Younger		
	Molyneux		Moran	
	Wheeler	White	Twentyman	
McNamara	Rowley	Liddell	Bimpson	A'Court
		O		
Fowler	Leek	Hawkings	Tebbutt	English
	Mills	Gale	Yeoman	
	Patterson		Collins	
		Elvy		
		NORTHAMPTON TOWN		

Cobblers gave their Second Division opponents a hard game and might have achieved a deserved draw if luck had not deserted Ben Collins. The full back had the misfortune to head into his own goal in the 74th minute of the game with the scores level.

THIS WAS TOUGH LUCK ON COBBLERS

DISAPPOINTED though the thousands of Northampton folk who visited Liverpool must have been, there was none so dejected as Cobblers' right-back Ben Collins. The tragedy of his own goal set Liverpool on the way to a 3-1 victory they did not deserve.

Collins told me afterwards: "That's the first time I've done it. It would have to be today; I'm afraid it cost us the match."

When Liverpool played Southend at Anfield in the previous round, their goal in the 1-1 draw was also deflected in by a defender.

For Collins the goal was an absolute tragedy, for he had played English International winger A'Court into obscurity.

I do not blame Collins for this goal in the accepted sense. He was between the devil and the deep, off balance, and the ball hit his head—rather than his head hit the ball.

This came when the Cobblers were well on top and defeat looked remote. A draw was a banker bet; a win was well within the bounds of possibility.

A gem of a move, the best of the game, saw Fowler centre perfectly for Hawkings to head home, the ball just striking the inside of the post inches above the ground.

Right to the final whistle, the Cobblers kept up their gallant attempt. It is to their credit that they never admitted defeat, not even when the score was 3-1 against them after Bimpson's goal.

One Liverpool director acclaimed the Cobblers as the best side seen at Anfield this season when asked how they compared with Second Division opposition.

Another came to the Cobblers' coach as it was about to leave and said: "Thank you for a good game. Get up to the top of that Third Division; you can do it and make the Second Division."

96

The cup dream was over. Only two years later, Bobby Tebbutt's promising league career was cruelly ended in a Fourth division game at Walsall when a fierce tackle shattered his right leg.

Local boy was capable of near genius

TEBBUTT'S INJURY COMES AS A GREAT BLOW NOW

THIS was the Cobblers' finest hour of the season, writes John Ashplant. When I predicted that they would hold league leaders Walsall, I did not anticipate the Cobblers winning so easily or with only ten men for 60 minutes of the game, and I must confess that when they went in at half-time with a 1—0 lead but reduced to ten men, I quite expected them to fold up during the final stages of the second half.

Every member of the side deserves credit for a magnificent rear-guard action, particularly Tony Brewer, whose skill saved the Cobblers during the only period when Walsall threatened to take charge. It's a tragedy that a fine victory should have to be won at the expense of Bobby Tebbutt's injury.

Bobby Tebbutt in goalscoring action.

Perhaps, in coveting crepe soled shoes, drainpipe trousers and a Tony Curtis hairstyle, I was influenced by what sociologists call the 'Youth Cult' that swept the country during the middle and late fifties.

Certainly the sprouting of hair under armpits coincided with 'Blue Suede Shoes' and 'Rebel Without Cause'. Sadly I was allowed one concession to the trappings of teenage rebellion - the flat top haircut once likened by Clive James to the 'front elevation of an aircraft carrier'.

In truth, I was wordly wise as a Trappist monk. The 'hothouse' culture of a Boys' Grammar School encouraged unhealthy, highly prejudiced attitudes,

97

particularly with regard to the opposite sex. Girls from the adjoining High School were a remote and alien species only ever referred to, through ignorance, in the most derogatory of puerile language. At the very mention of words such as knob or hole, entire formrooms became convulsed in paroxysms of hysterical laughter.

In the winter of 1957 I spent Wednesday evenings in front of the television watching the 'Perry Como Show' before sneaking out, no doubt whistling 'Magic Moments' on the way, to walk a girl home from her piano lesson. After five weeks of embarrassed posturing from a distance of several feet, somewhat tremulously, I plucked up the courage to hold her hand. A date followed. 'Jailhouse Rock' at the Granada. During a particularly tender scene I dared to venture a first kiss. Even this was prefaced by self conscious muttering. 'If t'were done when t'is done, t'were well t'were done quickly'.

Then closing my eyes and leaning clumsily sideways, inadvertently trapping her arm down the side of the seat, I planted a kiss somewhere between her right eye and left ear. Little wonder that the girl, fifteen going on twenty, abandoned the boy, sixteen going on ten, on the pretext of visiting the ladies, and never re-appeared.

In many ways I was relieved. I could concentrate once more upon matters of far greater importance - like football.

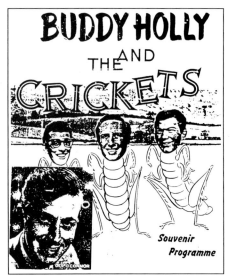

Souvenir Programme

During their tour of Britain in 1958, Buddy Holly and the Crickets performed at the De Montfort Hall, Leicester. Compere that evening was the former Northampton football fan of 1946, now becoming a star in his own right, Des O'Connor.

In January 1958, Matt Busby's Manchester United were heading inexorably for a third consecutive First Division title and the European Championship. Outstanding young players like Duncan Edwards, Eddie Colman and a certain Bobby Charlton, together with established internationals Roger Byrne and Tommy Taylor, had helped create a team that excited crowds all around the country. United swept into the European Cup semi finals following victory over Red Star Belgrade. Today we can speculate how much that side might have achieved and, as with the assassination of President Kennedy, remember with startling clarity how first we heard reports of the air disaster that claimed so many young lives. While researching this book, I spent several hours with Terry Bly, Peterborough's legendary goal scorer. He recalled a grief stricken young full back named Roy Lockwood from the flat upstairs breaking the news when both were playing in Norwich Reserves.

My own experience mirrored that of novelist H.E. Bates, a Rushden Town player of the twenties, although I was cycling home from my after school delivery round at the Home and Colonial Stores when I saw the newspaper hoarding.

Bates wrote; *"Late on a cold February afternoon, I was driving home from London when suddenly I saw, under the first lighted street lamps, one of those blue and yellow news placards .... MANCHESTER UNITED AIR CRASH. My immediate reaction was a mildly cynical one.... I am getting too old to be caught by newspaper screamers. At six o'clock, out of pure curiosity, I turned on my television set..... My eyes went deathly cold as I sat listening with a frozen brain to that cruel list of casualties ...."*

There was grief and tears throughout the football world and beyond. But as after Ibrox and Heysel, Bradford and Hillsborough, life went on.

Wellingborough recorded their most successful post-war season as runners up to Skegness Town in the Central Alliance.

Despite this considerable achievement, support at the Dog and Duck was disappointing, causing manager Tom McLain, (he of the chequered game against Norwich), to consider drastic team changes in a bid to improve attendances!

DOUGHBOYS ARE THE RUNNERS-UP

ANXIOUS to make sure of the Central Alliance runners-up position, the Doughboys soon got on top. They took the lead after 25 minutes and although Long Eaton equalised, Wellingborough soon made it 2—1. If Wellingborough won today it meant they are League runners-up and manager Tommy McLain took along two bottles of champagne to celebrate.

Wellingborough 4, Long Eaton

Manager's Comments in the programme against Derby County 'A' on Saturday March 29th 1958.

One thing I was downhearted about was the size of the 'gate' on such an occasion as last Saturday. It makes me wonder just what we have to do to attract support, for our playing record is good to say the least. Short of getting Diana Dors to play centre-forward I am at a loss for the answer. Our gallant friends the Supporters' Club came to our rescue yet again last week, and the Committee and myself are very grateful indeed.

T. McLain, *Manager/Coach.*

British Timken were runners up in the UCL which now included several local reserve sides and a re-established Stewarts and Lloyds.

Although Peterborough had no F.A. Cup success, losing a replay by the only goal at Torquay in the first round, the club unsurprisingly, collected the Midland League title again, prompting the all too familiar appeal in their programme notes.

1957-58	P.	W.	D.	L.	F.	A.	Pts
Kempston Rovers	32	28	2	2	135	39	58
B. Timken Duston	32	25	4	3	125	49	54
S & L Corby	32	24	3	5	82	46	51
St Neots Res.	32	19	1	12	102	76	39
Kettering 'A'	32	19	1	12	104	87	39
Northampton Town 'A'	32	16	4	12	105	75	36
Rushden Res.	32=	14	6	12	81	73	34
Bedford Avenue	32	16	1	15	99	78	33
Biggleswade Res.	32	13	2	17	64	66	28
Wellingborough Res.	32	11	5	16	60	69	27
Finedon Town	32	10	5	17	70	102	25
Wootton Blue Cross	32	8	7	17	59	80	23
Huntingdon United	32	8	6	18	67	121	22
Eynesbury Res..	32	8	6	18	50	99	22
Desborough Town	32	9	3	20	73	108	21
Higham Town	32	9	3	20	63	96	21
Raunds Town	32	4	3	25	61	138	11

Please endeavour to support us next Friday when the attractive Huddersfield Town will be our visitors, a good attendance could count much in our efforts to obtain election to the Football League, we hope you will show your interest by supporting this match.

Once more, however, 'Old Pals United' endured that the bottom clubs were safely re-elected and Peterborough's application was again unsuccessful.

Peterborough United 1957-58

(Back) Rigby, Shaw, Jacobs, Chadwick, Walls, Killin, Stafford, Cockburn.
(Front) Hails, Emery, Donaldson, Smith, Longworth.

Disappointed too were Northampton, whose failure to gain a position in the top half of the Third Division South, condemned the club to the newly formed Fourth Division.

And so were Kettering Youth United. Sunday evening selection meetings enlivened by singalong sessions to the Dansette and visits to a nearby 'Jug and Bottle' produced a team capable of winning both the District League and the N.F.A. County Cup. Resplendent in shirts bought with the proceeds

Season 1957–8						59th Season
LEAGUE – DIVISION III (SOUTH)						
		Played	Won	Drawn	Lost	Goals Points
1 Brighton and Hove Albion		46	24	12	10	88–64	60
2 Brentford		46	24	10	12	82–56	58
3 Plymouth Argyle		46	25	8	13	67–48	58
4 Swindon Town		46	21	15	10	79–50	57
5 Reading		46	21	13	12	79–51	55
6 Southampton		46	22	10	14	112–72	54
7 Southend United		46	21	12	13	90–58	54
8 Norwich City		46	19	15	12	75–70	53
9 Bournemouth and Boscombe Athletic		46	21	9	16	81–74	51
10 Queen's Park Rangers		46	18	14	14	64–65	50
11 Newport County		46	17	14	15	73–67	48
12 Colchester United		46	17	13	16	77–79	47
13 Northampton Town		46	19	6	21	87–79	44
14 Crystal Palace		46	15	13	18	70–72	43
15 Port Vale		46	16	10	20	67–58	42
16 Watford		46	13	16	17	59–77	42
17 Shrewsbury Town		46	15	10	21	49–71	40
18 Aldershot		46	12	16	18	59–89	40
19 Coventry City		46	13	13	20	61–81	39
20 Walsall		46	14	9	23	61–75	37
21 Torquay United		46	11	13	22	49–74	35
22 Gillingham		46	13	9	24	52–81	35
23 Millwall		46	11	9	26	63–91	31
24 Exeter City		46	11	9	26	57–99	31

of Saturday night whist drives at the Coop Hall, we contrived to lose both the league title play off and the County Cup final by the same 4-3 score.

Kettering Youth United 1957-58

Back Row: Essam, Thorley, Harris, Freestone, Bosworth, Draper.
Front Row: James, Bird, Stanley, Addis, Thompson, Lawman.

During the summer Bob Cooper and Brian Foster, opponents in Finedon Star Boys Club, Grant Cup final team, joined me for trials at Leyton Orient. They returned, Brian later keeping goal with distinction for Wellingborough's hugely successful sixties side. I stayed, seeking fame and fortune in the big city. At least my address was impressive - 38 Lancaster Gate.

101

During the summer, England, sadly deprived of its Manchester United stars, performed creditably in the World Cup finals held in Sweden. Undefeated in their qualifying group, the side held eventual champions Brazil to a draw, before losing to Russia in a play-off. At least one Englishman reached the final - Sweden's manager George Rayner, whose only British managerial post was at Skegness.

FLOODLIGHTS, MASCARA AND OLD RIVALRIES
1958-59

Night-time football is such an integral part of the modern game that it is difficult to realise that it was not until the early fifties that experts considered the possibility of widening floodlit entertainment, then limited to such popular sports as speedway and greyhound racing, to include soccer.

The F.A. Book for Boys of 1951-52 includes an enlightening chapter devoted to the subject. It contains a remarkable explanation of how much light would be required to provide sufficient illumination for night-time play.

"Now exactly how much light is required? The answer depends on many things but mainly on whether competition matches or practice games are intended. Light is measured in foot candles, or in 'lumens' per square foot - the terms mean very much the same thing. We will use the former, it is easily understood. For instance, 1 foot-candle is about the amount of light which we would get over a sheet of paper 1 square foot, each part of which was theoretically 1 foot from a standard candle. For practice games, somewhere about 3 foot-candles will be satisfactory, for club games, 5 to 7 foot-candles would be good, whereas for important matches 10 to 15 foot-candles would be more in line with the needs of the average ground".

That's much clearer isn't it?

Southern League Kidderminster Harriers were among the first clubs to install lights. Kettering visited for a fixture in 1952, attributing their heavy defeat to the problems of adjusting to the strange atmosphere - despite having taken the precaution of players wearing mascara to reduce the glare.

If footballers could have their choice of normal training routine, or mid-week floodlight. games, the floodlights would win every time, for everyone knows, match practice is unbeatable, as a means to football fitness.

Competition games always get more out of players than organised training sessions, no matter how strict, and how vigorous they are. The competition, the prestige of the individual, and the spectators, combine to give just that "edge" that training cannot give.

Were there grounds with floodlighting equipment in the immediate vicinity of Peterborough, it would be possible perhaps, for our supporters to see the team in action in mid-week, however there are not, therefore we can only look forward to the time when floodlit football grounds are commonplace.

A floodlit game always appears faster, and it is true, the lights make players go for the ball, which is an advantage, for to wait is fatal. This could help in our league matches, for there has been a tendency just recently to wait, instead of going in and getting the ball.

To hon. League Clubs, however, with a part-time playing staff, floodlighting is a boon, it enables players to train fully, and get in a weekly practice match like their big-brother Football League Clubs, where it is the custom to hold a Tuesday morning trial. Quite a number already have the equipment, and in addition they are raking in extra cash, by playing occasional games against Football League Clubs, Weymouth for instance in the past fortnight have played Tottenham Hotspurs and Swansea Town, and no doubt they will not only have earnt some extra money for the Club, but their players will have had the experience of playing against stronger opposition.

In the Peterborough United programme of December 11th 1954, 'Spotlight' focused on the advantages presented to non-league clubs by playing under floodlights.

British Timken staged a floodlit match against an all star eleven on November 8th 1955 winning 4-2 before a crowd of 3,000 at their Duston ground, but it was not until the sixties that most County sides began to acquire the facility. A notable exception was at Occupation Road where, shortly after

British Timken. Left to right : (back row) Johnny Wild (reserve), Maurice Collins, Bill Barron, Peter Pickering, Bobbie Scott (captain), Bob Clarke, Albert Johnson, G. Penn (acting trainer), (front row) Gordon Roberts, Arthur Dixon, Ray Powell, John McInnes, Gordon Inwood.

the commencement of the 1957-58 season, Corby Town announced its intention to construct floodlights.

On Monday February 17th 1958 an all star eleven, including several internationals, beat Corby 3-1 in the inaugural match, Jimmy Hagan scoring two goals.

At the end of March, the club took another momentous step when the board handed in its resignation from the Midland League, and early in April the Steelmen were elected to the North-Western zone of the reconstructed Southern League.

A new manager was appointed. England International Johnny Morris, who had played for Derby in their 1950 cup tie against Northampton before moving to Leicester City.

Johnny Morris

To the Football Public of Corby I would like to take this opportunity of thanking everyone concerned in giving me the chance to help in the Club policy of bringing good football to Occupation Road. The Morris family have already settled as if we were among the pioneers of this lovely town like some of you have been.

Since I came I have brought some new faces for you to see in action on Saturdays and along with the already signed lads I feel confident we shall have a good season.

From the word "go" this afternoon it will be football, football all the way, the same that I have been privileged to see from such great players as Peter Doherty, Wilf Mannion, Billy Steel, Tom Finney, Jimmy Delaney, Raich Carter and a few others.

Unfortunately I didn't have the privilege to see some of the "greats" that some of you saw. I am not saying we can play as those did but we can try to play a similar game with the same team spirit as they did and maybe one day out of our ranks we will find a great player or two for the future.

Yours in Sport,
JOHNNY MORRIS.

There was no shortage of optimism or civic support as the programme notes for their first league fixture on August 23rd indicate.

104

Unfortunately, results proved spectacularly inconsistent - a 5-1 league victory over Kettering was followed by a run of 8 consecutive defeats in which the side conceded 42 goals.

With only the top eleven clubs from the two zones due to comprise the Premier Division in 1959-60, the lowly Steelmen were consigned to Division 1.

Northampton's first season in Division 4 was memorable for Alan Woan's 32 goals, but blighted by F.A. Cup defeat by amateurs Tooting and Mitcham, (who were to take eventual winners Nottingham Forest to a replay in the next round).

	LEAGUE-DIVISION IV	Played	Won	Drawn	Lost	Goals	Points
1	Port Vale	46	26	12	8	110-58	64
2	Coventry City	46	24	12	10	84-47	60
3	York City	46	21	18	7	73-52	60
4	Shrewsbury Town	46	24	10	12	101-63	58
5	Exeter City	46	23	11	12	87-61	57
6	Walsall	46	21	10	15	95-64	52
7	Crystal Palace	46	20	12	14	90-71	52
8	Northampton Town	46	21	9	16	85-78	51
9	Millwall	46	20	10	16	76-69	50
10	Carlisle United	46	19	12	15	62-65	50
11	Gillingham	46	20	9	17	82-77	49
12	Torquay United	46	16	12	18	78-77	44
13	Chester	46	16	12	18	72-84	44
14	Bradford	46	18	7	21	75-77	43
15	Watford	46	16	10	20	81-79	42
16	Darlington	46	13	16	17	66-68	42
17	Workington Town	46	12	17	17	63-78	41
18	Crewe Alexandra	46	15	10	21	70-82	40
19	Hartlepools United	46	15	10	21	74-88	40
20	Gateshead	46	16	8	22	56-85	40
21	Oldham Athletic	46	16	4	26	59-84	36
22	Aldershot	46	14	7	25	63-97	35
23	Barrow	46	9	10	27	51-104	28
24	Southport	46	7	12	27	41-86	26

Port Vale, Coventry City, York City and Shrewsbury Town promoted to Division III.

Preparing for the 1958-59 season. Left to right Jim Hales, Jack Froggatt, Bob Wyldes and Maurice Marston lead a circuit of Kettering's new running track.

Kettering's players, their fitness enhanced by Froggatt's close season innovation of a running track around the ground, had begun the season in good form.

Yet another meeting with Peterborough in the F.A. Cup produced perhaps the most exciting encounter in their long history of cup competition.

Pre-match comments attributed to the Poppies player-manager brought swift riposte in the United programme, fuelling rivalry between the two clubs, whose senior sides had never competed in the same league since the war.

Froggatt will be with us today and we give him a personal welcome.

Some of the things he has said and written recently about United's strength have not gone down too well with some of us.

We do not believe that United are over-rated nor do we believe that the Southern League competition is better than the Midland League.

But this is F.A. Cup day and on the field or off we wish Froggatt and his men all the very best of luck.

```
Referee: Mr. T. JEPSON      PETERBOROUGH UNITED    Colours—Royal Blue Shirts.
         (Mansfield)                                White Shorts
  RIGHT                           WALLS                      LEFT
                    2             1              3
                 STAFFORD                     WALKER
                    4             5              6
                   SHAW         RIGBY        CHADWICK
        7           8             1             10      11
      HAILS       EMERY         RAYNER      SMITH, R.  McNAMEE


    BURROWS   TOSELAND     DRAPER     DADSWELL   MORROW
      11        10           c           8          7
         SMITH, T.        PLUMMER            FROGGATT
             6              5
           LOCKWOOD                       MARSTON
      LEFT     3                            2        RIGHT
                            ROBERTS
  Linesmen—Mr. G. H. Pegg              1
         Red Flag              KETTERING TOWN    Colours—Red Shirts, White
       Mr. J. Beswick                            Shorts
         Yellow Flag
```

In the event, Froggatt missed the tie at London Road, played before a crowd of 17,800, which ended in a 2-2 draw.

Alan Dadswell switched to right half in place of the injured player-manager and Savage came in at inside right.

(Those readers who enjoy coincidences will notice that Kettering's left back was the same Roy Lockwood who had broken the news of the Munich disaster to neighbour Terry Bly).

Peter Roberts

> ### Peterborough United 2   Kettering 2
>
> *This was another 'Torquay'. Having sprung into a 2-1 lead after being one down after only eight minutes, Peterborough dawdled towards what they thought would be a place in the second round of the cup.*
> *But the thousands of Peterborough supporters among the 17000 gathered at London Road on Saturday were shocked into near silence when, four minutes from the end of a pulsating game, the Poppies centre forward, Bill Draper, ran on to a beautiful pass from Hughie Morrow to slip the ball by a despairing Jack Walls.*

Ironically, Kettering's hero in that first game was none other than Peter Roberts, who had defied Lawton's attack in the Spalding match two years earlier.

Excitement was high for the replay, played the following Thursday afternoon. In Kettering, factories, classrooms and offices were emptied and the town resembled Goldsmith's 'Deserted Village'.

The attendance of 11,246 was just 280 below the ground record set for that infamous 1947 match.

Froggatt, returning from injury, put the record straight in his own, typically diplomatic, programme notes.

> A word on the contents of the Peterborough programme which stated that I had said that Peterborough were not the side they were cracked up to be. I was asked these questions along with a lot more and only half of what I said was printed in the programme. Surely not even the staunchest Peterborough supporters can say the opposition they face now-a-days is good enough for Posh. I do not deny Posh are a good footballing side but as most of their results prove they can get into a rut into thinking they are invincible against any non-league team. This kind of apathy can lead to disastrous results. Still I can but wish them a very happy day at Kettering and may the best team win; I can assure them we shall be all out to make the next round against Headington.
> Yours in Sport,
> JACK FROGGATT

Missing from the Poppies line-up was the unavailable Maurice Marston, replaced at full back by dependable former Posh player Brian Reynolds.

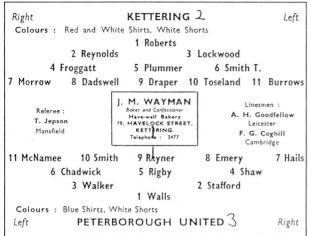

Right	KETTERING 2	Left
Colours : Red and White Shirts, White Shorts		

1 Roberts

2 Reynolds   3 Lockwood

4 Froggatt   5 Plummer   6 Smith T.

7 Morrow   8 Dadswell   9 Draper   10 Toseland   11 Burrows

J. M. WAYMAN
Baker and Confectioner
Have-well Bakery
70, HAVELOCK STREET,
KETTERING.
Telephone : 3477

Referee :
T. Jepson
Mansfield

Linesmen :
A. H. Goodfellow
Leicester
F. G. Coghill
Cambridge

11 McNamee   10 Smith   9 Rayner   8 Emery   7 Hails

6 Chadwick   5 Rigby   4 Shaw

3 Walker   2 Stafford

1 Walls

Colours : Blue Shirts, White Shorts

Left	PETERBOROUGH UNITED 3	Right

A goal four minutes from time had saved Kettering in the first game. The replay was dramatic in the extreme as the Poppies forfeited a two goal lead, Reynolds' unfortunate own goal equaliser taking the match into extra time. Billy Hails' scored Peterborough's winner with just nine minutes of play remaining.

A cruel blow for the Poppies

FATE struck a cruel blow to Kettering football yesterday afternoon. The Poppies suffered the sort of ill-luck that makes saints want to kick in stained glass windows. But in the cold light of a new day we calculate more clearly that Peterborough went home with no more than was justified, writes "The Friar."

The weird ironic twist is that they should have achieved it as they did—getting two gift goals at a time when they seemed able to do everything except score.

And the equaliser was the sort of goal one might not witness again in a lifetime of watching football — full-back Brian Reynolds beating his own 'keeper with a header that any forward would have been proud to deliver.

When this happened the Poppies were just five minutes from the next comfortable round against Headington. But as tired manager Jack Froggatt said last night: "That's football —one day it can be kind, the next cruel, you have just got to learn to live with it and move on to the next game without looking over your shoulder."

BRIAN'S INTENTION

Reynolds' explanation for THAT goal was that he had intended to head it out for a corner, but the ball was lower than he expected and in a flash the ball had hit his head and was in the back of the net.

Briefly the story of the tragic second half was that Kettering, leading by two great Bill Draper headers, were up against it and keeping an over-elaborate Posh side out. Then Denis Emery scored with a 71 minute shot which Roberts stopped on the line then allowed to screw under his prostrate body. Reynolds provided the extra time and a Peterborough winner seemed a formality— it came from Billy Hails nine minutes from the end.

THE winner! Billy Hails beats Roberts to the ball and puts Posh into the next round, nine minutes from the end of extra time. The goal that all Peterborough hails!

Consolation for Kettering came at the end of the season when, as runners up to Hereford, the club qualified as founder members of the Premier Division of the Southern League.

Now resident in London I missed the drama at Rockingham Road, but there were consolations. I saw the young Derek Dougan in Portsmouth colours at Highbury, veteran Stanley Matthews at Stamford Bridge, Bobby Moore's West Ham debut against Manchester United - and Peterborough's third round game at Craven Cottage.

Posh held the First Division side to a goal-less draw, Denis Emery completely overshadowing his Fulham counterpart - England's Johnny Haynes.

DENIS EMERY - SIMPLY THE BEST

In May 1993 readers of the Peterborough Evening Telegraph voted for the club's best player of all time.

BEST POSH PLAYER

33 — Denis Emery
24 — Tommy Robson
22 — Freddie Hill
14 — Tony Adcock
7 — Jim Hall
6 — Mick Halsall
5 — Mick Gooding
5 — Ken Charlery
4 — Derek Dougan
4 — Dave Gregory

Sadly, Denis was seriously injured in an horrific accident in 1962 which virtually ended his playing career. His statistics make interesting reading and, as Terry Bly's later testimony will confirm, beg questions about the failure of such an immensely gifted player to find a more illustrious club than humble Peterborough United.

EMERY STATISTICS		
Season	Appearances	Goals
1954/55	13	5
1955/56	46	28
1956/57	46	43
1957/58	46	51
1958/59	36	18
1959/60	18	17
1960/61	46	15
1961/62	19	14
1962/63	3	0
FA Cup: (35 appearances, 27 goals).		

United's star forward badly injured on way to Cup replay

THOUSANDS of Peterborough United fans were stunned on Monday morning by the news that the club's 28-year-old inside-forward, Denis Emery, had been taken to the Memorial Hospital with multiple injuries, following a car crash only three miles from the London-road ground.

Denis had been travelling from his Eynesbury home to report in readiness for that evening's all-important F.A. Cup replay against Colchester United at Norwich. But, while his shocked team-mates prepared for the match, he lay in hospital "critically ill."

Speculation that Emery must have been a troublemaker is firmly refuted by those that knew him well. In a newspaper article, written in March 1961, Denis recalls his early days in the game, recognising that lack of ambition probably cost him opportunities when attached to Tottenham Hotspur as a youngster.

The chance to join Arsenal was my last

by DENIS EMERY

LET'S get one thing straight at the start – I'm not a trouble maker. I've had my difficulties, but I've never made trouble for anyone. All I've ever done is stand up for myself and what I believe has been right.

It's no secret that things have not been too happy for me in recent seasons, but there has never been any question of trouble for trouble's sake, just a matter of sticking up for myself and standing by my principles.

OF COURSE, PETERBOROUGH HAS MEANT A GREAT DEAL TO ME, BUT FOR QUITE SOME TIME I WAS NOT CONTENTED AT LONDON ROAD.

I SUPPOSE IT STARTED ABOUT TWO YEARS AGO WHEN I HAD THE CHANCE TO FOLLOW GEORGE SWINDIN TO HIGHBURY AND PLAY FOR THE ARSENAL.

THE PETERBOROUGH CLUB, THROUGH MANAGER JIMMY HAGAN, WOULD NOT RELEASE ME, SO I MISSED THE CHANCE

All I asked for was a break

I'D HAVE GIVEN MY RIGHT ARM FOR THAT CHANCE, AND I COULD HAVE PLAYED WITH ONE ARM I WAS SO KEEN. I FELT IT WAS MY LAST CHANCE TO MAKE THE GRADE. OF COURSE, I MAY NEVER HAVE MADE THE TOP, BUT THE BREAK WAS ALL I ASKED FOR FROM ANYONE.

IT WASN'T MY FIRST CHANCE, FOR AS A YOUNGSTER I WAS WITH THE SPURS. I PLAYED YOUTH SOCCER AT MY HOME TOWN OF SANDY AND FOR AS LONG AS I CAN REMEMBER, WANTED TO MAKE SOCCER MY CAREER.

LATER I PLAYED FOR EYNESBURY ROVERS AND AS AN AMATEUR FOR SPURS IN THE LONDON MID-WEEK LEAGUE. AT THAT TIME I WAS WORKING FOR A COACHBUILDER IN BIGGLESWADE.

When I was seventeen, just before I went into the Army, I signed professional forms for Tottenham and played in the Metropolitan League side.

Then I sort of drifted away from White Hart Lane and towards the end of my service went back to Eynesbury on loan. I didn't bother too much about it then, but I guess I should have done.

They were still interested at Spurs because I got the chance to move to Chelmsford, at that time the club's nursery side. About the same time George Swindin asked me to come to London Road, and that's where I headed.

Success at Peterborough failed to generate more than passing interest from League Clubs, although an expected move to Arsenal, in the wake of former Posh Manager George Swindin was apparently blocked by his successor Jimmy Hagan.

Swindin confirmed in recent conversations, that he made Peterborough an offer for Emery but nothing came of the approach. He also confided that it remains a great personal regret that the inside forward was never afforded an opportunity to display his talents with a First Division club.

In a 'Memory Lane' feature from 1980, Emery reflects somewhat poignantly upon his playing career.

Denis Emery died just six years later from ulcerated colitis, at the age of 52.

Soccer legend is dead

PETERBOROUGH United's footballing legend, Denis Emery died early today in hospital.

Mr Emery (52), of Orchard Place, Eaton Socon, near St Neots died in Bedford General Hospital following an internal operation.

Today friends and former colleagues were "totally shocked" by the news.

Mr Emery joined Posh in 1954 it was his talented play that helped the club join the Football League in 1960.

However, the career of the inside forward came to a virtual end when he was involved in a near fatal car accident in 1962 on the way to the London Road ground.

Although he went on to play briefly for Bedford he began to drift away from football and for the last 20 years worked in a St Neots paper mill.

Ellis Stafford, who signed for Posh on the same day as Mr Emery and is currently the club's commercial manager said today: "He was a great man and an excellent player. He was the best player I have known at the club."

Former Posh player and manager Norman Rigby, who lives at Stanground, predicted Mr Emery could have become one of the country's top players if he had joined Arsenal in 1958 following an £8,500 bid.

Mr Emery leaves a wife, Joan, and two adult children.

Down memory lane
— 4. JAN. 1980 —

THIS WEEK . . . DENIS EMERY

THE footballing story of former Posh inside forward Denis Emery came to a tragic end when he was involved in a near fatal car accident on the way to the London Road ground in 1962.

Rated by many old observers as the most talented player in Posh's illustrious Football League debut side in 1960/61, he undoubtedly had a great future in the game.

During the season which was eventually to be his last in the league, Spurs and Preston had shown considerable interest in the lad.

Now living and working in Eaton Socon, near St Neots, Emery is understandably reluctant to recall the good times.

"Of course all my memories of Posh are good ones and I enjoyed tremendously playing in the championship team — it was really very good," said Emery.

"Posh were my entire football career — I never played for a club like them before and obviously never did afterwards.

"The accident finished me as a footballer. I was near death that day on the way to the ground and was never the same since, although I did stay on as a player for a couple of years, but never as a first teamer.

"It seems like such an incredibly long time ago to me now, all those good times at Peterborough . . . in fact football seems such a long way away.

"For the last ten years or so I have worked as a storeman at the paper-mill in St Neots. Nothing very special but it suits me.

"I have never had any involvement in the game whatsover since I left the Posh and have had no desire to," said Emery.

Synonymous with the remarkable achievements of Peterborough United during his eight year association with the club, he will certainly never be forgotten.

Peterborough United 1958-59 - Midland League Champions

Back Row: Stafford, Shaw, Rigby, Walls, Walker, Chadwick.
*Front Row: Hails, **Emery**, Rayner, Smith, McNamee.*

Shortly after their replayed cup game against Fulham, which was lost by a single goal, Posh entertained Sutton Town in the Midland League. As the fixture list indicates a more appropriate designation would be the North Eastern League. At that point of the season Peterborough were undefeated and hopeful that yet another application for football league status would be successful. Sadly, injury forced Andy Donaldson, scorer of many important goals since joining the club back in 1951, into retirement.

MIDLAND LEAGUE

Aug., 1968				F. A.
Sat.	23	Ashington	H	6—1
Mon.	25	Wisbech (Bancroft C.)	H	3—2
Sat.	30	Stockton	A	5—1
Sept.				
Mon.	1	South Shields	A	0—0
Wed.	3	Wisbech (Bancroft C.)	A	3—1
Sat.	6	Scunthorpe Utd.	H	5—0
Sat.	13	Scarborough	A	1—1
Sat.	20	Goole Town	H	5—1
Mon.	22	Maunsell C. (Semi-Final)		
		Northampton	A	2—0
Sat.	27	Blyth Spartans	A	5—1
Mon.	29	North Shields	A	3—1
Oct.				
Sat.	4	South Shields	H	2—0
Sat.	11	Gainsborough Trinity	A	3—1
Sat.	18	Blyth Spartans	H	6—1
Sat.	25	Sutton Town	A	2—0
Nov.				
Sat.	1	Walthamstow (Cup)	H	3—0
Sat.	8	South Africa		
		Touring Team	H	7—4
Sat.	15	Kettering (FA Cup)	H	2—2
Thur.	20	Kettering (Replay)	A	3—2
Sat.	22	Skegness	H	5—0
Thur.	27	Boston (E. Ang. Cup)	H	3—2
Sat.	29	Frickley	A	5—0
Dec.				
Sat.	6	Headington (F.A. Cup)	H	4—2
Sat.	13	Worksop	A	5—1
Sat.	20	Spennymoor Utd	A	7—1
Fri.	26	Grantham	A	2—2
Sat.	27	Grantham	H	7—1
Jan., 1969				
Sat.	3	Spennymoor Utd.	H	4—1
Sat.	10	Fulham (FA Cup)	A	0—0
Sat.	24	Fulham (FA C.-Replay)	H	0—1
Sat.	31			
Feb.				
Sat.	7	Worksop	H	7—0
Sat.	14	Sutton Town	H	
Sat.	21	Denaby Utd.	A	
Sat.	28	Frickley	H	
Mar.				
Sat.	7	North Shields	H	
Sat.	14	Gainsborough Trinity	H	
Sat.	21	Horden Colliery	A	
Fri.	27	Consett	H	
Sat.	28	Ashington	A	
Mon.	30	Consett	A	
April				
Sat.	4	Goole Town	A	
Sat.	11	Scarborough	H	
Sat.	18	Skegness	A	
Thurs.	23	Maunsell Cup Final		
Sat.	25	Denaby United	H	

To be arranged: Horden Colliery H, Stockton H, Scunthorpe A

Peterborough, remaining undefeated, won the Midland League Championship for the fourth successive year yet, almost inevitably, failed by a single vote to gain membership of the Football League.

CLUB CHATTER

Last Saturday brought our biggest win of the season, seven goals against Worksop without reply and again we hold pride of place in the Midland League. Ashington have been without Midland League games for the past two Saturdays and we now have a one point lead with one match in hand. Twenty Midland League matches played this season to date and still unbeaten; this is a record we can be proud of, how much longer can we keep it up.

The disappointing feature last Saturday was of course, the attendance. Taking into consideration the cold afternoon and the opposition, I suppose we ought not to complain but with attendance figures being one of our main items of propaganda for League status we do hope to maintain our gates at their previous high level. There is much speculation, as to our chances this year and we do hope that when we send our brochure out to the League Clubs very shortly we shall be able to produce figures which will enhance our prospects of obtaining the necessary votes and attendance figures will play a very great part in deciding who the League Clubs will support.

It has now been made known officially that Andy Donaldson is not to play football again. This great favourite with United supporters has been a grand player and we are all sorry he has found it necessary to hang up his boots. The Directors are mindful of his great services to this club and are giving consideration to making him a suitable reward at the end of the season.

Incidentally, Andy filled a very useful purpose last Saturday when he deputised on the line against Worksop. Will the local Referees' Association be seeking his services to help to fill their already meagre ranks?

Local Central Alliance sides, Wellingborough, Rushden and Rothwell continued to find the league demanding. Programme details from matches during the season indicate the composition of their sides.

WELLINGBOROUGH TOWN
Royal Blue and Gold Shirts, Black Shorts.

TAPP
(2) LLOYD, D.   (3) SMITH, C.
(4) CANDLIN   (5) SPENDLOVE   (6) McKAY
(8) BURN   (10) BRIGHT
(7) WHITEMAN   (9) CRUICKSHANK   (11) KENDELL

11 Chambers   10 Linnett   9 Marlow   8 Longhurst   7 Franklin
6 Worrall   5 Johnson   4 Traynor
3 Coleman   2 Kettley
1 Herbert

Colours : Blue Shirts White Shorts
Left   **ROTHWELL TOWN**   Right

CAVE   ADAMS   LAWRENCE   ROBERTS   HOLMES
DeBANKE   GOSS   LONG
DESBOROUGH   GIBBS
DRAPER

RUSHDEN (Green Shirts, White Shorts)

A rare photograph of the old Rothwell grandstand, (sited on the opposite touchline to the present building), before it was destroyed by fire.

1958-59	P.	W.	D.	L.	F.	A.	Pts
Dunstable Res.	34	25	7	2	150	34	57
Northampton Town 'A'	34	21	5	8	107	59	47
S & L Corby	34	22	3	9	101	56	47
St Neots Res.	34	20	5	9	88	63	45
B. Timken Duston	34	19	6	9	105	66	44
Shefford Town	34	19	6	9	95	60	44
Biggleswade Res.	34	20	3	11	73	73	43
Kempston Rovers	34	18	6	10	83	54	42
Kettering 'A'	34	13	7	14	91	75	33
Wellingborough Res.	34	14	4	16	99	70	32
Wootton Blue Cross	34	11	10	13	73	82	32
Rushden Res.	34	15	1	18	77	94	31
Desborough Town	34	12	5	17	85	103	29
Huntingdon United	34	10	2	22	62	115	22
Bedford Avenue	34	6	9	19	57	109	21
Finedon Town	34	7	5	22	72	142	19
Higham Town	34	5	4	25	50	130	14
Raunds Town	34	4	2	28	50	123	10

Desborough again failed to make the top half of a UCL table which saw Stewarts and Lloyds repeat the third place achieved in 1957-58.

THE FOOTBALL LEAGUE
AT LAST
1959-60

Peterborough United were justifiably proud of the season's achievement. Midland League champions once again, Jimmy Hagan's side completed further giant killing performances in the FA Cup, by toppling Shrewsbury, Walsall, and Ipswich

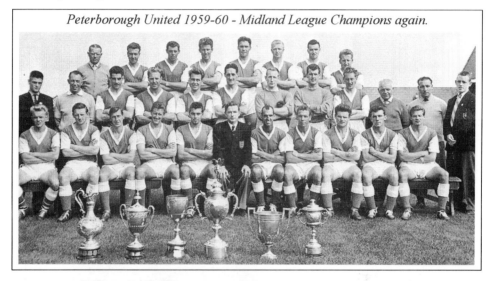

Peterborough United 1959-60 - Midland League Champions again.

Round 1

'Cup killers' do it with last kick

Peterborough 4, Shrewsbury 3

PETERBOROUGH was rocked by an explosion at 3.54 p.m. on Saturday. It was a thunderous salute by the fans to the part-time team which won its most dramatic giant-killing battle.

It was earned by a real-life performance that you would not credit in fiction.

Peterborough are the club who can't get into the Football League. Their players work on farms, in factories and offices during the week.

Shrewsbury are fourth in the Third Division, bidding for promotion. They train and plan full-time for Soccer success.

And twice in this tense First Round Cup clash which set the heart pounding and the nerves jangling, Shrewsbury were in front. They led 2—0 and 3—2.

Twice Peterborough drew level 2—2 and 3—3.

Underdogs

Then, with the second hand of the referee's watch sweeping round for the last time—relentlessly ticking away their chance of victory—the underdogs did it!

They pinched a page from the first fairy tale ever written about Soccer for schoolboys—the centre forward scored the winning goal !

With an anxious, excited crowd roaring them on, Peterborough swept down the right wing. Billy Hails curled a centre over the heads of the Shrewsbury defence.

It floated to centre forward Jimmy Rayner. His foot poised for a second, then it flashed the ball into the net—and Peterborough won.

Walsall were outclassed

Round 2

★ WALSALL 2 UNITED 3 ★

Rigby gets his reward

Round 3

THE 11 HEROES SHAME IPSWICH

Ipswich 2 Peterborough 3

☆ IPSWICH manager Alf Ramsey wants no star rating for his team after this defeat. Therefore it gives great pleasure to award all five to Peterborough.

There are no superlatives left to describe these non-League aristocrats who have become a Cup legend in their own time. But this was their finest hour.

Foolish Ipswich began like professors facing a tiresome class of teenagers.

They finished humbled and humiliated by the Soccer prodigies who rightly call themselves "The Posh."

Peterborough faced driving snow in the first half, nearly took the lead, then struggled.

Enter the first Peterborough hero, goalkeeper Tom Daley. Daley pounced on the ball like a tiger on a stag. But even he couldn't stop the Doug Millward shot in the 20th minute.

Enter the second hero—Peterborough outside left Peter McNamee, who swept upfield on the right. A cross, and centre forward Jim Rayner stabbed in the equaliser (41 min.).

JIM PLAYS ON

A minute later Peterborough left back Jim Walker collapsed making a strong tackle. He became Hero No. 3 when he played through the second half.

Thirty seconds after half-time Ted Phillips followed up a rebound to put Ipswich in front once more.

Enter eight more heroes. For the Phillips goal drew glorious response from the entire Peterborough team.

Ipswich were tackled and chased by a bunch of blue-shirted demons. Yet there was scarcely a foul.

McNamee again in the 54th minute. A swift pass to inside-right Dennis Emery, who flicked the ball into the far corner with an air close to contempt.

Three minutes to go and inside-left Ray Smith, a small man with a giant's spirit, swooped on a mistake by Ipswich centre-half Andy Nelson. A pass to Emery—and Emery, the Cup killer, doesn't miss from 10 yards.

At once the snow thickened into a blizzard. It was a magnificent final curtain for The Posh, and all football calls "Encore! Encore!"

But for Ipswich it was a shroud.

FOR nine seasons Norman Rigby has been the on-field inspiration of a club which during his captaincy has risen from scrap-heap obscurity to coveted luxury. Peterborough have now as good as received League status, which makes Rigby a happy man. Only last week, when the champagne corks were popping in the dressing room at Walsall, he was expressing doubts that it would happen in his Soccer lifetime.

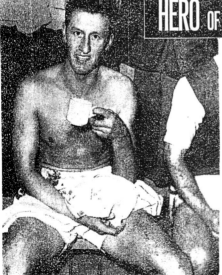

HERO OF THE DAY!

MEET the hero of yesterday's brilliant victory of Peterborough in the Cup—Dennis Emery.

He slammed in the goal that levelled the score at Ipswich and then, three minutes before the end, hit the winner.

Ten thousand fans from Peterborough cheered his feat and then two of them sent bottles of sherry into the dressing-room. Here is Emery enjoying their toast—from a cup.

Champagne? Not for "The Posh." They are saving that for the day when they beat a First Division side!

FOOTBALL ASSOCIATION CUP—FOURTH ROUND

SHEFFIELD WEDNESDAY
VERSUS
PETERBOROUGH UNITED

SATURDAY,
30th JANUARY, 1960
Kick-off 3.0 p.m.

OFFICIAL PROGRAMME PRICE 3d

Hillsborough

Round 4 took the Posh to Hillsborough and First Division Sheffield Wednesday. Ellis Stafford, Peterborough's long serving Yorkshire born full back, recalls the day with considerable pride.

"Sheffield United were at Bramall Lane the same afternoon hosting a crowd of some 30,000 for their game with Nottingham Forest, while Hillsborough attracted 20,000 more. Such occasions would be impossible today - grounds couldn't cope with the crowds, and crowds couldn't cope with the occasion. Yet in those days the police presence was often restricted to a handful of officers who sat on little folding chairs, backs to spectators, and watched the game".

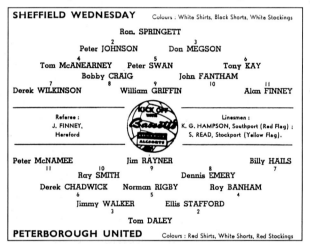

SHEFFIELD WEDNESDAY   Colours : White Shirts, Black Shorts, White Stockings

Ron. SPRINGETT

2 Peter JOHNSON   3 Don MEGSON

4 Tom McANEARNEY   5 Peter SWAN   6 Tony KAY

Bobby CRAIG   John FANTHAM

7 Derek WILKINSON   8 William GRIFFIN   10   11 Alan FINNEY

Referee :
J. FINNEY,
Hereford

Linesmen :
K. G. HAMPSON, Southport (Red Flag) ;
S. READ, Stockport (Yellow Flag).

11 Peter McNAMEE   10 Jim RAYNER   9   Billy HAILS 7

Ray SMITH   8 Dennis EMERY

6 Derek CHADWICK   5 Norman RIGBY   Roy BANHAM 4

3 Jimmy WALKER   2 Ellis STAFFORD

Tom DALEY

PETERBOROUGH UNITED   Colours : Red Shirts, White Shorts, Red Stockings

THEY'LL TAKE 20,000 TO SHEFFIELD, BUT CUP-HOLDERS WON'T

By ROY PESKETT

PETERBOROUGH, annually denied admission to the Football League, are expected to draw a bigger Cup crowd at Sheffield than are the Cup holders themselves who visit the same city in the same round.

Extracts from the Sheffield Wednesday Programme.

HEARTY GREETINGS to Peterborough United on their first visit to Hillsborough. Non-Leaguers they may be, but in recent weeks they have been given the attention and publicity usually reserved for VIPs and many a Football League club would be thankful if they could gain half as much boosting ! Good luck to them, we say, and may they achieve their ambition of Football League membership this year.

Peterborough have a good case. They have been champions of the Midland League for the last four seasons and last season were unbeaten dropping only four points of a possible 72. The team scored 137 goals against 26. They have a £90,000 stand : an average home crowd of about 15,000 : have achieved performances of distinction in the F.A. Cup in several seasons. This season they have beaten Shrewsbury Town, Walsall and Ipswich.

The playing pitch is first-class and in addition to modern lounges, refreshment bars, and even ladies' powder rooms, the club have their own dance hall on the premises. Lectures and concerts are on the progress plans.

Jimmy Hagan says that Peterborough have already spent £116,000 on ground improvements. All this seems fantastic when connected with a quiet cathedral city. Men of breath and vision are certainly at the helm.

They have the wholehearted backing of a Supporters' Club, which has more than 35,000 members, and, it has been stated, this body donates £1,500 a month to the football club—more than £55,000 in three years. Fixed assets are put at £113,000.

Manager Jimmy Hagan needs no introduction. The man who delighted crowds everywhere during his 20 years' service with Sheffield United and who has given Wednesdayites plenty of anxious moments, had excellent credentials for the job he took over some 18 months ago.

115

Two goals in the final twelve minutes brought Peterborough to eventual fourth round defeat.

WHAT A FANTASTIC FIGHT BY POSH!

Sheffield Wed. 2, Peterborough 0

PETERBOROUGH UNITED—greatest non-League club in football—are out of the Cup. . . . But what a fantastic battle ! What a thundering, thrill-soaked, backs-to-the-wall fight proud Posh put up before they capitulated to the team from the First Division.

For 79 minutes, before two superb goals by Sheffield's half-pint Scottish inside left Bobby Craig finished them, Peterborough's defence shut out the Wednesday wonders.

For 79 minutes centre-half Norman Rigby, goalkeeper Tom Daley, wing-halves Roy Banham and Derek Chadwick, and full-backs Ellis Stafford and Jimmy Walker lived up to Peterborough manager Jimmy Hagan's before-the-match boast : "We are a good team—a very good team, fit to play anyone. . ."

Aided by centre-forward Jim Rayner, who played back for most of the match as an extra half-back, the Hagan-Peterborough plan gradually unfolded through the golden murk of Hillsborough : "Play for a draw . . . get Wednesday to Peterborough."

This was Hagan's briefing—and how nearly Peterborough pulled it off under those fog-wreathed floodlights.

Gradually, however, as the legs and muscles of the Peterborough players grew more and more leaden under the ceaseless siege of their goal, Wednesday began to find the gaps.

But it was not till the 34th minute of the second half that Alan Finney, Wednesday's skipper and outside left, finally broke the Peterborough wall.

For a long time Wednesday had been prisoners of their own foolish tactics. They dribbled and dribbled and dribbled instead of moving the ball with swift incisive passes.

Then Finney, the straightest running forward on the field, showed the way. With 11 minutes to go he flashed down the right wing—he played there for most of the second half—in a dazzling dribble.

Pulling the entire Peterborough defence out of position, he slipped the ball inside to Bobby Craig.

Craig suddenly pivoted and crashed a tremendous right-foot drive which glanced off a defender, hit the inside of a post and ricocheted into the net.

The 20,000 Peterborough fans who had made the journey by train, coach, and car were still slack-jawed with horror when three minutes later the now unstoppable Finney repeated the medicine.

He dribbled the ball on a hairpin before pushing in again to Craig. This time the 5ft. 4in. Scot "dummied" past two defenders before cracking the ball past the Peterborough goalkeeper, who was spreadeagled helplessly in the Sheffield slush.

The Non-League record of Giantkilling 1952-60

UNITED'S CUP RUNS

In response to many requests by Posh supporters Sports Standard has prepared the following chart which shows United's progress in the F.A. Cup competition since the 1952-53 season when their run of "giant killings" first started —

1952-53
1st qual. round — Symingtons (A). Won 5-2. 2nd qual. round — Spalding (A). Drew 2-2. Replay — Spalding (H), Won 3-0. (8,100). Divisional final — Corby (A). Drew 0-0. Replay — Corby (H). Won 5-3 (9,843). 4th qual. round — Bedford (H) Won 2-1 (15,327 record). 1st round — Torquay (H). Won 2-1 (12,948). 2nd round — Bristol Rovers (H). Lost 0-1 (15,280).

1953-54
4th qual. round — Grays Ath. (H). Won 4-1 (11,200). 1st round — Hitchin (A). Won 3-1. 2nd round — Aldershot (H). Won 2-1 (16,717 record). 3rd round — Cardiff (A). Lost 1-3.

1954-55
4th qual. round — Boston (H). Lost 1-2 (16,558).

1955-56
4th qual. round — Ilkeston (A). Won 3-1. 1st round — Ipswich (H). Won 3-1 (20,601 record) 2nd round — Swindon (A) Drew 1-1. Replay — Swindon (H). Lost 1-2 (16,000).

1956-57
4th qual. round — Corby (A). Won 5-1. 1st round — Yeovil (A). Won 3-1. 2nd round — Bradford (H). Won 3-0 (18,000). 3rd round — Lincoln (H). Drew 2-2. (22,000 record). Replay — Lincoln (A). Won 5-4. 4th round — Huddersfield (A). Lost 3-1.

1957-58
4th qual. round — Wolverton (H). Won (13,200). 1st round — Torquay (H). Drew 3-3 (17,800). Replay — Torquay (A). Lost 0-1.

LAST SEASON
4th qual. round — Walthamstow (H). Won 3-0 (14,700). 1st round — Kettering (H). Drew 2-2 (17,800). Replay — Kettering (A). Won 3-2. 2nd round — Headington (H). Won 4-2 (16,855). 3rd round — Fulham (A). Drew 0-0. Replay — Fulham (H). Lost 0-1 (21,600).

THIS SEASON
4th qual. round — Bury Town (H). Won 8-1 (9,922). 1st round — Shrewsbury (H). Won 4-3 (16,321). 2nd round — Walsall (A). Won 3-1. 3rd round — Ipswich (A) 2 ? ? 2
22,000 *26,000 2 - 0*

Peterborough's spirited and skilful performance finally helped to convince the footballing establishment that the club could hold its own in the elevated company of the Fourth Division.

SATURDAY, MAY 28, 1960

PETERBOROUGH IN DIVISION IV
The 'Posh' are in after 21 years

by ALAN HOBY

FOR 20 years Peterborough United have been trying to break into League football. And for 20 years "The Posh"—as they are called by their proud and patient fans—have had their application thrown out by the shameful "jolly old pals" act of the League clubs.

But yesterday—at the 21st time of trying—Peterborough enjoyed their "finest hour."

For at 11.41 a.m. the big clubs, at their annual meeting in London, elected the brave and indomitable "Posh" to membership of the Football League.

Final Midland League Table, 1959-60

	P	W	D	L	F	A	Ps
Peterboro'	32	23	6	3	108	37	52
N. Shields	32	22	5	5	76	27	49
Ashington	32	19	7	6	90	40	45
S. Shields	32	16	8	8	65	41	40
Blyth Sp.	32	13	10	9	74	51	36
Stockton	32	12	8	12	53	66	32
Goole	32	13	5	14	62	78	31
Consett	32	13	4	15	54	65	30
Spennymoor	32	12	6	14	47	57	30
Horden	32	12	5	15	46	62	29
Gainsboro'	32	7	14	11	41	60	28
Skegness	32	9	9	14	50	64	27
Scarboro'	32	9	8	15	48	65	26
Worksop	32	10	4	18	41	70	24
Sutton	32	5	11	15	44	76	23
Denaby	32	8	6	18	44	68	22
Frickley	32	7	6	19	54	70	20

117

There they would join Northampton Town.

The season proved a watershed for the Cobblers. Dave Bowen, now a Welsh international right half, had always retained domestic links with the town and returned from Arsenal as player-manager. Results took time to improve, a decidedly low spot being the 7-1 FA Cup defeat at Torquay, but by the end of the season the side had achieved sixth place and omens were good for the following year. Winger Jack English, a Cobbler since 1949 and

	LEAGUE-DIVISION IV	Played	Won	Drawn	Lost	Goals	Points
1	Walsall	46	28	9	9	102-60	65
2	Notts County	46	26	8	12	107-69	60
3	Torquay United ..	46	26	8	12	84-58	60
4	Watford	46	24	9	13	92-67	57
5	Millwall	46	18	17	11	84-61	53
6	Northampton Town ..	46	22	9	15	85-63	53
7	Gillingham ..	46	21	10	15	74-69	52
8	Crystal Palace ..	46	19	12	15	84-64	50
9	Exeter City	46	19	11	16	80-70	49
10	Stockport County	46	19	11	16	58-54	49
11	Bradford	46	17	15	14	70-68	49
12	Rochdale	46	18	10	18	65-60	46
13	Aldershot	46	18	9	19	77-74	45
14	Crewe Alexandra	46	18	9	19	79-88	45
15	Darlington	46	17	9	20	63-73	43
16	Workington Town	46	14	14	18	68-60	42
17	Doncaster Rovers	46	16	10	20	69-76	42
18	Barrow	46	15	11	20	77-87	41
19	Carlisle United ..	46	15	11	20	51-66	41
20	Chester	46	14	12	20	59-77	40
21	Southport	46	10	14	22	48-92	34
22	Gateshead	46	12	9	25	58-86	33
23	Oldham Athletic ..	46	8	12	26	41-83	28
24	Hartlepools United	46	10	7	29	59-109	27

Walsall, Notts County, Torquay United and Watford promoted to Division III.
Peterborough United elected in place of Gateshead.

scorer of 125 goals, was released, injury ended Bobby Tebbutt's league career and Peter Kane joined Bowen's former club for £10,000.

In the summer of 1959 Johnny Morris had strengthened his Corby Town side by signing Henry Cockburn. The former Manchester United and Peterborough player was not as influential as hoped and the side struggled once again, despite centre forward McKay's 27 goals, (following 34 in the previous season). Even a 9-0 victory over Bexleyheath in the final league game failed to gloss over the disappointment of another poor season, which included an humiliating 2-1 F.A. Cup defeat at Rushden.

The club's new floodlights, however, provided opportunities for innovation. A cup competition, involving Boston United, Worcester City and visitors for the inaugural match, Peterborough United, (whose own floodlights became operational in February 1958), began at Corby on October 5th when over 4,000 spectators watched Posh win by 5-0.

CORBY TOWN

versus

PETERBOROUGH

MONDAY, OCTOBER 5th, 1959
Kick-off 7.15 p.m.

FOOTBALL HISTORY WILL BE MADE TONIGHT!

FIRST EVER MATCH OF THE
MIDLAND FLOODLIT CUP COMPETITION

CORBY TOWN versus PETERBOROUGH UNITED

Tonight is the first match of this new Floodlit Cup Competition and the Directors, Officials and myself are very pleased and proud that Corby Town sponsored this Competition, as we felt that there was a need for floodlit competitive football in the Midlands.

I give a very warm welcome to our renowned opponents, Peterborough United, this evening, and I trust you all see a match worthy of the occasion.

118

In November, former player Tommy Hadden, who with fellow stalwart Jack Connors had recently enjoyed a testimonial, returned to the club as first team trainer. It proved a fortuitous appointment.

Tommy Hadden

PREMIER DIVISION Final Table—Season 1959/60							
	P.	W.	D.	L.	F.	A.	Pts.
Bath City	42	32	3	7	116	50	67
Headington Utd	42	23	8	11	78	61	54
Weymouth.....	42	22	9	11	93	69	53
Cheltenham T...	42	21	6	15	82	68	48
Cambridge C...	42	18	11	13	81	72	47
Chelmsford C...	42	19	7	16	90	70	45
Bedford Town..	42	21	3	18	97	85	45
King's Lynn ..	42	17	11	14	89	78	45
Boston Utd. ..	42	17	10	15	83	80	44
Wisbech Town..	42	17	10	15	81	84	44
Yeovil Town ..	42	17	8	17	81	73	42
Hereford Utd ..	42	15	12	15	70	74	42
Tonbridge	42	16	8	18	79	73	40
Hastings Utd. ..	42	16	8	18	63	77	40
Wellington Tn. .	42	13	11	18	63	78	37
Dartford	42	15	7	20	64	82	37
Gravesend & N.	42	14	8	20	69	84	36
Worcester City .	42	13	10	19	72	89	36
Nuneaton B. ..	42	11	11	20	64	78	33
Barry Town ..	42	14	5	23	78	103	33
Poole Town ..	42	10	8	24	69	96	28
KETTERING ..	42	9	10	23	60	90	28

Kettering's Premier status was short-lived as a disastrous season brought FA Cup defeat at Margate, (of the lower division), and eventual relegation.

One game at Rockingham Road, however, on February 20th 1960, enabled over 3,000 spectators to spot a number of future stars in the North v South Schoolboy International Trial.

NORTH	SOUTH
D Roper (Bradford)	A Dewis (Coventry)
J Hickton (Chesterfield)	S Winsall (Kettering)
R Thompson (Don & Dearne)	**R Wills (Northampton)**
J Smithurst (Derby)	D Pratt (Bristol)
P Madeley (Leeds)	P Turner (West Ham)
R Lee (Sheffield)	S Vale (West Bromwich)
D Pleat (Nottingham)	K Colsell (Swindon)
D Walker (Mid-Cheshire)	**R Harris (Hackney)**
R Hewitt (Manchester)	A Hodgetts (West Bromwich)
W Atkinson (Seaham)	**B Fry (Bedford)**
D Thwaites (Stockton)	J O'Rourke (Barking)

Right   **KETTERING TOWN**   Left

Colours :   Red and White Shirts, White Shorts

1 ROBERTS

2 MARSTON   3 GROOME

4 FROGGATT   5 BAXTER   6 SMITH (TERRY)

7 MORROW   8 HAMILTON   9 DRAPER   10 NEALE   11 BURROWS

11 LOVE   10 DICKSON   9 McINNES   8 THOMPSON   7 GIBSON

6 DENIAL   5 KYLE   4 ATKINSON

3 ADAMS   2 BEAVON

1 PETERS

Colours :   Gold Shirts, Black Shorts

Left   **HEADINGTON UTD.**   Right

Another hopeful youngster appeared in Headington United's colours on September 5th 1959. Ron Atkinson, later manager at Kettering and much later at Manchester United, Aston Villa and Coventry.

119

Kettering's reserve side was the best of the Central Alliance contingent - a distinction equalled by Wellingborough's second string in the UCL.

1959-60	P.	W.	D.	L.	F.	A.	Pts.
Dunstable Res.	34	24	7	3	131	52	55
Kempston Rovers	34	23	7	4	104	43	53
Shefford Town	34	22	4	8	110	51	48
St Neots Res.	34	23	1	10	92	42	47
Wellingborough Res.	34	22	2	10	70	41	46
Northampton Town 'A'	34	19	5	10	114	63	43
Rushden Res.	34	16	7	11	89	80	39
S & L Corby	34	18	1	15	93	84	37
Raunds Town	34	15	4	15	65	81	34
Kettering 'A'	34	13	7	14	74	82	33
Wootton Blue Cross	34	14	5	15	71	84	33
Biggleswade Res.	34	14	2	18	88	79	30
Desborough Town	34	13	1	20	61	92	27
Finedon Town	34	11	5	18	72	83	27
Huntingdon United	34	9	3	22	65	115	21
Bedford Avenue	34	5	5	24	50	102	15
Higham Town	34	3	6	25	52	130	12
B. Timken Duston	34	3	6	25	35	130	12

CENTRAL ALLIANCE

Division 1—South

	P.	W.	D.	L.	Goals F.	A.	Pts.
Bourne Town ...	32	26	5	1	106	43	57
Grantham	32	24	2	6	85	31	50
St. Neots Town	32	21	3	3	106	59	45
Long Eaton U.	32	18	4	10	67	44	40
Ely City ..	32	18	3	11	74	42	39
KETTERING R.	32	13	9	10	83	67	35
Stamford	32	12	8	12	73	66	32
Rushden Town..	32	12	8	12	60	66	32
Rothwell Town.	32	12	8	12	56	71	32
Derby City. A...	32	11	8	13	58	69	30
Nuneaton Res..	32	11	6	15	56	70	28
Wellingboro' T.	32	10	6	16	54	71	26
Potton Utd. ..	32	9	7	16	51	68	25
Wisbech T. Rs.	32	10	4	13	66	86	24
Rugby T. Res.	32	8	4	20	50	88	20
Anstey Nomads	32	5	6	21	50	98	16
Corby Town R.	32	5	3	24	47	103	13

Kettering's club handbook refers to a remarkable achievement by long serving Bobby Wyldes.

Bobby Wyldes

Bobby Wyldes was born in Southport and came to Kettering at the age of four. After leaving Stamford Road School he played for Kaycee for six years. After serving in the Royal Navy he played alongside his brother at Desborough. He then moved to Luton Town making thirty first team appearances in three seasons. Now playing for the Poppies he has appeared in every position, including goalkeeper.

I had spent my first London season commuting two or three times a week up and down the Central Line to Leyton, and a second, crossing the river to Selhurst Park. One April evening in 1960 I absorbed the terrible truth that I was unlikely ever to pursue a career as a full-time professional footballer. Gentlemanly Arthur Rowe, he of Spurs 'push and run' fame and by then assistant manager of Crystal Palace, broke the news in kindly fashion after an 'A' team game at Folkestone.

"Go to college son," he said, "and then get a proper job. You can always make a few shillings on the side playing football."

Although the words hurt beyond belief at the time they were both wise and prophetic. He even bothered to write a personal note - brief but sincere.

Dear Dan,

good luck!

Sincerely, Arthur Rowe.

In September I entered Teacher Training College in the King's Road, Chelsea. A new chapter began.

GOALS, MORE GOALS
AND
TERRY BLY
1960-61

The season of 1960-61 again belonged to Peterborough United. Any fears that they would be overawed in their new league were quickly dispelled in the opening game against Wrexham, when a 3-0 win included a first goal for close season signing, centre forward Terry Bly.

● "Posh" Peterborough United, new boys of the Football League, beat Wrexham 3—0 in their opening match in Division Four—and the fans went home happy.

● Attendance at the game, 17,564, was greater than any other in Divisions Three and Four, and was as good as that drawn by Proud Preston of Division One.

● Manager Jimmy Hagan shared in the general joy but said his men would need to speed up if they hope to be able to make League progress.

Jack Walls

EMERY SHOWS THE WAY

Peter McNamee

Peterborough 3, Wrexham 0

THE "Posh" are off to a dream start in their first ever League campaign. But for a long while I thought they would have to struggle to hold on to an oh, so slender goal lead.

Up to the last quarter of an hour, Wrexham looked worth a point in a high-standard game in which there was hardly a foul to be seen.

But Peterborough finally crushed the tenacious Welshmen with splendid goals from Peter McNamee (seventy-five minutes) and former Norwich Cup hero Terry Bly (eighty minutes).

Can the "Posh" measure up to Fourth Division football—so different from the Midland League they have known for too long?

On this showing I think they will.

Terry Bly

Now we are 'in', and the big question is: "Can we keep up our form and reach the Third Division?"

Well, as one of the old hands with 'Posh', I am sure we will make a go of it. And I like to think that one day I might be in a promotion-winning side.

The Midland League championship is very nice, but the gilt goes off the gingerbread after five years of winning the same competition. I say that with all due respect to a fine League.

Apart from those regulars who were colleagues of mine in our Midland League championship runs, we have some new chums in Terry Bly, John Anderson and Dick Whittaker, all of whom have had plenty of League football experience—in the case of Anderson and Whittaker, in the First Division.

As Billy Hails records in a magazine article from those early days in the Fourth Division, the side was largely George Swindin's Midland League team.

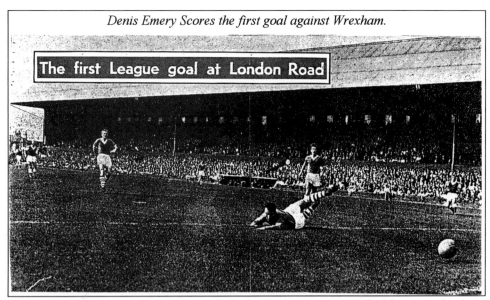

Denis Emery Scores the first goal against Wrexham.

The first League goal at London Road

In early September, Peterborough helped create a remarkable record when visiting Selhurst Park for a Fourth Division fixture against Crystal Palace. The crowd of 36,478 witnessed a fine Posh victory over Arthur Rowe's side.

SUPER POSH

Crystal Palace 0, Peterborough 2

NOW WE KNOW! The Posh are too good for the Fourth Division.

This wasn't just a game of football—it was the emotional experience of a lifetime. And 36,478 people rammed themselves into a boiling pot of excitement and glorious confusion called Selhurst Park to live through it.

This is a record for a fourth division game, and also for a league game at the ground.

I wish you'd been there, you people who want to make soccer an armchair game!

Two months before the Cup rounds start here were the ingredients of a dozen ties all rolled into one.

Great football, incidents piling up like cars at a traffic light that won't turn green, and an atmosphere you could see rising above these frenzied fans like smoke from chimneys.

Arthur Rowe's push-and-run, pushed and probed all they knew.

But does South London realise how good this Palace team is? Angry fans stamped their feet and yelled for the boot.

If I had my way I'd have given it to them — in the pants.

Peterborough, in their first visit to London, took the town by storm—Hailstorm.

After only five minutes right-winger Billy Hails sent 36,000 nervous systems tingling like telephone cables with a goal so soft and smooth we wondered if it had really happened.

Dennis Emery, the man who owes his start in football to Arthur Rowe, put Peter McNamee through to make it 2—0.

OUT OF PLACE

LUCKY PETERBOROUGH! They'd seen it all before in their great Cup battles of the past. They raised their game to the mood of the crowd.

Palace, unused to it, couldn't.

● It was a game that had no place in the Fourth Division. Here was first-class football played by a couple of teams that won't linger long in the lower reaches of the Football League, I'll wager.

Personalities? There were none in this £9,000 Peterborough bunch of heroes.

Their defenders were magnificent. Skipper Norman Rigby, so cool, so efficient pulled his men out so well that nearly always the Palace raiders had to shoot from outside the penalty area.

The meeting of the county's top sides at London Road on October 8th provided one of the season's most exciting games. 22,959 watched a weakened Cobblers, deprived through injury of amateur international centre forward Laurie Brown and tenacious wing half Roly Mills, squander a 3 goal lead.

The reporter had the fore-sight to predict a happy ending for both sides.

Peterborough U. 3,   Northampton T. 3

PETERBOROUGH and Northampton for promotion! That's my firm conviction after seeing this exciting drawn Derby game, witnessed by a record crowd of 22,959 spectators at London Road. If there are any Fourth Division clubs capable of playing better football than these two, I just can't wait to see them in action.

A tussle between United skipper Norman Rigby and the Northampton leader Mike Deakin.

The game had everything, including plenty of skill, many thrills, and the quickest goals I have seen.

Northampton's two in three minutes staggered Peterborough, and when a third went in 17 minutes later it looked to be the complete knock-out. Instead of which Peterborough came out full of fight to reduce the lead in the first minute of the second half.

Shortly afterwards Northampton lost their left winger, Tom Fowler, for the remainder of the game.

This unquestionably upset the rhythm of an attack which had previously terrorised a none-too-surefooted Peterborough defence.

Whether Fowler's absence made all that difference to the result is questionable, in view of the second-half skill and determination of the home players.

Northampton, having struck quick blows through Derek Leck and their go-ahead untiring Mike Deakin, proceeded to play football which one seldom sees in these circles.

It was Fowler who scored their third and what appeared to be crushing goal.

What happened in the second half bore no relation to what had gone before. Peterborough sprung into life and two goals by Peter McNamee set the crowd roaring for the equaliser, which came within a minute of McNamee's second through that other favourite, Dennis Emery.

By the time Northampton and Peterborough met in their return game in February, Posh were virtual champions and duly recorded a 3-0 victory.

THE return battle of the two League teams of Northamptonshire got under way at the County Ground, Northampton, this afternoon with the Posh and Cobblers both trying to secure three points from their two Division IV clashes.

The previous game—in October, 1960—resulted in a 3-3 draw after Northampton had held the upper hand with a first-half three-goal lead.

Peterborough have not made many changes since that time, but the Cobblers have made several. The Cobblers included their 20-year-old centre-forward Mike Everitt, signed this week from Arsenal, and the youngest man on the field was their goalkeeper, 19-year-old Norman Coe.

COBBLERS

Coe

Phillips   Claypole

Cooke   Gale   Mills

Spelman   Brown   Everitt   Moran   Fowler

•

McNamee   Smith   Bly   Emery   Hails

Ripley   Rigby   Rayner

Walker   Whittaker

Walls

POSH

Posh make it 134 and Bly makes it 52

<table>
<tr><td colspan="9">Division IV</td></tr>
<tr><td></td><td></td><td></td><td></td><td></td><td colspan="2">Goals</td><td></td></tr>
<tr><td>Peterborough</td><td>46</td><td>28</td><td>10</td><td>8</td><td>134</td><td>65</td><td>66</td></tr>
<tr><td>C Palace</td><td>46</td><td>29</td><td>6</td><td>11</td><td>110</td><td>69</td><td>64</td></tr>
<tr><td>Northampton</td><td>46</td><td>25</td><td>10</td><td>11</td><td>90</td><td>62</td><td>60</td></tr>
<tr><td>Bradford</td><td>46</td><td>26</td><td>7</td><td>12</td><td>82</td><td>72</td><td>59</td></tr>
<tr><td>Millwall</td><td>46</td><td>21</td><td>8</td><td>17</td><td>97</td><td>86</td><td>52</td></tr>
<tr><td>York C</td><td>46</td><td>21</td><td>9</td><td>16</td><td>80</td><td>60</td><td>51</td></tr>
<tr><td>Crewe</td><td>46</td><td>20</td><td>9</td><td>17</td><td>61</td><td>67</td><td>49</td></tr>
<tr><td>Workington</td><td>46</td><td>21</td><td>7</td><td>18</td><td>74</td><td>76</td><td>49</td></tr>
<tr><td>Darlington</td><td>46</td><td>18</td><td>13</td><td>15</td><td>78</td><td>70</td><td>49</td></tr>
<tr><td>Aldershot</td><td>46</td><td>18</td><td>9</td><td>19</td><td>79</td><td>69</td><td>45</td></tr>
<tr><td>Stockport</td><td>45</td><td>18</td><td>9</td><td>18</td><td>56</td><td>63</td><td>45</td></tr>
<tr><td>Doncaster</td><td>46</td><td>19</td><td>7</td><td>20</td><td>76</td><td>78</td><td>45</td></tr>
<tr><td>Oldham</td><td>46</td><td>19</td><td>7</td><td>20</td><td>79</td><td>88</td><td>45</td></tr>
<tr><td>Southport</td><td>46</td><td>19</td><td>6</td><td>21</td><td>69</td><td>67</td><td>44</td></tr>
<tr><td>Rochdale</td><td>46</td><td>17</td><td>8</td><td>21</td><td>60</td><td>66</td><td>42</td></tr>
<tr><td>Wrexham</td><td>46</td><td>17</td><td>8</td><td>21</td><td>62</td><td>56</td><td>42</td></tr>
<tr><td>Gillingham</td><td>44</td><td>16</td><td>11</td><td>17</td><td>62</td><td>64</td><td>41</td></tr>
<tr><td>Carlisle</td><td>46</td><td>13</td><td>13</td><td>20</td><td>61</td><td>79</td><td>39</td></tr>
<tr><td>Accrington</td><td>45</td><td>16</td><td>7</td><td>22</td><td>72</td><td>86</td><td>39</td></tr>
<tr><td>Exeter C</td><td>46</td><td>14</td><td>10</td><td>22</td><td>66</td><td>94</td><td>38</td></tr>
<tr><td>Mansfield</td><td>45</td><td>16</td><td>5</td><td>24</td><td>71</td><td>78</td><td>37</td></tr>
<tr><td>Barrow</td><td>44</td><td>12</td><td>10</td><td>22</td><td>47</td><td>76</td><td>34</td></tr>
<tr><td>Hartlepools</td><td>46</td><td>12</td><td>8</td><td>26</td><td>71</td><td>103</td><td>32</td></tr>
<tr><td>Chester</td><td>46</td><td>11</td><td>9</td><td>26</td><td>61</td><td>104</td><td>31</td></tr>
</table>

NOT content with being divisional champions in their first season, Posh were cheeky enough today to shatter the whole Football League's scoring record of 128—and the record-breaking one was also Terry Bly's fiftieth of the season

The fact that Barrow were meanwhile prevented from becoming the only side to complete a double over the champions paled into insignificance before these feats.

Watching Posh make history was Mr. Len Shipman, a member of the League Management Committee, who was to present the Fourth Division Championship Trophy to skipper Norman Rigby after the game.

Peterborough: Walls; Whittaker. Walker; Rayner. Rigby, Ripley; Hails, Emery, Bly, Smith, McNamee.

Barrow: Coglan; Robinson. Cahill; Staniforth. McEvoy. McGlennon; Howard, Clark, Lowes, Robertson. Kemp.

Referee Mr. K A Collinge (Barnsley).

In their final league game, champions elect Posh trounced Barrow 6-2, creating a new Football League record of 134 goals, Terry Bly netting his 52nd of the season.

Terry Bly's 50th goal of the season, against Barrow, in the final league match of the 1960-61 season.

League success was accompanied by the now obligatory Cup run, Posh accounting for Portsmouth in the third round, before losing 2-1 at Aston Villa in a replayed fourth round match before a crowd of 64,500.

Finale!

HAILS WINS
IT BY 70 sec.

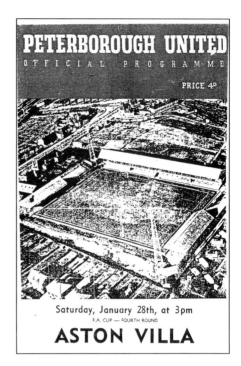

PETERBOROUGH UNITED
OFFICIAL PROGRAMME

PRICE 4ᴅ

Saturday, January 28th, at 3pm
F.A. CUP — FOURTH ROUND

ASTON VILLA

Portsmouth 1 Peterborough 2

FOURTH DIVISION Peterborough are convinced they are capable of reaching the semi-final of the F.A. Cup this year—if they get a home match in today's fourth-round draw.

Portsmouth would be the last to disagree. For only a brilliant performance by Portsmouth goalkeeper Dick Beattie in the second half stopped the score from mounting to a humiliating 4—0.

Then, when substitute outside-left Alex Wilson headed Portsmouth's equaliser in the 78th minute, the 1—1 score line was outrageous flattery to the home side.

But, as they have often done before, Peterborough staged a breath-taking finale.

Seventy seconds from the end outside-right Billy Hails delicately stopped a centre from inside-left Ray Smith near the edge of the penalty area.

Hails beat former England star Jimmy Dickinson with insolent ease and crashed the ball past Beattie as the cameramen's flash-bulbs popped to record Pompey's fall.

Right half Keith Ripley scored Peterborough's first, this time only seven seconds from half-time, with Beattie clawing desperately at the 30-yard shot which went just inside a post.

Terry Bly's goalscoring exploits during Norwich City's run to eventual F.A. Cup semi-final defeat in 1959 attracted national attention. Perhaps most memorable were the two that

Referee—Mr. A. W. LUTY (Leeds)	**Peterborough United**			Colours—Red White Shorts
	WALLS.			
RIGHT WHITTAKER			WALKER	LEFT
RAYNER 2	BANHAM 5		RIPLEY 3	6
HAILS 7	EMERY	BLY 9	SMITH 10	McNAMEE 11
McPARLAND 11	WYLIE 10	HITCHENS 9	O'NEILL 8	MACEWAN 7
	THOMSON 6	DUGDALE 5	CROWE 4	
LEFT	LYNN 3		NEAL 2	RIGHT
		POTTER		
Linesmen—Mr. R. A. Bedford (Red Flag) Mr. W. A. Marriott (Yellow Flag)	**Aston Villa**		Colours—Light Blue Shirts White Shorts	

contributed to a 3-0 third round victory over Manchester United at Carrow Road. But the following season the goals mysteriously dried up, despite him returning to the ground after training for additional shooting practice. On joining newly promoted Peterborough he was concerned that he might never rediscover his goalscoring touch. He needn't have worried. His record 52 goals during 1960-61 is unlikely ever to be surpassed.

Recalling the season, Bly revealed his debt to the wing play of Billy Hails, with whom he developed an almost telepathic understanding.

126

"He was probably responsible for 40 of my goals," he said. Then added significantly, "But Billy would no doubt say that Denis (Emery) had supplied him with the ball in the first place." The Emery-Hails-Bly triangle was certainly effective and with outside left Peter McNamee, less predictable than Hails but immensely gifted, and inside forward Ray Smith, formed the league's most formidable strike force as the huge goal tally demonstrates.

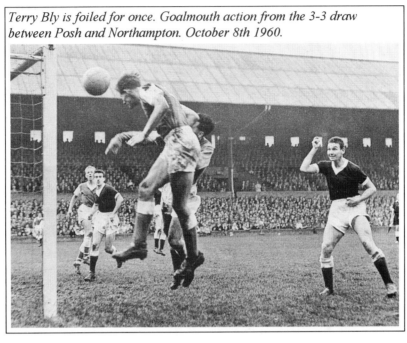

Terry Bly is foiled for once. Goalmouth action from the 3-3 draw between Posh and Northampton. October 8th 1960.

Bly in goalscoring form in a rare defeat at Crewe, November 12th 1960.

127

Peterborough United 1960-61. Fourth Division Champions at the first time of asking.

Bly's recollections of the managerial team at Peterborough during that period emphasise the important role played by trainer and former player Johnny Anderson, whose cheerful, ebullient personality and vast knowledge of the game did much to promote team spirit. His party piece on away coach trips was to regale the players with wildly exaggerated accounts of his goal for Manchester United in the 1948 F.A. Cup final against Blackpool. (The Observer report of the match, refereed by local official C.J. Barrick, bears testimony to the quality of the goal - if not the goalkeeping).

> *"Then, to seal up victory, Anderson from right half and 35 yards scored with the sort of shot that boys dream of. I suppose it should have been saved."* April 25th 1948

Jimmy Hagan, England and Sheffield United.

Manager Hagan, in stark contrast, cut a rather dour, unsympathetic figure, his training methods distinctly at odds with those expected from one of the game's great ball-playing inside forwards. Sessions generally consisted of endless lapping of the pitch with hardly a glimpse of a football.

There was little communication with the players, either individually or collectively. Bly's previous manager, Archie McCauley, had insisted that each player understood his particular role in the side, ensuring that it operated as a cohesive unit.

128

Fortunately there were so many talented players in Hagan's team that they simply went out and played, instinctively, the attacking football that masked any tendency to defensive frailty.

Jim Walker, the Sheffield born full back and survivor of the Midland League side, remembers an incident which removed any doubts about the manager's own footballing ability.

It was a rare occasion when the first team players were each practising with a ball. Hagan stood in the centre circle, dressed in blazer, slacks and ordinary brown leather shoes. When he demanded the ball, the entire squad fired them at him, fiercely with no love lost, from all quarters of the pitch. As balls approached, the former international adjusted his position and killed each one dead, before turning to face the next. When he had finished, the footballs lay in a circle around him, none farther than 2 feet away. Even the sceptical Denis Emery was heard to say admiringly, "He'll do!"

Although overshadowed to some extent by the newcomers, Northampton Town achieved third place, thus gaining promotion for the first time in the Cobblers' history. Earlier in the season the club had joined the rapidly expanding floodlit fraternity

	LEAGUE - DIVISION IV			Played	Won	Drawn	Lost	Goals	Points
1	Peterborough United	..	..	46	28	10	8	134-65	66
2	Crystal Palace	..	..	46	29	6	11	110-69	64
3	Northampton Town ..	..	..	46	25	10	11	90-62	60
4	Bradford	..	..	46	26	8	12	84-74	60
5	York City	..	..	46	21	9	16	80-60	51
6	Millwall	..	..	46	21	8	17	97-86	50
7	Darlington	..	..	46	18	13	15	78-70	49
8	Workington Town	..	..	46	21	7	18	74-76	49
9	Crewe Alexandra	..	..	46	20	9	17	61-67	49
10	Aldershot	..	..	46	18	9	19	79-69	45
11	Doncaster Rovers	..	..	46	19	7	20	76-78	45
12	Oldham Athletic	..	..	46	19	7	20	79-88	45
13	Stockport County	..	..	46	18	9	19	57-66	45
14	Southport	..	..	46	19	6	21	69-67	44
15	Gillingham	..	..	46	15	13	18	64-66	43
16	Wrexham	..	..	46	17	8	21	62-56	42
17	Rochdale	..	..	46	17	8	21	60-66	42
18	Accrington Stanley	..	..	46	16	8	22	74-88	40
19	Carlisle United	..	..	46	13	13	20	61-79	39
20	Mansfield Town	..	..	46	16	6	24	71-78	38
21	Exeter City	..	..	46	14	10	22	66-94	38
22	Barrow	..	..	46	13	11	22	52-79	37
23	Hartlepools United ..	..	..	46	12	8	26	71-103	32
24	Chester	..	..	46	11	9	26	61-104	31

Peterborough United, Crystal Palace, Northampton Town and Bradford promoted to Division III.

with a fixture against Arsenal, who included former player Peter Kane in an impressive line up.

GRAND FLOODLIT OPENING MATCH

NORTHAMPTON TOWN FOOTBALL CLUB

SOUVENIR PROGRAMME 6d.

Northampton

Brewer

Claypole   Phillips

Cooke   Gale   Mills

Olah   Leck   Deakin   Wright   Fowler

Henderson ' Bloomfield Kane Herd Clapton

Groves   Sneddon   Docherty

McCullough   Wills

Kelsey

Arsenal

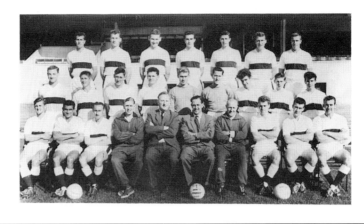

Northampton Town 1960-61

So marked was the improvement in Kettering's fortunes that by the end of April a quick return to the Premier Division of the Southern League seemed certain, possibly as champions.

A remarkable run included FA Cup successes over Corby, Stamford, St. Neots, Boston Utd, Wycombe Wanderers before eventual defeat by 4-2 at Third Division Reading.

There was a draw in the penultimate game against Poole Town, when a controversial late equaliser ensured that once again a league title would be decided in the last match of the season.

Reading

Meeson

Goodall   Vallard

Walker   Davies   Evans

McIlvenny   Whitehouse   Lacey   Norton McLuckie

Walden Humphries McGill Shaw Murrow

Armour   Quigley   Froggatt

Harding   Marston

Smethurst

Kettering Town

Fantastic scenes at Poppies' ground

KETTERING TOWN 2,   POOLE 2

THE most fantastic scenes broke out in the closing minutes of last night's game with Poole at the Rockingham Road ground, writes "The Friar."

I don't expect I will ever know the answer to the most controversial question of the season: was that last-minute shot by Sammy Savage a goal?

Savage appeared to net the equaliser in the last minute, but goalkeeper Brown insisted that the ball did not enter the net and that it hit the side netting.

Sammy Savage was certain. "It was a goal all the way." But before he could explain exactly what happened, Kettering officials coaxed him away.

Frank Brown, the Poole goalkeeper, was in no mood to see anyone. But it became clear on the field that Brown was extremely annoyed with the referee's decision to award a goal.

Kettering forwards replied that the ball went through and under the net, though there was no way for the ball to get either through or under the netting.

Then two supporters claimed that the ball outside the net was a spare ball which had been returned to the field after being kicked out of the ground.

REFEREE

I tackled referee C. A. Sharpe, of Welwyn Garden City. "I awarded a goal. There's nothing more to it than that," he said. Why, then, did the Poole players surround you and hold up play for four minutes? "Does that matter? I've nothing more to say."

130

CAN THE POPPIES DO IT?

THE LAST SOUTHERN LEAGUE MATCH OF THE SEASON
ROCKINGHAM ROAD GROUND
TOMORROW, WEDNESDAY, MAY 3rd —

KETTERING TOWN v.
CAMBRIDGE UNITED
Kick-off 6.45 p.m
ADMISSION AS USUAL

The fixture list had contrived to bring together the two top sides, Kettering and Cambridge United, (once Abbey United of the UCL), for a game which Kettering won comfortably 3-0.

The Poppies side included Bernard Shaw, formerly of Peterborough United, Ted Smethurst, probably the club's most highly rated goalkeeper and a certain gangling centre forward, signed from local club Emmaneff, called John Ritchie.

Poppies need one point

KETTERING Town need one point from tomorrow's home encounter with Cambridge United to be the Southern League's Division One champions, writes "The Friar."

A large crowd is expected to see this top-of-the-table tussle between the teams which have won promotion to the Premier Division.

Kettering must get at least one point. If they lost by the odd goal, for instance, they would lose the championship title by 0.2564 of a goal.

The Kettering team will be chosen from 13 players: the team which drew last night with Poole, plus John Storey and Jimmy Morrow.

The team is: Smethurst; Marston, Storey, Quigley, Froggatt, Armour, Smith; Morrow (H), Morrow (J), Shaw, Savage, Ritchie, Pearson.

The kick-off is at 6.45 pm

Poppies celebrate with champagne after winning the championship 1960-61

Back Row: Marston, Storey, Shaw, Savage, Armour, Morrow H.
Middle Row: Ritchie, Burton, Smethurst, Froggatt, Quigley, Morrow J.

Ted Smethurst

131

Johnny Morris's final season at Corby was hardly covered in glory. An early FA Cup exit against Kettering and a mid table position contributed to a decidedly mediocre record for the player manager. In 116 matches played during his 3 seasons in charge the Steelmen won 41, drew 21 and lost 54.

1960-61	P.	W.	D.	L.	F.	A.	Pts
Shefford Town	32	25	2	5	108	38	52
Corby Reserves	32	24	2	6	109	46	50
Bletchley Town	32	21	5	6	87	41	47
Kempston Rovers	32	21	4	7	99	53	46
St Neots Reserves	32	19	4	9	105	55	42
S & L Corby	32	14	8	10	83	71	36
Wootton Blue Cross	32	15	4	13	62	62	34
Desborough Town	32	14	6	12	74	77	34
Dunstable Reserves	32	15	3	14	75	78	33
British Timken Duston	32	14	5	13	68	71	33
Rushden Reserves	32	12	5	15	53	66	29
Finedon Town	32	11	4	17	74	104	26
Biggleswade Reserves	32	10	3	19	67	81	23
Bedford Avenue	32	8	6	18	47	90	22
Wellingborough Reserves	32	7	3	22	40	76	17
Higham Town	32	3	5	24	50	104	11
Raunds Town	32	4	1	27	49	137	9

At the end of the season, Rushden, Wellingborough, Rothwell, Kettering Reserves and Corby Reserves ended their flirtation with the Central Alliance and rejoined Desborough in the United Counties League.

I had seen very few local games during the season, having spent most Saturdays playing College football in what my father called 'the smoke'.

When I read of the excesses of 'Swinging London' in the early sixties I have to remind myself that I was there - at its throbbing heart, living in the King's Road. I may as well have been in Keynsham - spelt K-E-Y .... as our most decadent pastime was to while away hours listening to Radio Luxembourg. A legacy of this is an unerring ability to recall the names of obscure singers and songs from the period, to the intense irritation of family and friends.

A further indulgence was to spend a shilling or two at Annabel's Cafe, directly opposite the College in the Fulham Road, where Chelsea youngsters Bert Murray, Bobby Tambling and a smoothie with an Italian haircut called Venables, gathered after training.

There they sat, huddled over coffee cups, oblivious to us students, Tel no doubt planning tactics for the 1998 World Cup, while I hid behind a treatise on Child Psychology, silently cursing their talent.

SUPER TED, BIG CLIFF
1961-62

Promoted Peterborough achieved a creditable fifth place in the Third Division in 1961-62. Almost inevitably, the season was enlivened by an FA Cup run. Victory over Colchester in Round 1 was achieved without Denis Emery, injured in the car crash when driving to catch the team coach for the replayed match, held at Carrow Road, Norwich. New striker George Hudson, signed from Accrington Stanley, scored a hat trick.

THE OLD POSH TOUCH!

PRAISE Posh Peterborough. Even without star forward Dennis Emery, injured in a car crash, they strode into the second round of the Cup with a great attacking display against Colchester at Norwich last night.

Three first half goals were more than enough to win this second replay of a tie which lasted 300 minutes.

Peterborough hardly missed Emery. Manager Jimmy Hagan said before the kick-off: "The boys will fight doubly hard tonight."

| Peterborough | ... | 3 |
| Colchester | ...... | 0 |

After 11 minutes Hudson pounced on an accurate centre by Roy Senior to put the Posh ahead. Colchester fought back hard, but 20 minutes later Hudson struck again.

This time Bly gave him the chance and 'keeper Percy Ames was helpless to save.

Goal No. 3 fell to Hudson with a brilliant right-foot shot from 18 yards.

Again it was Bly, the Cup-tie leader discarded by Norwich, who made the goal. And Peterborough had virtually booked their ticket for Torquay.

Colchester, without centre-forward Martyn King—under FA suspension

HE WAS RIGHT. Ray Smith, Emery's stand-in at inside-right, and right-winger Billy Hails ripped the Colchester defence wide open in the first half.

Hefty George Hudson, signed a month ago from Accrington, grabbed a first half hat-trick in 33 minutes, and Colchester were out for the count.

Hudson was billed at inside-left in the programme, but for most of the time he formed a twin-shooting spearhead with Terry Bly, the one-time Norwich star, who revelled on his former home ground.

The charismatic George Hudson, idolised by fans at both Peterborough and Northampton.

Torquay were accounted for in Round 2 setting up the possibility of yet another giant killing at St James Park Newcastle.

Newcastle were duly defeated by a single goal. Terry Bly, who scored the winner, remembers the result as a travesty. Newcastle spurned dozens of chances during a one sided first half and at half time Posh manager Hagan gave the centre forward a rare piece of advice.

133

"Play up alongside their centre half and wait for the mistake."

Bly waited. A long ball cleared the marking defender, giving him a clear run at goal. Even then his badly mis hit shot deceived goalkeeper Dave Hollins and trickled over the line for the only goal of the game. Contemporary reports tell a different story however, and I suspect Terry's account is modest in the extreme!

Peterborough's 'iron man' defender Ollie Hopkins, hero of FA cup success at Newcastle.

PETERBORO GO AGAIN!

BLY HUMBLES THE JADED GIANTS

WHEN it comes to Cup football, Bly's the name. And Peterborough are the team. Terry Bly, who spearheaded Norwich's great Cup triumphs in 1959, set the Posh dreaming of a money-spinning run with a golden goal against Newcastle at St. James's Park, yesterday.

NEWCASTLE 0, PETERBOROUGH 1

TERRY BLY is the poshest of the Posh's 11 heroes who will undoubtedly be the toast of the town today.

Ace goalscorer Bly shot Third Division Peterborough into the fourth round of the Cup after humiliating proud Newcastle in the first half and then surviving a terrific battering designed to drive them into the ground.

But if Bly gets the goalscoring credit, Peterborough wingers Billy Hails and Roy Senior earn high marks for some blinding shots.

Disallowed

Only five minutes after the start skipper Ivor Allchurch had a goal disallowed for off-side.

The referee turned down an appeal that winger Tuohy had forced the ball over the line and with the minutes ticking out goal-keeper Jack Walls appeared from nowhere to save what looked a certain goal by centre-forward John McGuigan.

After this shameful defeat what does the future hold for such a famous club as Newcastle? They haven't been on the winning side since mid-November.

This tie got off to a cracking start, with Newcastle every much as dangerous at Peterborough, but as the game wore on the visitors were much the better team.

The Newcastle attack simply could not get into gear and failed to master Peterborough's offside tactics.

They fell victims to this trap at least half a dozen times in the first half hour.

Never give up Peterborough survived Newcastle attacks to come back.

In a breakaway with inside-right Ray Smith and left-half Keith Ripley Bly blasted home the winner in the 74th minute.

While this spelt tragedy for Newcastle the fruits of victory could not be denied to Peterborough.

THE MAYOR WAS CHEER LEADER

Players read the Sunday paper's headlines proclaiming a famous victory with no small embarrassment. Revealing too, is Bly's recollection that from leaving London Road early on the morning of the match, to returning that evening, the only refreshment offered to the players was the half-time cup of tea!

134

The Fourth Round brought manager Hagan's old club Sheffield United to London Road.

THE FANS AT BRAMALL LANE STILL TALK ABOUT 'SIR JAMES'

THERE was a mixed reaction among Sheffield United supporters when it was known that the "Blades" had been drawn against Peterborough United. They would have preferred to meet "Posh" at a much later stage in the F.A. Cup competition. United's supporters have a leaning towards Peterborough because it is managed by their former idol, Jimmy Hagan.

He is considered one of the finest forwards ever to wear the red and white striped shirt, and some United fans when they speak of him refer to him as "Sir James." United are under no misapprehension as to the task that confronts them. They remember the great fight Posh · put up at Hillsborough against a Sheffield Wednesday team which at that time were fourth from the top of Division I.

There was no fairytale ending. Sheffield United won 3-1.

Peterborough v Sheffield United

Back Row: Walker, Whittaker, Rayner, Walls, Ripley, Hopkins. Front Row: Hails, Smith, Bly, Hudson, McNamee

At the end of the season, Bly moved on to Coventry where Jimmy Hill's direct interventionist style of management earned the centre forward's lasting admiration. Sadly the feeling was not reciprocated, Hill deciding that although Bly had continued to score goals at Highfield Road he required a "more skilful kind of player". Coventry signed George Hudson, Bly's team mate at Peterborough and later a folk hero at Northampton.

Terry moved on to Notts County, and eventually into non-league football at Grantham.

135

Jimmy Hill, footballing legislator, manager and TV pundit, portrayed in a Brentford programme from 1949.

Today Bly remains a committed football man, and a keen follower of the modern game. (In the summer of 1994 he predicted with unnerving accuracy that Norwich's Chris Sutton would defy the doubters and continue his goalscoring habits with new club Blackburn Rovers. It takes one to know one!)

Despite gaining meagre financial rewards compared with the fortune earned by today's players, he expresses no regrets, save that of doubting that he could ever put as much back into the game as he'd taken out.

"We were the lucky ones", he says without irony. "I got paid for doing something I loved - something I'd have done for nothing .... A lot of fun's gone out of the game today, and there was no bitterness either. Terry Branston would kick lumps off me all afternoon and we'd still be friends at the end. Especially if I scored ...."

Kettering Town, now managed by former Steelman Wally Akers, had joined the floodlit fraternity. On Monday October 9th 1961 the club entertained Alf Ramsey's Ipswich Town for the inaugural match. The game, which gave supporters an opportunity to see the season's eventual First Division champions, was attended by FIFA President Sir Stanley Rous.

KETTERING'S floodlights were switched on last night by Sir Stanley Rous, president of FIFA --and another milestone in the history of the Poppies was marked.

After a short concert by Munn and Felton's (Footwear) Band, the two teams lined up to receive Sir Stanley, who was accompanied by Kettering chairman, Mr. John Nash. After the National Anthem, Sir Stanley gave a quick wave of his hand and the floodlights went on full power.

Sir Stanley after being introduced by Mr. Nash, was presented to the players and officials.

Two minutes later, John Ritchie scored Kettering's first goal "under the lights."

Sir Stanley Rous signals for Kettering Town's floodlights to be switched on. Club chairman John Nash watches.

Kettering sparkle under new lights

RAZZELL IMPRESSES SUPPORTERS

KETTERING TOWN 2,   IPSWICH TOWN 2

WHAT a dainty dish to set before the coveted gentry of the Football League! Poppies' chairman, Mr. John Nash, had told supporters: "We are out to impress. We have good lights, a good ground, a good team and good opposition."

And Kettering did what they were asked to do—impress. They held a strong-looking Ipswich side to a 2—2 draw. And though it would be only fair to say that Ipswich did not pull all the stops out—they shied away from a hard tackle on occasions—Kettering gave their most impressive game of the season.

Virtually every man in the Poppies team managed to give a good account of himself and so reduce the overwhelming odds. After the break new boy Derek Razzell took over the reins at centre-forward with Ritchie moving to inside-right and Bernard Shaw dropping back to right-half.

Razzell looked good and gave Kettering the hope for added punch in the forward line.

THE LEAD

Kettering took the lead after only two minutes when from a Golding corner Shaw just failed to connect, but Ritchie converted from close in at his second attempt. Then Morrow improved Kettering's score in the 60th minute with a shot to which Bailey could only get his fingertips.

Ipswich replied with two goals in thirty seconds during the second half. Crawford crashed the ball home after the burly Phillips had hit the ball against Smethurst, and the Ipswich leader added another with a header which had the home 'keeper completely beaten.

Most entertaining Ipswich player was Ted Phillips, who gave a great display of power shooting. Kettering, however, had several players worthy of mention. Shaw and Curran excelled in the attack, while each and every defender played his heart out.

Kettering Town: Smethurst; Marston, Lawson; Parsons, Froggatt, Armour; Morrow, Shaw, Ritchie, Curran, Golding. Razzell played in second half.

Ipswich Town: Bailey; Carberry, Compton; Thrower, Laurel, Nelson; Stephenson, Moran, Crawford, Phillips, Leadbetter.

Attendance: 5,400.

Just weeks later Third Division Swindon were visitors for a replayed FA Cup First Round fixture. The first game had produced a dramatic finale. With ten minutes left and Swindon coasting to a comfortable 2-0 victory, Poppies Supporters Club Secretary Reg Abbott was disconsolately making for the exit. Cheers from excited Kettering supporters heralding winger Norman Golding's goal, lured him back to witness a belated penalty equaliser, calmly taken by Terry Curran.

In truth, Kettering, who included both Jack Froggatt and former Leicester City colleague Johnny Morris, had been outplayed by a young Robins side which contained future First Division stars Ernie Hunt and Mike Summerbee. The Poppies hero was goalkeeper Ted Smethurst who earned the following accolade in the Evening Telegraph.

Ernie Hunt

THE HERO

But, as all England knows by now, Ted Smethurst was the real hero. Swindon supporters, who stood and applauded at the interval and final whistle, will remember his display for years to come.

For Kettering's supporters Smethurst's display was just another of those great efforts which he has achieved time and time again since he joined the club.

I go along with all the tributes such as: "He won the 'Pink 'Un' Biscuit all on his own" and "He should be given the Freedom of the Borough."

137

Super Smethurst

The replay was more evenly contested until another Curran penalty in the 61st minute gave Kettering the lead. Curran added another before John Ritchie, soon destined to move into more elevated circles at Stoke City, put the result beyond doubt with a third just eight minutes from time.

As Bryan Potter's article informs, the Poppies had been given an ideal incentive to beat Swindon. The second round draw paired Kettering with old rivals Northampton Town for the first time since 1904-05 when the Cobblers had won 2-0.

THIS WAS NO FLUKE...

WHAT a tremendous fillip to Kettering, and, indeed, Northamptonshire soccer the Poppies provided last night. Poppies' chairman John Nash echoed the thoughts of us all when he said: "A 3—0 win was more than we dared hope for."

There was very little Cup luck about this staggering result. It was as clear cut as the score suggests, and during the second half an outsider would have been justified in asking: "Who is supposed to be the League side out there?"

'Hampden'

The Kettering fans, and those who made themselves "supporters for the night," provided their own little "Hampden roar" to mark those three moments of ecstacy when the Poppies scored. Their delight was not merely derived from the achievement of beating a Third Division side, but also from the realisation that a county FA Cup derby with the Cobblers was the prize that had been won.

This is a clash to capture the imagination of the most reluctant fan.

Last night's glory went to goal-scorers Terry Curran and John Ritchie, and the man who worked for all three, Norman Golding.

Of course we salute the whole side for this heart-warming success. But I must also spotlight the tremendous efforts of half-backs Bernard Shaw, Jack Froggatt and George Armour.

In my book it was they who provided the drive in that 20 minute spell of Kettering pressure after the interval which broke the back of Swindon's resistance.

Two young Poppies' forwards, Terry Curran left and John Ritchie right discuss tactics with manager Wally Akers.

While manager Akers discussed tactics with his players, one ET correspondent urged fans to give the club their wholehearted support.

To the Sports Editor

QUITE a lot has been said of Kettering Town Football Club recently. Let us hope much more will be said of them (in their favour) after the FA Cup clash tomorrow with the Cobblers.

Admission charges increase, poor performances recently (excepting, of course, the Swindon replay), poor gates, especially the eight and a half thousand for the Swindon game, which was at least four thousand below the generally expected gate, are a few, of the quibbles.

Let us forget all these to-morrow, and hope that all those would-be supporters find their way to the County Ground to give their vocal support to a team who have the opportunity of making history this year by repeating the Swindon act.

Kettering Town 1961-62

Back Row: Marston, Morris, Armour, Froggatt, Smethurst, Lawson. Front Row: Morrow, Shaw, Savage, Curran, Golding.

The match, played before 18,825 spectators, proved a triumph for Cobbler Cliff Holton, who scored all the goals in Northampton's 3-0 victory.

Holton, a member of the Arsenal side humbled back in 1958, had joined the Cobblers from Watford after the start of the season. So popular was he at Vicarage Road, scoring 42 league goals during 1960-61, that supporters demonstrated against the transfer, threatening to boycott matches.

139

A hat-trick on his debut at Crystal Palace began a goalscoring sequence that produced 36 in the season, beating Ted Bowen's club record set in 1929.

Holton's hat trick goal against Kettering.

This is the goal that clinched the Cobblers victory. Cliff Holton (white shirt), puts a tame shot just out of Ted Smethurst's reach and Jack Froggatt, right, looks on helplessly as the ball glides past the Kettering keeper to give Holton his hat-trick.

Defeat at Port Vale ended the FA Cup run but the Cobblers completed the season in a commendable eighth place. New signing John Reid, a skilful playmaker from Bradford City, added composure to midfield. Youngster Barry Lines from Bletchley filled the wing vacancy created by the absence of legendary Tommy Fowler, who had moved to Aldershot. Fowler's passing comment, recorded in Frank Grande's 'The Cobblers', sums up the

Northampton Town 1961-62

Back Row: Jennings, Osborne, Spelman, Leck, Branston, Coe, Foley, Brodie, Woollard, Robson, Mills, Bowen, Payne.
Front Row: Everitt, Moran, Holton, Reid, Lines.

philosophy of the fine footballing journeyman - 'You have to go where the work takes you'. This after 16 years, 564 games and 90 goals in a Cobblers' shirt.

Another young winger, Geordie Tommy Robson, scored on his debut against Peterborough, the club he was to represent later in a league career which embraced both Chelsea and Newcastle.

Corby Town 1961-62

Back Row: Smith, Rodgers, Parsons, Williams, Harris, Fisher, Hadden. Front Row: Liddell, Kearns, Kelly, Rennie, McCorkindale.

Corby Town, under new manager Tommy Hadden, made a memorable start to the season with a thirteen match unbeaten run.

The Steelmen included Peter Kearns, who had played for Wellingborough before joining Plymouth Argyle in 1956, together with Barry Parsons and John Rennie, survivors from Hadden's Midland League team. Andy Easton arrived in the new year from Bedford, followed shortly by Tommy Crawley who soon made his mark scoring 13 goals in 16 games. Kearns top scored with 32, but the side had to be content with sixth place - its best yet.

Rothwell Town celebrated a return to the UCL by opening a new grandstand, built to replace its fire damaged predecessor, in the first fixture of the season against near neighbours and arch rivals Desborough. The game was my first for 'Ar Tarn', managed by former player and ex-Poppy Bob Wyldes. Just as we were about to leave the dressing room before kick off the player-manager gave us the definitive, often repeated, team talk.

"Keep the high balls high
And the low balls low.
If we score first
We're one up."

Rothwell Town, pictured prior to their opening game of 1961-62 v old UCL rivals Desborough.

Back Row: Worrall, Freestone, Smith, Rogers, Rothe, Dadswell, Squires.
Front Row: Nutter, Linnett, Garvie, Marlow, Franklin.

Desborough Town

Back Row: Coe, Smith, Swann, Chisholm, Dawkins, Grant, Pratt
Front Row: Simmonds, Joyce, Wyldes, Addis, Chambers.

We lost 3-0 to a Bones side led by John 'Charlie' Marlow, a prolific goal scorer at United Counties level and destined to achieve cult status in the league during the sixties.

Such was his enthusiasm for the game that his diligence ensured a home match with championship rivals, Wisbech Reserves, was probably the only game in England to beat appalling weather conditions. Unfortunately, postponement of the Fenmen's first team fixture persuaded manager Jesse Pye to divert his entire senior side to Cecil Street, where it duly inflicted defeat upon Marlow's team.

Rothwell never regained the initiative and Wisbech went on to win the championship by a convincing margin.

Unable to get home from college as usual on Friday evening, I arranged to hitch-hike from London to Fenland Park on the Saturday morning of the match for Desborough's away fixture. Six hours and eight lifts later, I arrived at the ground on a British Sugar Corporation lorry, minutes before kick off. It was hardly worth the effort. We were tormented by former Cobbler's winger, Hungarian international Bela Olah, who scored four times as Wisbech won 6-0.

1961-62 Division 1	P.	W.	D.	L.	F.	A.	Pts
Wisbech Reserves	30	24	4	2	112	38	52
Wellingborough Town	30	21	5	4	95	43	47
Kettering Reserves	30	19	3	8	73	46	41
Dunstable Town	30	14	8	8	69	48	36
Bletchley Town	30	15	5	10	64	48	35
Rothwell Town	30	15	4	11	91	63	34
Rushden Town	30	13	5	12	64	46	31
Corby Reserves	30	13	4	13	69	64	30
St Neots Reserves	30	10	5	15	58	64	25
Potton United	30	9	7	14	53	72	25
Wolverton Town	30	11	2	17	62	73	24
Desborough Town	30	11	1	18	58	77	23
Bletchley United	30	10	3	17	49	70	23
S & L Corby	30	6	7	17	51	114	19
Shefford Town	30	7	4	19	49	83	18
Wootton Blue Cross	30	7	3	20	49	108	17

Still we had a dubious consolation on the return journey, stopping at Peterborough's Corn Exchange for a concert by Helen Shapiro's cousin, the imaginatively named Susan Singer.

Runners up Wellingborough Town, had achieved a notable 4-3 Senior Cup victory over Corby in December 1961, including in their side the nucleus of the team that would dominate the league during the early sixties.

NORTHANTS. SENIOR CUP — FOURTH ROUND

'DOUGHBOYS' v. CORBY TOWN

SATURDAY, 16th DECEMBER, 1961.   KICK-OFF 2-15 p.m.   ISSUE No. 10
OFFICIAL PROGRAMME 2d. (Issued by the Supporters' Club)

THE TEAMS AND OFFICIALS

RIGHT   *4*   LEFT

WELLINGBOROUGH TOWN

Royal Blue and Yellow Shirts, Black Shorts.

TAYLOR

(2) PATENALL   (3) HAYWARD

(4) LLOYD, M.   (5) WOODING   (6) YOUNG

(7) HAMILTON   (8) BURN   (9) DAWSON   (10) MILLER   (11) LOASBY

Referee :

R. A. LONG
(Northampton)

Linesmen :

Red Flag
L. Homer (Duston)

Yellow Flag
D. G. Patchett (Wollaston)

(11) McCORKINDALE   (10) KEARNS, P.   (9) KELLY   (8) ROBINSON   (7) LIDDELL

(6) RENNIE   (5) PARSONS   (4) RODGERS

(3) HARRIS   (2) FISHER

WILLIAMS

CORBY TOWN

White Shirts, Black Shorts.

LEFT   *3*   RIGHT

NEXT HOME GAMES

Sat., Dec. 23rd—U.C.L. Div. 2, Reserves v. BRITISH TIMKEN (DUSTON). Kick-off 2-15 p.m.
BOXING DAY—U.C.L. Div. 1, FIRST TEAM v. DESBOROUGH TOWN.   See Local Press.

(advertisement badge: THE CENTRE FOR SMART HAIRDRESSING — VIC HUCKLE, SHEEP STREET)

(Football supporters could complete their entertainment by moving from the Dog and Duck to the Lyric Cinema to enjoy one of British Cinema's classic offerings).

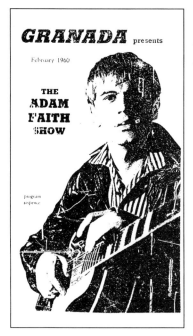

The 'star' of the film had himself appeared live at Kettering's Granada Cinema only a year earlier in one of the many 'bandshows' which featured the leading pop singers of the day.

MONDAY, 18th DECEMBER — FOR SIX DAYS

Adam Faith   **Sidney James**
Carole Lesley
"**WHAT A WHOPPER**"
(2-15)   5-35   8-50   (Certificate 'U')

Meanwhile in faraway Chile, Brazil retained the World Cup overcoming Czechoslovakia 3-1 in the final. England were the only home nation to qualify, reaching the quarter finals before losing to the eventual champions.
In the semi-final stage, Brazil beat Chile 4-2 before 76,594 while the Czechoslovakia v Yugoslavia match attracted 5,890. Feranc Puskas, once a famous Hungarian, represented Spain, but failed to inspire his adoptive country to the glories of 1953, the team finishing bottom of its qualifying group.

THE GREAT FAITH
1962-63

Late on Christmas night, 1962, I stepped into the street outside our front door clutching my newly acquired Johnny Mathis LP, ironically entitled 'Warm', and promptly skidded on the frozen pavement. The record slipped from its sleeve and fell crashing to the ground, littering the gleaming slabs with pieces of black vinyl. The big 'freeze' had begun.

Corby groundsman Fred Loak during the big freeze.

Seasonal powdery snow was transformed in hours. Streets, gardens and football pitches became enveloped in a heavy layer of smoky, grey-brown ice, which lingered defiantly until late Spring.

From Boxing Day to early March only a handful of matches could be played.

At least two county sides can look back on this rather unusual season with satisfaction.

Northampton Town won the Third Division championship, securing the title on May 11th 1963 with victory over county rivals Peterborough.

COBBLERS THE CHAMPS

4—0 win over Posh settles title issue

Peterborough v Northampton

THE Cobblers are Third Division champions. At Peterborough this afternoon they smashed Swindon's last hopes and put the title beyond doubt by crushing county neighbours Posh 4-0.

DIVISION 3	P	W	D	L	F	A	W	D	L	F	A	Pts
Northampton T	46	16	6	1	64	19	10	4	9	45	41	62
Swindon T	46	18	2	3	60	22	4	12	7	27	34	58
Port Vale	46	16	4	3	47	25	7	4	12	25	33	54
Coventry C	46	14	6	3	54	28	4	11	8	29	41	53
Bournemouth	46	11	12	0	39	16	7	4	12	24	30	52
Peterboro' U	46	11	5	7	48	33	9	6	8	45	42	51
Notts Co	46	15	3	5	46	29	4	10	9	27	45	51
Southend U	46	11	7	5	38	24	8	5	10	37	53	50
Wrexham	46	14	6	3	54	27	6	3	14	30	56	49
Hull C	46	12	6	5	40	22	7	4	12	34	47	48
Crystal P	46	10	7	6	38	22	7	6	10	30	36	47
Colchester U	46	11	6	6	41	35	7	5	11	32	58	47
QPR	46	9	6	8	44	36	8	5	10	41	40	45
Bristol C	46	10	9	4	54	38	6	4	13	46	54	45
Shrewsbury T	46	13	4	6	57	41	3	8	12	26	40	44
Millwall	46	11	6	6	50	32	4	7	12	32	55	43
Watford	46	12	3	8	55	40	5	5	13	27	45	42
Barnsley	46	12	6	5	39	28	3	5	15	24	46	41
Bristol R	46	11	8	4	45	29	4	3	16	25	59	41
Reading	46	13	4	6	51	30	3	4	16	23	48	40
Bradford	46	10	9	4	43	36	4	3	16	36	61	40
Brighton & HA	46	7	6	10	28	38	5	6	12	30	46	36
Carlisle U	46	12	4	7	41	37	1	5	17	20	52	35
Halifax T	46	8	3	12	41	51	1	9	13	23	55	30

Initially, the strike force of Holton and new signing Alec Ashworth from Luton spearheaded the attack, sharing 21 goals in ten games. Holton moved to Crystal Palace and was succeeded by a brave, dashing centre forward, who quickly became a great favourite at the County ground - Frank Large.

Another to make his Cobblers debut during the season was seventeen year old Graham Carr, who deputised at Bournemouth for Terry Branston. The centre half had been injured during a match at QPR the previous week by a supporter brandishing a bottle!

Northampton Town 1962-63

Back Row: Osborne (Sec), Cockroft, Reid, Branston, Brodie, Leck, Large, Jennings (Trainer)
Front Row: Hails, Mills, Smith, Bowen (Manager), Foley, Lines, Everitt.

Ironically, the Northampton team that clinched the championship included Billy Hails and Ray Smith, former stars from Peterborough's Midland League and Fourth Division title winning sides.

Inevitably that great Posh side had begun to break up. Relative newcomer Terry Bly moved on to Coventry City while long-serving Norman Rigby went back into the Midland League with Boston United.
In October, Jimmy Hagan, the architect of Peterborough's more recent successes, left the club in rather sad circumstances - sacked, allegedly for 'incidents involving players'.

Jack Fairbrother returned to the club as manager in December, surprising supporters by releasing Hudson to join Coventry shortly before the end of the season. Perhaps he already knew who the centre-forward replacement would be.

There were no cup exploits, a brief run in which Notts County were beaten at Meadow Lane ending in third round defeat at Derby, although the team did achieve fifth place in the league.

The long winter adversely affected both Kettering and Corby's fortunes. A legacy of the freeze-up required that the Poppies, well placed to challenge for the Southern League Premier title, should play the final 12 games in 29 days. It is hardly surprising that results were mixed and the side had to settle for eventual fourth place.

Defeat at Boston United, with Norman Rigby in commanding form, brought FA Cup disappointment. A surfeit of football probably contributed to an apathetic response by Kettering fans, who gave scant support to the team in those crucial end of season games. Nothing, however, excused the pitifully low attendance for Jack Froggatt's testimonial game against Portsmouth. A poor reward for such a great player.

THAT'S IT CHAPS!

. . . . so said Jack Froggatt on Monday night as he put his boots up for the last time. Jack, who has seen action with England, Portsmouth, Leicester and Kettering, played his last game of football at Kettering in his own benefit — when the Poppies lost 4—3 to Portsmouth.

Only 1,800 supporters turned up to say farewell to Froggatt — but he capped an excellent career by laying on one of Kettering's goals and scoring another against his old club.

Jack is now manager of a Portsmouth hotel.

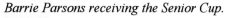
Barrie Parsons receiving the Senior Cup.

Corby Town also suffered a deterioration of form following the long enforced break, destroying fragile hopes of promotion from the Southern League Division 1. Leading scorer Peter Kearns moved to Aldershot in a record £2500 deal, returning to Occupation Road with his new club for a testimonial match for Barrie Parsons and John Rennie.

The Steelmen completed the season on a high note, beating Northampton Town's championship team 2-0 in the final of the Northants Senior Cup. The winning side included much travelled Bobby Laverick, late of Everton, Chelsea, Coventry and Brighton, and former Cobbler David Laird, who scored Corby's second goal.

Barrie Parsons was a stalwart in Corby teams from 1956 until his injury enforced retirement ten years later. His inspiring performances brought numerous offers from league clubs, the most publicised being a 'name your price' approach from Norwich City in 1958. Barrie stayed with the Steelmen, living on in his home town until his premature death when a benefit game was held for his bereaved family. The programme contained this tribute.

> **BARRIE PARSONS — A STEELMAN**
> In 1954 Manager Wally Akers coaxed 17 year old Barrie, then playing for Uppingham and Corby Boys Club, to join his then highly successful "A" team. By the next year Barrie was a regular reserve team player and in fact made his first team debut, still as an amateur, on 16th April, 1956, in a Midland League match at Gainsborough. The "Trinity" at that time were one of the strong teams of the League and although Barrie's debut was not a winning one, neither was it a losing one, and Corby did well to share four goals on this occasion. Barrie's team mates that day were: Jimmy Brown, "Tanner" Allen and Jimmy Baird, John McLachlan, Jack Connors (and Barrie himself), Tommy Davies, Jimmy Adam, Russell Green, Alf Hornby and Charlie Adam. Green and C. Adam were the Corby scorers. Barrie signed professional forms in May, 1956 and made his Professional debut for Corby Town on 29th December that year at *Outside Right* against Frickley Colliery and received his first winning bonus! In 1957/58 season Barrie became a first team regular and went on to make around 400 appearances before injury forced his premature retirement at the end of 1965-66.

I still recall with affection his regular Saturday night double act (with Rothwell full back Neil Rothe), at the Angel Hotel, Kettering in that pre-karaoke age, when they treated the patrons to a towering rendition of 'The Northern Lights of Aberdeen', in the final minutes before closing time.

The other title winning County side was Wellingborough Town, who won the UCL championship for the first time in the club's history. It was probably poetic justice. In February 1962 'The Northamptonshire Advertiser' devoted a whole page to the efforts of the backroom staff at the Dog and Duck.

Like most players, I was generally disinterested in the contribution made by such dedicated groups of helpers, content instead to don carefully pressed shirts in freshly swept dressing rooms, to tread newly mown grass with whitewashed lines, to collect folded notes in sealed brown envelopes. Belated thanks!

THE GREAT FAITH

These men wait for a star to rise again

Wellingborough Town FC is certainly one of the county's oldest clubs and it has always had an energetic management. Sometimes it has been a committee, sometimes a player manager. The Doughboys' present committee have comparatively only recent associations with the club they represent.

A passion for soccer

Their longest serving member is the chairman, Mr. Harold Blunt, a shoe worker in his fifties with the club and football very much at heart. Chairman for the past seven seasons, Harold developed his love for the game when he played as an inside-forward with the old Wellingboro' Sunday School League until a knee injury put him out of the game for good.

the secretary, Mr. Norman Lovell. Norman is the club's unofficial historian and statistician. Officially he sometimes runs the line, generally keeps the minutes, and always fixes the fixtures.

He plays an essential and enthusiastic part in the run-

Harold Blunt, Chairman of Wellingborough Town

ning of the club. So does the treasurer, Mr. Brian Rose, who manages to steer the club on an even financial course; keeps a weather eye open to the future and a firm but liberal grip on the purse strings. He, of course, has very considerable help from the Supporters' Club and without them the Doughboys couldn't really survive a week.

No change this time

Come hail or rain, the gatemen, Messrs. Bob Dexter, Rowland Percival, A. Jones and Sam Parsons (vice-president) are on duty. This is where there is a great need for a sense of humour. Gates are low at present and have been for a long time. "A fortnight ago I took 4s 6d gate money and the customers turned up

with £1 notes," cracked Bob.

Others who help to keep the players on their feet include committee men Alec Porter and Stan Goosey, chief scout, Mr. Roy Freestone, formerly a Doughboy himself; Mr. Eddie Mallin, ready to do anything at any time; trainer Frank Holman always ready with the magic sponge and a timely word of advice as only an old and seasoned ex-player can give it.

And we mustn't forget Mr. Charlie Johnson, who has seen them all come and go with more than fifty years' service at the Dog and Duck to his credit. One time player, Charlie is now a very active pensioner who almost lives at the Dog and Duck.

Officially he is the groundsman. That means painter, carpenter and greenkeeper.

He is also stoker, sees that the baths are ready for the players and a hundred and one other jobs fall to his willing hands.

Although Mr. Jack Kingston is not an active member of the committee, he is the most active supporter the Doughboys have ever had. In his eighties, Mr. Kingston still has his season ticket for 1896, when Wellingborough played in the Midland League—and he has regularly bought a season ticket ever since. Although a pensioner, Mr. Kingston never takes advantage of the old age concession at the gate. He believes in really supporting the club.

A worthy champion

The main support behind the Supporters' Club has always been Mr. Rowley Mitchell. Mr. Mitchell, at present vice-chairman is an active supporter and a worthy champion of the Doughboys. He has been there as long as the rest of the committee can remember. Mr. Mark Leach, the chairman, has a good committee to work with him.

Charlie Johnson, the club's groundsman, painter, carpenter and greenkeeper.

If the parent club is in need—and they generally are—the treasurer, Mr. Dennis Humphries, can usually find the necessary money to keep them going. Secretary Fred Coles keeps an eye on the official business and one way and another the rest of the committee lend a hand.

It might be to broadcast the half-time scores or music over the relay system, sell programmes or competition tickets, or the very important task of sustaining spectators, players, officials and the Press with steaming hot cups of tea from a near bottomless urn at the interval. This is where the women take an active part.

Both clubs are indivisible. Take away the parent club and what are the Supporters left with to support? Take away the Supporters' Club and Wellingborough Town Football Club would cease immediately.

A common interest

Their common interest is football. Their ambitions a ground for Wellingborough, and someday to see them playing League football again. The Doughboys once enjoyed a day of glory when teams like Arsenal were numbered among their opponents and players like Fanny Walden, later to be a mainstay of Tottenham, dominated the field.

They want to see their star rise again.

149

And so it did as everyone at Wellingborough had plenty to celebrate during the sixties.

Early season victory over rivals Rushden Town assumed great significance as the season dragged on to its belated climax.

October 1962 was the month when even the quality newspapers wrote of "the world holding its breath". Russian ships, carrying nuclear missiles, were bound for Cuba. American warships had been given orders to intercept and attack. I went to a party in Notting Hill Gate convinced that the end of the world was nigh -

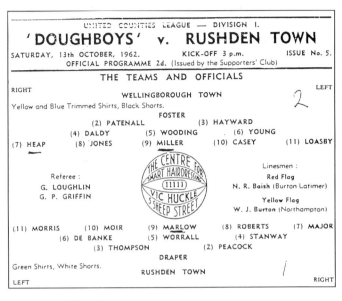

UNITED COUNTIES LEAGUE — DIVISION I.

'DOUGHBOYS' v. RUSHDEN TOWN

SATURDAY, 13th OCTOBER, 1962.   KICK-OFF 3 p.m.   ISSUE No. 5.
OFFICIAL PROGRAMME 2d. (Issued by the Supporters' Club)

THE TEAMS AND OFFICIALS

RIGHT   LEFT

WELLINGBOROUGH TOWN

Yellow and Blue Trimmed Shirts, Black Shorts.

FOSTER

(2) PATENALL   (3) HAYWARD

(4) DALDY   (5) WOODING   (6) YOUNG

(7) HEAP   (8) JONES   (9) MILLER   (10) CASEY   (11) LOASBY

Linesmen :

Referee :   Red Flag
G. LOUGHLIN   N. R. Baish (Burton Latimer)
G. P. GRIFFIN   Yellow Flag
W. J. Burton (Northampton)

(11) MORRIS   (10) MOIR   (9) MARLOW   (8) ROBERTS   (7) MAJOR
(6) DE BANKE   (5) WORRALL   (4) STANWAY
(3) THOMPSON   (2) PEACOCK

DRAPER

Green Shirts, White Shorts.

RUSHDEN TOWN

LEFT   RIGHT

perhaps even imminent. In a room full of joss sticks and pretty girls the talk was not of the chances of seduction but the odds against survival. We sat around a radio set in the early hours of the morning listening to each news flash with a sense of foreboding, until ... "The Russian ships have changed course ...." Reprieved, a collective sigh of relief exhaled from every corner of the so-called civilised world. Someone put on a record they'd bought the previous day by an unknown group from Liverpool. "Love Me Do". And the party began at last.

Terry Murray, a former Eire international, led Rushden to second place.

1962-63 Division 1	P.	W.	D.	L.	F.	A.	Pts.
Wellingborough Town •	26	22	2	2	94	24	46
Rushden Town	26	21	2	3	80	29	44
Desborough Town	26	16	4	6	76	44	36
Wisbech Res.	26	15	4	7	90	60	34
Bletchley Town	26	13	5	8	64	54	31
Wolverton Town	26	13	2	11	73	54	28
Corby Res.	26	10	7	9	65	63	27
S & L Corby	26	10	3	13	67	90	25
Rothwell Town	26	8	6	12	41	60	22
Dunstable Town	26	5	8	13	50	56	18
Northampton Town 'A'	26	5	8	13	39	62	18
St Neots Res.	26	6	4	16	52	89	16
Potton United	26	5	6	15	36	75	16
Kempston Rovers	26	2	1	23	26	93	5

The Doughboys won the league, but not without controversy, the late signing of former Corby player McCorkindale provoking a bitter response from runners up Rushden.

Doughboys, Champions 1962-63

Back : McCormick, Patenall, Lloyd, Foster, Hayward, Young, Holman, Ramscar
Front: Casey, Jones, Wooding, Blunt (Chairman), Miller, Heap, Loasby

DOUGHBOYS ARE UCL CHAMPIONS

MAKING his last official appearance as chairman of Wellingborough Urban Council, Mr. Howard Deighton presented the United Counties League Championship Cup to the Doughboys at the Dog and Duck last night. The club had clinched the Division One title for the first time in their history over the weekend.

WELLINGBOROUGH Town are the new champions of the United Counties League. They became Division One title holders yesterday when Rushden lost 4—0 to Bletchley and so failed to get the two points they needed to maintain their challenge.

The Doughboys moved a point in front of Rushden on Saturday when they defeated Potton 4—0 and they still have one game remaining—against Northampton "A" at the Dog and Duck tomorrow night.

The championship trophy will be presented after the match by league chairman Mr. F. C. A. Dunmore. This will be the first time Wellingborough have had their name on the trophy although Wellingborough Redwell, who joined up with the Town club on moving to the Dog and Duck, won the championship in 1910.

Before that Wellingborough Reserves won the championship in 1895 when they played in the Northamptonshire League—the forerunner of the UCL.

But Wellingborough's success may not be very well received at Rushden.

The programme notes at Newton Road yesterday deplored the signing of McCorkindale by the Doughboys after

centre forward Miller was suspended.

The notes continued: "We would not have thought a club with a long record of victories over the past 15 months would have stooped to this means. It does no credit and is a sad reflection on their opinion of other players on their books if they can't call on someone in the reserves to fill the gap."

"Doughboy's" comment: "Wellingborough have had one of the toughest seasons of their existence and have fought every inch for this championship. Eight away games ended a marathon season culminating in what I consider the undeserved suspension of Miller, one of their star players. They were left with no alternative than to sign McCorkindale."

DOUGHBOYS RECEIVE THEIR TROPHY

At the Dog and Duck, 1962. Wellingborough v Desborough. The author looks on from a safe distance as Bobby Wyldes leaps to attack the ball. Dennis Jones and Dennis Casey wait to pick up the pieces.

Desborough Town's third place was its highest since 1950. The club also achieved a notable first when, on March 17th, it staged the first Sunday match to be held in England between two sides with professional players.

DESBOROUGH ROUND OFF GOOD YEAR

DESBOROUGH completed their league programme on Wednesday with a fine win over Wolverton and so take third position in the league chart their highest place since 1950.

This week the club have had one of their busiest period with games on every day Sunday included except Thursday. As a result of winning two cup ties two extra games will have to be played next week, the final of the K.A.L. Munton Cup and the Harborough Charity Cup.

SUNDAY MARCH 17th

DESBOROUGH TOWN V
BLETCHLEY TOWN UNITED

Todays game is the first to be held in England on a Sunday between two sides with professional players. We hope it will be a success from both the players and spectators point of view. Next Sunday we travel to Rushden and hope as many as possible will make the journey to cheer us in this top of the table clash. We regret that all seats have now been taken on the official bus.

Division 2 produced the unusual situation of the British Timken sides, Daventry and Duston, occupying the two top positions.

1962-63 Division 2	P.	W.	D.	L.	F.	A.	Pts.
B. Timken Athletic	32	24	5	3	111	35	53
B. Timken Duston	32	22	6	4	111	40	50
Bedford Avenue	32	23	2	7	114	51	48
Higham Town	32	18	6	8	73	48	42
Wootton Blue Cross	32	18	4	10	102	65	40
Wellingborough Res.	32	18	4	10	94	63	40
Biggleswade Res.	32	16	4	12	66	60	36
Bletchley Res.	32	13	6	13	58	68	32
Rushden Res.	32	10	7	15	47	58	27
Rothwell Res.	32	11	4	17	75	95	26
Raunds Town	32	11	4	17	49	84	26
Wolverton Res.	32	10	3	19	58	79	23
Corby 'A'	32	9	5	18	57	103	23
Dunstable Res.	32	9	4	19	68	90	22
Kettering 'A'	32	8	5	19	61	93	21
Finedon Town	32	7	4	21	55	123	18
Eynesbury Res.	32	7	3	22	66	110	17

152

UPS AND DOWNS
1963-64

Manager Dave Bowen sprang a surprise before Northampton's first ever season in the Second Division when he resigned, seeking a break from the game. John Kurila became entangled in a contractual dispute after playing in Canada during the summer, and was prevented from rejoining the Cobblers, signing instead for Bristol City.

Joe Kiernan may leave Roker Park for Peterborough

Joe Kiernan was the only new face in the squad. The Scot had found first team opportunities limited at Roker Park, Sunderland and, following speculation that he might join Peterborough, finally chose Northampton.

Joe now confesses that, after a night out on the town with Graham Carr, Tommy Robson and others, the decision was a mere formality.

There had been considerable disappointment amongst Sunderland fans when Kiernan was released. He starred in a highly successful youth side, earning rare praise from Sir Matt Busby after a particularly impressive performance against Manchester United. Words that Kiernan recalls with characteristic modesty but immense pride.

Sunderland wing-half moves

JOE KIERNAN, Sunderland's promising wing-half, was transferred to newly-promoted Northampton Town today for a substantial fee.

Twenty-year-old Kiernan, skipper of the Sunderland Reserve team, was on the transfer list at his own request.

Three appearances

The Scot's senior appearances were limited because of the grand form of his fellow countryman, Jimmy McNab.

Signed as a schoolboy from Coatbridge, he played three times in the first team — at Southampton, home, to Oldham, when he scored twice in a 7-1 win, and in a friendly against Bangu of Brazil.

A tough-tackling, constructive player, Kiernan should greatly help Northampton in their first season of Second Division soccer.

He is Jock Kiernan, 17 year old Sunderland left half and skipper who in Busby's words, "addressed the ball and stroked it forward like a veteran."

More masterful throughout at Sunderland
INSPIRED IN ATTACK AND RESOLUTE IN DEFENCE
Sunderland 0, Northampton T. 2

BY whipping Sunderland—pride of the north-east —in front of more than 39,000 Roker Park fans, the Cobblers proved conclusively that they will be a force to be reckoned with in the Second Division. The manner in which the victory was accomplished was deserving of the cheers they received from the unbiased crowd.

The Cobblers completely dominated the first half. Quicker on the ball they outplayed the Sunderland defence. Reid and Smith provided the inspiration while Lines, in one of his most dominating moods, and Hails proceeded to pull the home defence apart so that Sunderland could count themselves extremely fortunate not to be more than two goals down at the interval.

Sunderland disappointment turned to disbelief in August when the young wing half returned to

153

Wearside, leading the Cobblers to a remarkable 2-0 victory in their second game of the season.

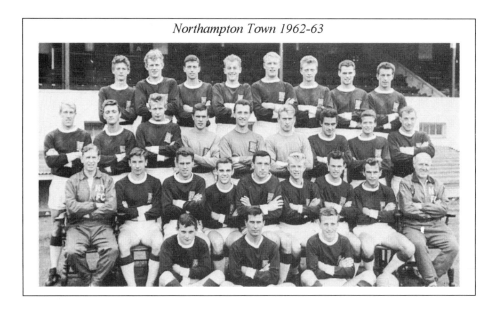

Northampton Town 1962-63

After a spectacular start, however, Joe found it difficult to settle into the side, was dropped and spent several months languishing in the reserves. But what reserves! The team included ex-youth internationals, Don Martin, Carr, Jim Hall and Brian Etheridge, together with John Mackin, Robson and Billy Best.

Kiernan enjoyed his football, regained form and would have been restored to the first team earlier, had caretaker manager Jack Jennings shared reserve trainer Joe Payne's confidence in his ability.

Critical changes in personnel eventually occurred, most significantly Dave Bowen's return as manager after his brief sabbatical. Goalkeeper Brian Harvey joined from Blackpool, Bobby Brown from Watford, while John Reid moved to Luton for £13,000. Kurila returned from Bristol City, adding his own brand of steel to the half back line.

The return fixture with Sunderland was played on a frozen pitch - (Desborough's game was postponed and we had the rare opportunity to watch a Saturday league match). An inspired choice of footwear by manager Bowen sent his team out in baseball boots. While the opposition slithered and floundered, the surefooted Cobblers skated around them to register a fine 5-1 victory.

Another revenge for Joe Kiernan, now recalled to the side and, with John Kurila as his 'minder', beginning to establish himself as both a major talent and marketable asset for the future.

THOSE UNFORTUNATE FANS! WHO STAYED AWAY MISSED THE SIGHT OF JAUNTY **JOE KIERNAN** GIVING A SUPERB EXHIBITION OF WING HALF PLAY, OF DETERMINED TACKLING — AND ASTUTE PASSING,

FIVE-FLUSHED COBBLERS GET RIGHT SPIRIT

NORTHAMPTON TOWN 5. SUNDERLAND 1

By David Jones

★ PLAYING enterprising football, the Cobblers sent promotion-chasing Sunderland to their biggest defeat of the season on the deep-frozen County Ground this afternoon. The Cobblers dominated play for much of the game and their attack —with Barry Lines once more in deadly form — completely upset the North Easterners.

NORTHAMPTON TOWN
Harvey
Foley   Everitt
Leck   Branston   Kiernan
Hails   Martin   Large   Kane   Lines

Mulhall   Crossan   Sharkey   Herd   Usher
McNab   Hurley   Harvey
Irwin   Ashurst
Montgomery
SUNDERLAND

Referee: Mr. W. J. Gow (Birmingham).

KIERNAN PUTS LIFE INTO NORTHAMPTON

Northampton 2, Southampton 0

MANAGER Dave Bowen laughed at his critics after a glorious mud revel by left-half Joe Kiernan had sparked Northampton to victory. It took courage to drop Derek Leck and bring in 20-year-old Kiernan, who has disappointed since being bought from Sunderland last summer. But Bowen's confidence was justified.

Kiernan never put a foot wrong and was as happy as a hippo as he surged through the sticky going which slowed other players almost to a standstill at times.

It was Northampton's power in the half-line which swung the game. And it took one of this strong trio to open the scoring.

John Kurila did the trick with a 25-yard drive that left Tony Godfrey standing.

David Paton, Southampton's third choice centre-half, made a fine first team debut.

He refused to let Northampton's busy forwards fluster him and gave a display which suggested that Southampton must have a surplus of good centre-halves.

Bobby Hunt missed one or two chances for Northampton, but redeemed himself by settling the result near the end after Kiernan had fashioned a move that spreadeagled the Southampton defence.

Further evidence of Bowen's ability to recognise and cultivate local talent, already apparent with Lines, Martin, Mackin and Etheridge, was displayed when former Walgrave Amber and Kettering winger Harry Walden joined from Luton in exchange for Billy Hails.

At the end of their first season in Division 2 the Cobblers finished in a commendable 12th place. Even so, few could have realised that greater glories awaited in 1964-65.

Peterborough United

Back Row: Sissons, Cooper, Duff, Rankmore, Pearce, Singleton.
Front Row: Moulden, Horobin, Dougan, Graham, McNamee.

Hudson's replacement at centre forward for Peterborough United proved to be the enigmatic, former Portsmouth and Blackburn player, Derek Dougan. Aston Villa manager Joe Mercer released the Irish international during the close season and Jack Fairbrother beat off competition from numerous clubs to make the prestigious signing. Another international, Welsh U23 player, Frank Rankmore joined from Cardiff City, (managed by former Posh boss George Swindin).

Excitement over the new signings was clouded somewhat by the departure of the great Denis Emery, who moved to non-league Bedford Town.
The season proved disappointing, early FA and League Cup exits and inconsistent league form contributing to manager Fairbrother's resignation in February. Johnny Anderson held the fort, as he had done previously, before Gordon Clark was appointed from Sheffield Wednesday.

The season finished on a high note when champions elect Coventry City were beaten 2-0 at London Road before a crowd of 26,307.

In stark contrast to rivals Northampton's continuing success, words from the Kettering Town handbook reflect bitterly upon a season which brought relegation from the Premier Division of the Southern League.

THE 1963-64 SEASON

WITHOUT DOUBT, this season will be remembered as one of the worst in the Club's history. Gates were on average the lowest since the war ; we were once again relegated to the first division ; the football played fell far below expectations of the players on the Club's books. The inability to achieve one away victory from 21 games had disastrous effects. All of the above combined to give the Club the biggest bank overdraft it has ever had. A sad story indeed. ..

156

Yet at the outset, the signing of star forward Harry Hooper, (joining ex-Leicester winger Derek Hogg), had given manager Wally Akers considerable grounds for optimism.

Derek Hogg

Harry Hooper signs on.

In 1994, an old style West Ham shirt with a collar and large Hammers badge was marketed as the 'Harry Hooper' shirt. Harry had achieved 'Folk Hero' status at Upton Park during the fifties.

The Kettering side also included ex-Cobbler Bobby Tebbutt and former Doughboy, Barry Daldy.

League form was disastrous but, strangely, the FA Cup offered respite. After Grantham, led by former Posh player Jim Rayner, were beaten 3-1, Millwall were drawn at Rockingham Road in the first round proper.

Tommy Lawton had returned to Kettering as care-taker manager following the enforced resignation of Wally Akers. The Poppies drew 1-1, and faced the dubious pleasure of travelling to The Den in Cold Blow Lane for the replay.

'WE DID ENOUGH TO WIN'—LAWTON

● Tommy Lawton, even after a lifetime in the game, said: "One of my happiest days in football.

I DREAD to think what may happen if Millwall lose the replay at the Den tonight. The dockers are likely to be very angry indeed.

But Millwall have only to repeat the dreadful performance they put up at Kettering to deserve all the insults they get.

Their ineptness in front of goal, their slackness in the tackle, and their general lack of enthusiasm allowed struggling Southern League Kettering to dominate the match.

And I agreed with Tommy Lawton, Kettering's care-taker chief, with his after-match verdict: "We played with heart, and I felt we did enough to win."

After Pat Terry had slipped Millwall into a thirteenth-minute lead, the Londoners seemed to consider that was enough.

And against Kettering's tide of tigerish attacks it was inevitable that the Millwall defence would crack.

It did. With ten minutes to go, centre half Brian Snowdon, in a rare old panic, put the ball past his own goalkeeper.

Tonight could be quite a night.

The Millwall side had future Manchester United star Alex Stepney in goal, but he was beaten by a brave header from Daldy and two tremendous drives by wing half Armour, giving Kettering a dramatic 3-2 victory.

157

Millwall sink as Last Post rings out

LEFT-HALF George Armour, 26-year-old steel worker, was the uncrowned king of Kettering last night. Twice Armour's right foot went bump in the night—and Millwall crashed out of the Cup.

Two goals from Armour and one from 21-year-old right-winger Barry Daldy shot Kettering into a second round tie with Oxford United.

Tommy Lawton, one of England's greatest centre-forwards, who is now Kettering's acting manager, said: "I'm proud of these boys. This is one of my happiest days in football.

"They gave the lot. In fact our goalkeeper, Ted Smethurst, played throughout the second half with concussion."

Armour told me: "I started work at seven this morning and took the afternoon off. I'll be back at work tomorrow morning at seven."

Barry Daldy heads Kettering's second goal past Alex Stepney the Millwall goalkeeper

The second round brought a visit to old Southern League adversaries Oxford, formerly Headington United, and now of the Fourth Division.

Kettering lost 2-1 but, in a 1988 interview with 'ET' reporter Tony Smith, Lawton recalls an unfortunate refereeing decision that may well have denied his team a place in the 3rd Round draw.

In the Second Round, the Poppies lost 2-1 away to Oxford United which had Tommy seething from the bench. "We were absolutely robbed. Our winger Derek Hogg got the ball in his own half, went past two players and flashed it into the net. But the ref, incredibly, had given offside. I ask you — I was so livid. It would have put us 2-1 up."

Oxford, and wing half Atkinson, went on to reach the quarter finals, their run including a 5th Round victory over Blackburn Rovers, then second in Division 1.

KETTERING DESERVED THAT GOAL BY HOGG

OXFORD U. 2, KETTERING 1

TOMMY LAWTON, Kettering's manager, told me he thought Kettering were mighty unlucky to go out of the Cup. And I agree with him.

Said Tommy: "Oxford's second goal was scored because of a completely stupid defensive mix-up. Longbottom just had to tap the ball in.

"But Derek Hogg's shot which went into the net soon afterwards should have been a goal. He moved past a couple of defenders before shooting."

But the referee disagreed. He had seen another Kettering player standing well offside as Hogg moved forward.

Unlucky Kettering did most of the attacking in the second half and their forwards were often checked unnecessarily by the Oxford defence.

Frankly, Kettering deserved a draw.

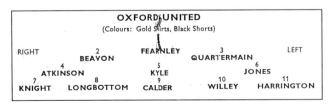

OXFORD UNITED
(Colours: Gold Shirts, Black Shorts)

RIGHT						LEFT
	2 BEAVON		FEARNLEY		3 QUARTERMAIN	
	4 ATKINSON		5 KYLE		6 JONES	
7 KNIGHT		8 LONGBOTTOM	9 CALDER		10 WILLEY	11 HARRINGTON

I began my teaching career in Corby in September 1963.

Picking a school football team has seldom been harder - every playtime, 300 'tanner ball players' displayed their skills on the yard and the problem was always which 289 to leave out.

Most evenings I stayed behind after school, not to fill in endless record sheets, but to join the boys in tennis ball matches that went on until dusk. Then, flushed and sweaty, I hastened down Studfall Avenue to the Town Centre to catch a bus home.

Sadly, today's young teachers can find little time for such 'extra curricula' activities.

Many of the boys sought to emulate the great Jim Baxter or Denis Law - but others adopted a more local persona. Strikers became Tommy Crawley or Arthur Hukin, (whose 'Tommy and Arthur Show' together amassed 77 goals in the Steelmen's 1963-64 season).

Manager Tommy Hadden discusses tactics with Tommy Crawley, Bill Rodgers, Hugh Curran, Arthur Hukin and Alan Alexander before Corby's tie with Bristol City.

Defenders identified with new full back Davy Pollard, while those with an eye to recognise genuine star potential favoured former Manchester United youngster Hughie Curran.

I suppose dozens of my pupils were amongst the 5,000 spectators at Occupation Road for the FA Cup tie against a Bristol City team which included international centre forward, John Atyeo.

Experienced Bobby Laverick missed the match through suspension, his place taken by local boy, Jimmy Stanley.

After taking the lead through Crawley, Corby succumbed to three break away goals and, as one post match newspaper headline proclaimed,
'City went through on a prayer'.

The league campaign ended in disappointment too. Injury to Crawley, who made only two appearances out of the last seventeen fixtures, and the inevitable loss of the talented Curran - transferred to Millwall for £3,000 - deprived the club of its two most influential performers at a crucial time.

Only four points were taken from the last six fixtures, Corby were displaced at the top of the table, and finished in eventual 5th place.

After losing the UCL title to neighbours Wellingborough in the last game of the previous season, Rushden went one better in 1963-64 by winning the championship for the first time in 26 years.

Rushden Town UCL Champions

Back Row: Dyte, Cowper, Peacock
Middle Row: DeBanke, Draper, Marlow, Coleman
Front Row: Pipes, Stanley, Major, Corbyn, Clipston

Player manager John 'Charlie' Marlow's side included former Cobbler, Bob Peacock, (whose father Ron played alongside trainer Len Pipes in the 1947 FA Cup match against Kettering), and Cobblers 'A' team goalkeeper from 1953, John Draper. Captain Peter De Banke had been a Rushden stalwart since the mid fifties, while winger Alan Major once scored 8 times in a Corby reserve victory over Raunds.

THE United Counties League trophy, draped in the club's green and white colours, took pride of place at Rushden Town FC's annual dinner last night.

During the evening tributes were paid to the team which had brought the trophy back to Rushden after a lapse of 26 years and also to the people behind the scenes.

Mr. W. Wiseman, vice-chairman of the United Counties League and secretary of Corby Town FC, described the club's championship success as a fine achievement and wished members every success for the future.

He recalled some of the encounters between Rushden and his club from which the Russians had emerged as very worthy opponents.

Speaking about the championship, Mr. Wiseman said: "The best things come to the best clubs in the end."

Rushden's chairman Mr. C. C. Cox, said, in his opinion, the United Counties League had a promising future. A manager in a higher grade of football admired the way in which it was run, he told the 200 people present.

A good job of work had been done by player/manager John Marlow, who, in his first year had seen the team win the championship, said Mr. Cox.

Rushden celebrate UCL title win

1963-64 Division 1	P.	W.	D.	L.	F.	A.	Pts
Rushden Town	32	23	4	5	91	33	50
Holbeach United	32	22	5	5	95	35	49
Biggleswade Town	32	22	2	8	100	63	46
Wellingborough Town	32	18	8	6	81	46	44
Rothwell Town	32	17	6	9	79	58	40
Corby Res.	32	17	4	11	60	45	38
Desborough Town	32	17	4	11	82	68	38
Eynesbury Rovers	32	15	3	14	77	82	33
Wisbech Res.	32	14	1	17	73	95	29
B. Timken Athletic	32	10	6	16	68	82	26
Wolverton Town	32	10	6	16	79	98	26
Bletchley Town	32	10	5	17	71	86	25
Northampton Town 'A'	32	9	6	17	73	84	24
Peterborough Athletic	32	8	8	16	63	76	24
Potton United	32	8	5	19	53	80	21
St Neots Res.	32	8	2	22	50	89	18
S & L Corby	32	5	3	24	43	118	13

I had joined Rushden from Desborough at the beginning of the season, together with old Kettering Youth colleague Barry Stanley and full back John Coleman, but Hayden Road was never a favourite ground and I returned to 'Ar Tarn' in October. Those few months, however, provided ample examples of manager Marlow's decidedly idiosyncratic style of management.

On one occasion, the Thursday evening training session before a Saturday cup tie with Wellingborough, he brought a box into the dressing room containing a brand new green and white strip. He then summoned inside forward Albert Moir.

"Put it on Bertie. Let's see what it looks like."

Albert was happy to oblige and paraded up and down the room to the raucous delight of team mates. 'Charlie' allowed him his moment of glory, before delivering the 'Coup de grace' in his characteristic Desborough drawl.

"Right! Now tairk the bugger awf - you're dropped on Satdy." And he was.

But 'Charlie' got results, and his record, both as goalscorer and manager, speaks eloquently enough.

BOOKED FOR THE
FIRST DIVISION
1964-65

There was no better place to be during the 1964-65 season than at the County Ground, Northampton. The irresistible blend of keen, enthusiastic youngsters and wise old heads, cobbled together on Bowen's shoestring budget, and urged on by a fervent crowd, had swept the team to the top of the Second Division.

BOWEN BUILDS £290,000 SIDE

NO wonder Northampton directors are delighted with their master-builder Dave Bowen. For manager Bowen has constructed his conquering side for a mere £16,000 . . . a crazy figure compared with their current value of £290,000.

In five years of slogging, with only a bankful of buttons, busy Bowen has pieced together a squad that has risen from the graveyard of Division Four to the gates of Division One.

Just look at the cash chart of the men who drew 1—1 at Norwich last Saturday.

PLAYER	COST	VALUE
B. Harvey	£4,000	£35,000
T. Foley ..	£1,000	£20,000
M. Everitt.	——	£20,000
D. Leck ..	£1,000	£15,000
T. Branston	——	£45,900
J. Kiernan.	£2,000	£45,000
T. Walden .	——	£15,000
D. Martin .	——	£15,000
B. Brown ..	——	£15,000
K. Leck ..	£8,000	£15,000
T. Robson .	——	£50,000
	£16,000	£290,000

Goalkeeper Bryan Harvey was inspired. The defence, marshalled by newly capped Eire International Theo Foley, bolstered by fearsome

Scots babe in £40,000 class

He's 'another Baxter'

FIVE years ago Joe Kiernan, a bright-eyed 15-year-old, went to England.

Like so many of our boys taken up by the English soccer baby-snatchers, he might have become homesick. But the Coatbridge lad, nephew of Tommy Kiernan, former Celtic star, stuck it out—and is now worth over £40,000 ! That is the offer Sheffield Wednesday made for him.

Manager David Bowens, who looks like creating a record of taking Northampton from the English Fourth Division to the First in five years, tells the young Scot's story

"Believe me when I say that Kiernan, now 20 years old, is the greatest left-half in England. We were made an offer of well over £40,000, but he is essential to our promotion drive and won't be allowed to leave.

WATCHED

"I got his transfer for a moderate fee from Sunderland towards the end of last season, and the youngster has become one of the key men in our race for the First Division. I have seen your Jim Baxter, of Rangers, and have no hesitation in claiming that Kiernan is in the same class.

Terry Branston and ably supported by Everitt and Cockcroft were mean in the extreme. Midfield had perfect balance. Kiernan's sublime skills blossomed alongside the tenacious Kurila and ungainly, yet deceptively effective, Derek Leck.

The forwards were sharp and potent. Wingers Lines, Walden or Robson provided ideal service for strikers Martin, Hunt, Brown, Livesey and former Cobbler Ken Leek, latterly returned from spells at Leicester, Newcastle and Birmingham.

Joe Kiernan, Cobblers stylish wing half evades a challenge from Coventry centre half George Curtis, to cross with his 'sweet' left foot,.

As the campaign drew to a close, a catalogue of famous club names left Northampton with reputations somewhat tarnished.

Northampton Town 1964-65

Back Row: Osborne, Carr, Kiernan, Leck, Harvey, Branston, Brown, Martin, Everitt, Payne. Front Row: Walden, Foley, Bowen, Hunt, Robson.

Many of those matches were played on midweek evenings, for which I remain eternally grateful. Otherwise I might never have seen the game that in many ways epitomised the Cobblers great season. The Bolton Wanderers team included internationals, Hopkinson and Hill - and future Manchester City and England star Francis Lee. When Bolton were awarded a penalty,

163

Lee's shot struck the diving Harvey's legs and flew over the bar. The crowd, crushed shoulder to shoulder around the ground, raised arms aloft and responded with a spontaneous chorus of 'Harvee, Harvee!' And, in the excitement, a footballing friend experienced unforgettable moments of pure delight. He accidentally returned his hand between the buttons of his female neighbour's coat. The girl, a complete stranger, responded wordlessly by slipping hers through the lining of his mac and into his trousers. The smiles on their faces were not entirely due to events on the field, where the Cobblers recorded a vital 4-0 victory. Consummation was mutually achieved, he assures me, at the very blast of the final whistle at which both were then swept away on the tide of departing supporters, never to meet again.

A foot in time...

Penalty! But Harvey's foot stops a Bolton score.

NOW BOOKED FOR FIRST DIVISION

BURY 1, NORTHAMPTON TOWN 4

IT IS THE FIRST DIVISION FOR THE COBBLERS NEXT SEASON.

They could not have ended their promotion campaign with a more convincing and commanding display than this stylish victory over Bury today. They controlled the game throughout and, although falling back on defence in the closing stages, they never looked like losing their grip.

The Cobblers' forward line has rarely moved with more fluency and their defence was as sound as ever, giving a good omen for next season.

Two goals in the first 14 minutes saw the Cobblers off to a flying start. Kiernan scored the first with a shot from 20 yards which went in off the post and Brown notched the second with a shot which the Bury goalkeeper just failed to stop.

Durrant, the Bury left-winger, put the Lancashire club back in the game with a well-taken goal after 21 minutes, but the Cobblers increased their lead again when Martin scored six minutes before the interval.

Martin clinched the match for the Cobblers after 58 minutes when he raced through a bewildered Bury defence to head in a free-kick taken by Kiernan.

On visits to the County Ground in more recent years, observing tiny groups of spectators standing yards apart on sparsely populated terraces, he would wistfully recall that far off evening.

And I thought nothing transcended football!

Promotion was assured on April 17th when a Bury side, including future internationals Colin Bell and Alec Lindsay, were beaten 4-1 on their own ground.

In the final game of the season the legendary Jimmy Dickinson made a farewell appearance, when a 1-1 draw enabled Portsmouth to secure the point

164

needed to avoid relegation to the Third Division.

The Cobblers, however, were heading for Division 1, an achievement acknowledged by the manager in a Players Promotion Souvenir. The booklet also contains the thoughts of the crop of local players who contributed to the success of 1964-65.

Among those offering congratulations was Cobblers Fund raiser Bob Calder, the former Poppies manager, who had left Kettering in rather acrimonious circumstances at the beginning of the Lawton era in 1956.
Optimism abounded.

DAILY DIP AND COBBLERS BOBBERS COMPETITIONS
COMPETITION OFFICE

On this most auspicious occasion, we would like to add our heartiest congratulations to our Manager and Players on their most meritorious performance, by bringing First Division Football to Northampton. I feel certain that speaking on behalf of all our Agents and also the Competition Office Staff, Edwina Cockerill, John Linnell and myself, we have been richly rewarded in return for the financial help we have given to the Club through you, the Agents, whose help is much appreciated.

We will be continuing our efforts as usual throughout the Summer, and Agents are required for our New " Armchair Bingo " Competition. Please call at the Competition Office, we will be pleased to welcome you.

Yours sincerely,

BOB CALDER,

Competition Organiser.

1964	SECOND DIVISION			
Aug.	24	Middlesbro'	(27,121)	0 1
	29	Manchester	(20,845)	2 0
Sept.	1	Middlesbro'	(17,028)	1 1
	5	South'ton	(13,989)	0 2
	8	Newcastle	(15,365)	1 0
	12	Huddersfield	(12,984)	3 2
	15	Ipswich T.	(13,518)	0 0
	19	Coventry C.	(30,069)	1 0
	26	Cardiff City	(12,278)	1 0
	29	Ipswich T.	(14,886)	3 2
Oct.	3	Preston N.E.	(15,593)	2 2
	7	Portsmouth	(12,262)	3 3
	10	Charlton	13,552)	1 0
	17	Leyton	(8,533	2 2
	24	Bury	(11,324)	2 0
	31	Crystal P.	(21,331)	2 1
	7	Norwich C.	(16,774)	0 0
	14	Rotherham	(11,273)	1 1
	21	Swansea	(13,427)	2 1
	28	Derby Co.	(17,367)	2 2
Dec.	5	Swindon T.	(9,486)	2 1
	12	Newcastle	(41,340)	0 5
	19	Manchester	(12,665)	2 0
	26	Bolton W.	(24,269)	0 0
Jan.	2	South'ton	(15,245)	2 2
	16	Huddersfield	(7,359)	0 2
	23	Coventry	(18,741)	1 1
Feb.	6	Cardiff City	(7,650)	2 0
	13	Preston N.E.	(14,010)	2 1
	20	Charlton A.	(8,958)	1 1
	27	Leyton O.	(13,537)	2 0
Mar.	2	Bolton	(15,515)	4 0
	13	Crystal Pal.	(17,350)	1 1
	20	Norwich C.	(25,517)	1 1
	23	Swindon T.	(17,686)	2 4
	27	Rotherham	(19,488)	1 0
Apr	3	Swansea T.	(10,536)	2 1
	10	Derby C.	(17,917)	2 2
	17	Bury	(6,800)	4 1
	19	Plymouth	(10,281)	2 5
	20	Plymouth	(19,718)	3 1
	24	Portsmouth	...	Home
May	1	F.A. Cup-Final		

FIRST TEAM APPEARANCES & SCORERS

		F.A. Cup	F.L. Cup	Lge.			F.A. Cup	F.L. Cup	Lge.
Harvey	...	1	4	41	Best	...			4
Foley	...	1	4	41	Hunt	...		2	15
Everitt	...	1	3	38	Martin	...		2	19
Cockcroft	...	1	1	6	Livesey	...	1	4	25
Leck	...	1	3	41	Brown	...		1	19
Branston	...	1	4	34	Hall	...		2	6
Carr	...			7	Etheridge	...		1	9
Keirnan	...	1	4	40	Leck	...	1		12
Kurila	...		1	1	Lines	...		1	9
Walden	...	1	4	38	Robson	...	1	3	35
Walton	...			1					

SCORERS

		F.L. Cup	Lge.				Lge.
Brown	...		13	Leck	...		3
Martin	...	3	13	Branston	...		2
Robson	...		13	Everitt	...		2
Hunt	...	2	4	Kiernan	...		2
Foley	...	1 1	3	Etheridge	...		1
Leck	...		3	Hall	...		1
Livesey	...	1	3	Walden	...	1	1
				Opponent	...		1

165

IT has been six years since I came back to Northampton to manage the Cobblers, after ten years with Arsenal. It was a very proud day for me as I was, at this time, the youngest manager in the Football League. I had previously played for the Cobblers from 1947-50 before being sold to Arsenal.

The club, at this period, was in the Fourth Division of the Football League and things were a little depressing after tasting the marble hall of Highbury. I had been advised by many so called authorities to forget Northampton as their footballing future was nil.

The challenge appealed—and the jeremiahs contemplated—but we did succeed and the footballing world was astonished when, in three years, we were in the Second Division. However, this was not the end because, after two more years, we are now in the First Division. So Northampton Town F.C. have made history by achieving, for the first time, the meteoric rise from the fourth to the first in five years.

This has been accomplished by great team spirit throughout the club which has generated from the ground staff boys right through to the Chairman.

No words can express my appreciation to the players for their magnificent efforts. They have lived for the progress of the club and have spent hours at practising to play the game to set patterns, even at the expense of their own particular abilities. Many more hours have been spent at team meetings, analysing their own performances and working on their opponents weaknesses.

They have dedicated themselves to an objective and succeeded—and it has been the greatest joy of all my footballing career to have been associated with the club and its wonderful players in this historic era.

DAVE BOWEN.

Promoted from

Division IV. —	1960-61
Division III. —	1962-63
Division II. —	1964-65

DON MARTIN

BORN Corby on the 15th February, 1944. Played football for the local county and district schools.

Joined Northampton Ground Staff from school in 1959. Played for England Youth team on several occasions in England and abroad in 1961-62 season.

Signed full-time professional for Northampton in July, 1962.

Made League debut on the 15th December, 1962, against Carlisle.

Dave Bowen has helped me most in my football career up to now.

The most memorable match in season 1964-65 was when we gained promotion against Bury.

Height, 5' 11¾". Weight, 11st.

The club has just given me a club house and I am looking forward to playing for the Cobblers for many years to come, yes, in Division One!

BARRY LINES

BORN Northampton May 1942. Played for North Bucks Schoolboys, joined Bletchley Town Football Club 1958, played for Bletchley United F.C. before signing for Northampton Town, September, 1960.

Made First team debut October, 1960 against Wrexham (Football League Cup). Made League debut against Hartlepools, November, 1960.

I have since lost my place to Tom Robson, but I promise that I shall fight to regain it, as I too want to play in Division One.

BRIAN ETHERIDGE

Represented Northampton Town and County Schoolboys before joining the ground staff of Northampton Town F.C. at the age of 15.

After progressing through Colts side to Combination team, was capped for the England Youth team against Scotland at Peterborough.

Played in the 1962 Youth International tournament in Rumania and toured Israel with professional youth team, gaining eight caps and skippering the England amateur youth team on five occasions.

Made League debut while still an amateur, against Notts County at Meadow Lane.

Signed professional forms for Northampton Town on return from Israel and made professional debut against Halifax Town at the " Shay."

Made F.A. Cup debut against Sunderland at Roker Park and home League debut against Middlesbrough.

I have got over my knee injury and hope to play in the First Division with the Cobblers.

HARRY WALDEN

BORN Walgrave, Northamptonshire, played for local village team after leaving school, joined Kettering at the age of 17, made about 50 first team appearances in a two and a half year stay. Fortune was still with me when I signed for Second Division Luton Town. Made debut for them at Norwich. After staying at Luton four years I moved across to my local team, Northampton Town. It was a great break from a relegated side to a team promoted to the First Division.

The match I really enjoyed last season was the evening match against Bolton. I feel that win was the one that put us in the First Division.

JIM HALL

BORN locally on 21st March, 1945, attended Northampton G.S. where rugby was the main sport.

Began football career with Holy Trinity F.C., Northampton Town League side. At the age of seventeen joined the Cobblers as an amateur, and graduated via the Youth and Colts side onto the ground staff.

In 1962-3 season gained three Youth International caps, playing against Wales, Ireland and Scotland, and at the end of the season signed professional forms for Northampton.

Playing at inside left made Football League debut against Charlton at the Valley on the Easter of 1964. Made League Cup debut against Portsmouth the following season and at the end of last season went on the club's first tour abroad to Czechoslovakia.

ROLAND MILLS

BORN Daventry June 22nd, 1933. Joined N.T.F.C. at the age of 14 years, under the management of Bob Dennison. Made debut in the First team at Colchester when I was 17. From then I played about 300 games in the First team.

Took over assistant trainers job at the beginning of last season, when we gained promotion to the First Division.

I have enjoyed my playing years with Northampton and hope to be associated with them for quite some time to come. I would like to take this opportunity of wishing the lads as much success in the coming seasons as the one just concluded.

167

Peterborough United enjoyed a return to national prominence after several barren years, when reaching the 6th Round of the FA Cup. After victories over Salisbury, QPR and Chesterfield, Arsenal were drawn at home in the 4th Round.

The January day was bleak and chill - fitting weather for the funeral of Sir Winston Churchill. That same afternoon, Desborough Town were Peterborough bound for a fixture against United's 'A' Team at the Brotherhood Sports Ground, a short distance from London Road.

Posh fans, initially mistaking our coach for Arsenal's, jeered good naturedly. During our game, played in front of six men and a dog, it was extremely disconcerting to hear 30,056 disembodied voices roar in unison as you retrieved the ball for a throw in.

Posh make history as casual Arsenal go out

PETERSOROUGH 2, ARSENAL 1

WONDERFUL, wonderful Peterborough. The club with a Cup giant-killing history as striking as the entrance hall of Arsenal's palatial headquarters, sent the Gunners reeling from the FA Cup in this fourth round match.

Records are there to be broken and Posh, playing in the fourth round for the fifth time, sent the record book pages flipping over with this fantastic performance which put them into the fifth round for the first time.

Peter McNamee, who earlier in January completed ten years with the London Road club, scored the winning goal four minutes from the end for a dramatic finish.

A ground record of 30,056 were thankful that Posh had managed to hit back and equalise when Arsenal appeared to be taking control. But Arsenal's hopes of a replay went by the board as

McNamee glided into the area and clipped the ball past teenage goalkeeper Tony Burns to persuade hundreds of frenzied young fans to invade the pitch and dance with delight.

The winning goal started from an Arsenal attack. Frank Rankmore, United's centre-half and the best man on the field, headed the ball well clear and it passed from McNamee to Barnes before going into the six-yard box for McNamee.

Peterborough had the best of the first half, but were a goal down when John Radford snapped up a chance from Eastham's right-wing corner just before half-time.

Arsenal were on top in the second but Derek Dougan, who gave Scottish international Ian Ure a nightmare afternoon, scored an equaliser from Vic Crowe's pass.

As expected, Oliver Conmy played a deep lying game to allow Crowe to shadow Eastham. As a result, Eastham was never able to move forward and Arsenal's attack was subdued.

Yet Arsenal, probably through Eastham's casual style, never really put themselves about until the last minute when they fought to try for a late equaliser.

Then Willie Duff covered himself with glory. He dived to block a shot from Radford as nine Arsenal men stormed into the attack. The rebound went to Baker whose snapshot—it was his only effort at goal all afternoon—sent Duff flashing across the goal to make another sensational save.

Both Peterborough teams were inspired - Posh recorded their first ever victory over a First Division side, with Peter McNamee sole survivor from the Midland League team, scoring the winning goal.

THIS is Posh's proudest moment. Richly do they deserve their success. It is the first time these legendary F.A. Cup giant-killers have reached the fifth round, and the first time they have beaten a First Division side on the way.

Now, they are only three matches away from Wembley, and the most glittering prize in English football. This is, of course, wishful thinking, but whatever happens now, nothing can take the glory of Saturday's moment of victory away from Peterborough United.

It was no fluke—Posh won on merit. They rose magnificently to the big occasion. Arsenal did not, and their disappointed supporters, baying for blood after the match, took defeat hard.

Peterborough had a special affection for Arsenal—even before the match. Arsenal were one of the clubs that helped secure Posh's election to the Football League, and entertained Peterborough officials on the day of the meeting.

This is a wry turn of fate and, while immediate memories may be bitter, the long-term effect of the match will surely help to seal the ties of goodwill between the two clubs.

The 'A' team, fielding an entire Football Combination side, won 5-2.

Swansea were defeated in a replayed 5th round tie at the Vetch Field. The quarter final took United to Stamford Bridge to face a Chelsea side which included Bert Murray and Terry Venables.

Chelsea players watch opponents 'Posh' in training prior to their quarter final tie.

IN ROUND SIX FOR FIRST TIME   **F.A.CUP SPECIAL**

PETERBOROUGH UNITED 1964-65

Back row: B. Wright, O. Hopkins, F. Rankmore, W. Duff, K. Smith (now Crystal Palace), T. Singleton.
Front row: I. Crawford, P. Deakin, D. Dougan, O. Conny, P. McNamee.
Insets: V. Crowe, R. Barnes, G. Birks, H. Orr.

Vic Crowe is stretchered off.

Gallant Peterborough, giant-killers in the past, met their match in Chelsea in the quarter-finals of the F.A. Cup. But they fought, even though after two minutes they lost their captain and right-half Vic Crowe because of a groin injury. Here he is being carried off.

Peterborough supporters in the crowd of 63,635 watched in horror as influential skipper Vic Crowe was stretchered off with the game only two minutes old.

Crowe returned to score a consolation goal but, as reporter Alan Curling's account indicates, it was very much a question of what might have been .

169

I MUST have looked the picture of misery A gloomy face, a long black overcoat and I was deep in thought. Then Ron Barnes, Posh's winger said "Cheer up. This was the sixth round, not the first."

Ron was putting on a brave face after United's 5—1 defeat at Stamford Bridge on Saturday and we were in the Posh dressing room after the game.

But even cheerful Ron could not move that air of disappointment.

It was disappointment not so much in defeat but in the way Dame Fortune had frowned so cruelly upon Posh in their first appearance in the sixth round of the Cup.

The scene was set at 3 o'clock. The gates were locked and over 63,000 people had paid £17,000 officially (and several had paid over the odds!) to see this game. Peterborough United from the Third Division were all set after extragant preparations to make their effort against the First Division leaders.

Two minutes later, it — to all intent and purposes — was all over. Vic Crowe, Posh's captain and the most vital man in the side, fell awkwardly making his first tackle of the game and was carried off on a stretcher. He returned later, but his absence had taken its toll on disorganised United.

Chelsea whipped in three goals in four minutes as Ron Cooper and then Willie Duff made mistakes under the strain of Chelsea's powerful attacking.

SHATTERED

But don't incriminate any of these players for their mistakes. Their world was shattered when Crowe went off. His strong skilful play was not all that was missed. United needed his leadership, his generalling of the side.

It was cruel luck for Posh, but all credit to them, they kept the party clean, they fought all the way and they gave as good as the got — even with Crowe at a quarter-pace — all through the second half.

Chelsea (and who can blame them?) cashed in on Posh's misfortune with four goals in the first half-hour.

Crowe's return brought a cheer and then the biggest roar of the day came as the skipper prodded the ball into the net from McNamee's cross just before half-time.

STAR MEN

Posh had a good second-half. Deakin and McNamee, backed by some good play by Orr, carved some big holes in Chelsea's defence and First

BY ALAN CURLING

Division men had to play well to contain Peterborough.

These three were Posh's star men and with a full side, I'm sure Peterborough would have made it an interesting and close battle.

Chelsea's youngsters, to my mind, look good enough to take a couple of the big honours this season — possibly the League Cup and the F.A. Cup. No-one on the field looked better than skipper Venables, although he would certainly have been more contained by a full Posh side.

Chelsea snatched a rather fortunate goal in the last minute of the game but by that time Peterborough's disappointment was completed.

All their preparations had not, however, been wasted. They proved — even to the London side's supporters — that they can play good football, they have plenty of skill and were worthy of the Cup

THE VITAL STATISTICS

THE TEAMS

Chelsea: Bonetti; Hinton, Harris; Hollins, Mortimore, Boyce; Murray, Graham, Bridges, Venables, Tambling.

United: Duff; Cooper, Birks; Crowe, Rankmore, Orr; Barnes, Conmy, Dougan, Deakin, McNamee.

Referee: Mr. J. Parkinson (Blackburn).

THE SCORERS

Chelsea: Tambling (11 and 14 mins.), Hollins (12), Bridges (31), Murray (89).

United: Crowe (43 mins.).

THE CROWD

63,635.

Receipts — £17,486.

history they have made this season.

Full marks to all the lads. All the supporters were just as disappointed as they were

I certainly was — and, according to Ron Barnes, I looked it!

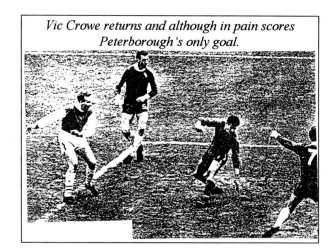

Vic Crowe returns and although in pain scores Peterborough's only goal.

The side completed a memorable season in eighth place - promotion probably the price of cup success.

170

One of Peterborough's stars during the cup run was inside forward Ollie Conmy, a close season signing from Huddersfield. The Irishman's form was impressive enough to attract interest from Eire and he was chosen - appropriately on St Patrick's Day - to represent his country against Belgium in Dublin.

Ollie Conmy

Ollie remembers reporting at Dublin's Gresham's Hotel on the evening before the match, surprised to find no sign of other team members or manager Johnny Carey. Disconcerted, he ordered himself a meal in the restaurant, ate alone, put the bill on account and went to bed. It was breakfast before he met team mates, but Carey was still conspicuously absent. When eventually the former Manchester United Cup Final colleague of Posh hero, Johnny Anderson, appeared, it was to deliver a memorable pre-match team talk - 'Keep the score down.'

Conmy earned five caps in all and a fitting tribute to one of Peterborough's finest midfield players appeared in the programme issued on the occasion of his testimonial game against Leicester City.

Kettering failed in their bid to regain the Southern League Premier status forfeited during 1963-64. New player-manager Dick, 'call me Boss', White had played in the Liverpool cup side victorious over the Cobblers back in 1958.

Ollie Conmy is one of the thinkers in the game, a qualified coach, he passed his certificate with the Football Association in 1969 he now spends many hours coaching the youngsters of Western Star youth club. Looking to the future he says that he will probably make use of his qualification and concentrate on coaching when his playing days are through.

But he is not preparing to hang up his boots just yet he says he is enjoying his football this season as much as at any time in his career. For the lad from Ireland who likes family life and lives in Peterborough with his Yorkshire wife Rosalie and three year old daughter Lisa there are still two ambitions to fulfill, "a promotion medal with Posh and maybe another International cap".

The team began the season well, but a poor run-in condemned the club to a lowly final position - the attendance for the last home match against Dover, 311, was the lowest then recorded for a post-war Southern League fixture at Rockingham Road.

171

POPPIES' MANAGER SAYS CALL ME 'BOSS'—NOT DICK

KETTERING Town's professionals started full-time training this morning. Before leaving the Rockingham Road ground for Northampton Road recreation ground—where they are to do their training—the players were addressed by the Poppies' new manager, Dick White, writes "The Friar".

He made it clear that there would have to be discipline in the team. "So, from the start, you will call me 'boss' and not "Dick", he said.

He outlined the club's new policy of going full-time and demanded 100 per cent effort from the team.

Legendary goalkeeper Ted Smethurst, hero against Swindon, was dropped after 190 consecutive league appearances, replaced by local youngster Gordon Livsey, and moved on to Rugby Town.

Gordon Turner

Ken Evans

Former Luton player Gordon Turner joined the club from Wisbech in exchange for Norman Bleanch, and another Kettering boy, Ken Evans, eventually won a regular place in the side.

The FA cup paired the Poppies with Millwall in a First Round repeat of the previous year's fixture. However, there was no happy return for Kettering who were beaten 2-0.

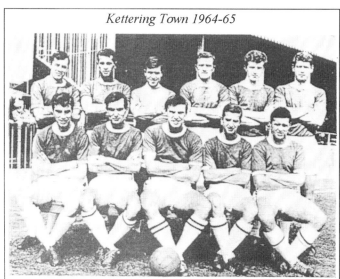
Kettering Town 1964-65

Back Row: Dodge, Norton, Smethurst, White, Davey, Ramshaw.
Front Row: Salmon, Kerry, Bleanch, Wyld, Hooper.

Popular players full back Rex Norton and winghalf Ralph Ramshaw had joined the Poppies from Loughborough College. Rex still teaches locally but Ralph was tragically killed in a flying accident while serving with the RAF in Cyprus, in 1971.

The club's 'A' side had a marvellous season, however, winning the UCL Division 2 and scoring 151 league goals in the process. Dick Underwood netted 54, included two sixes, one five, one four and three hat tricks.

John Ritchie

Another local centre forward, former Poppy John Ritchie, was hitting the headlines in his second season at Stoke City.

Kettering's lean season was in contrast to rivals Corby Town, who at last gained promotion to the Southern League's Premier division.

Captained by former Peterborough and Eire full back Dick Whittaker, the Steelmen attained the fourth promotion place following an extended winning run during March.

Tommy Crawley top scored with 37 goals, while local boy Maurice Goodall replaced Arthur Hukin at centre forward. Former Poppy George Armour joined John Rennie and Barrie Parsons to complete a home grown half back line.

The side again suffered an early exit from the FA Cup, this time at home to the 4th Division strugglers Hartlepool United, who won 3-1.

PROMOTION FOR STEELMEN

CORBY TOWN 3, DEAL TOWN 0

IT was champagne all round in the Corby dressing room after the Steelmen had clinched a victory that gave them promotion to the Premier Division of the Southern League for the first time, writes Steelman.

What a pity they did not end in a blaze of glory!

For, although Corby defeated the visitors by a comfortable three-goal margin, it was not one of their better performances. Poor finishing and an excellent display by Lennie Long in the Deal goal, kept the score down.

Early in the second half, Corby appeared to be struggling to consolidate their position as the better team.

Throughout the first half they attacked non-stop and only a series of misses and incredible saves by Long kept the interval margin down to a single goal.

Deal, who tended to keep the ball too close—especially in defence—brought on a lot of the trouble to themselves. But Corby were slow to take advantage of this and all the forwards missed scoring chances before a Tommy Crawley free-kick gave them the lead in the 30th minute. Left-half Russell was penalised for handling and, from the edge of the area CRAWLEY drove the ball through a crowd of players.

Deal's spasmodic second half raids looked dangerous but they could not press home an equaliser.

Promotion was eventually secured in the 60th minute with a picture-book goal. Alex Garden sent GOODALL through with a perfect pass.

SOUTHERN LEAGUE
First Division

	P.	W.	D.	L.	F.	A.	P.
Hereford U	42	34	4	4	124	39	72
Wimbledon	42	24	13	5	108	52	61
Poole T	42	26	6	10	92	56	58
Corby T	41	24	7	10	88	53	55
Stevenage T	41	19	13	9	93	42	51
Hillingdon Bor	41	21	7	13	105	62	49
Merthyr Tyd.	41	19	9	13	70	58	47
Burton Alb	42	20	7	15	83	75	47
Crawley T	39	20	5	14	78	46	45
Gloucester C	40	17	10	13	76	65	44
Canterbury C	40	13	15	12	71	47	41
Kettering T	42	14	13	15	74	64	41
Ramsgate Ath	42	16	8	18	51	59	40
Dover	42	14	10	18	54	59	38
Hinckley Ath.	40	12	8	19	54	81	32
Trowbridge T.	40	13	4	22	67	101	30
Ashford T.	41	11	8	22	60	93	30
Barry T	41	10	7	24	46	103	27
Deal T	42	7	13	22	61	127	27
Gravesend	40	9	7	24	56	97	25
Tunbridge W.	40	9	5	26	49	106	23
Sittingbourne	42	7	5	30	57	104	19

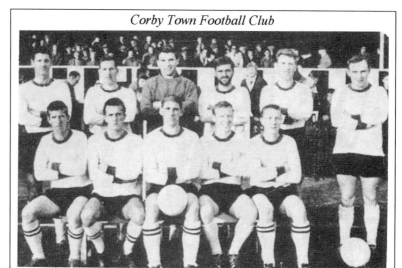

Corby Town Football Club

Back Row: Whittaker, Rennie, Alexander, Jagger, Armour, Pollard
Front Row: Stenhouse, Garden, Goodall, Grassam

Wellingborough Town won the UCL championship for the second time in three seasons losing only one game, to runners up Rothwell Town, who finished a massive 11 points behind.

A measure of the Doughboys superiority was evident in an 8-1 victory over reigning champions Rushden, goalkeeper Brian Foster netting from the penalty spot. The incident refuelled long standing rivalry between the clubs and prompted an explanatory response from manager McCormick in the programme the following week.

1964-65 Division 1	P.	W.	D.	L.	F.	A.	Pts.
Wellingborough Town	30	25	4	1	97	24	54
Rothwell Town	30	18	7	5	81	47	43
Bletchley Town	30	18	6	6	81	37	42
Holbeach United	30	16	6	8	79	50	38
Desborough Town	30	15	5	10	84	65	35
Corby Res.	30	12	7	11	62	66	31
Potton United	30	12	6	12	40	42	30
Wisbech Res.	30	12	3	15	71	82	27
Rushden Town	30	9	8	13	62	59	26
Wolverton Town	30	9	8	13	53	65	26
B. Timken Athletic	30	8	9	13	63	78	25
S & L Corby	30	8	7	15	68	85	23
Northampton Town 'A'	30	9	3	18	50	88	21
Biggleswade Town	30	8	4	18	51	81	20
Peterborough Athletic	30	8	4	18	50	83	20
Eynesbury Rovers	30	7	5	18	40	83	19

The impression seems to be abroad that we sought to humiliate Rushden by allowing Brian Foster to take the penalty. Let me correct this – nothing was further from our minds as the move was planned some weeks previously, so that if the opportunity arose, it would enable the Doughboys' claim the unique record of every player in the side having scored.

Wellingborough Town 1964-65

Back Row: Blunt, Miller, Chapman, Wooding, Foster, J Daldy, McNamee, Kightley, Holman.
Front Row: Newman, B Daldy, Hayward, McCormick, Casey, Franklin, Harper

1966 AND ALL THAT
1965-66

1965-66 was the season when Northampton breathed the rarefied air of the First Division. The Cobblers began their league campaign at Goodison Park, amid speculation that the team would be hopelessly outclassed. After all, the side included four players, Leck, Lines, Branston and Everitt, who had played in the Fourth Division days.

BOWEN RAPS CRITICS

NORTHAMPTON'S superbly fit and under-rated young men go into First Division battle at Goodison Park on Saturday with this fierce and proud assurance for manager Dave Bowen :—

"Boss, you know we would go through agony for you. We will not let you down."

Arsenal-reared Bowen, the demanding Welshman who has driven Northampton from the Fourth to the First Division in five years, admits his players' attitude is the most satisfying thing that has ever happened to him.

"I've been having a bit of a go at them, letting them know who is boss. It was only a minor point, but I sensed the lads thought I was being hard.

Then one of them got up and stressed the team's loyalty. As the others nodded their agreement I felt very humble. No manager could ask for greater backing."

Despite Bowen's pre-match optimism, a 5-2 defeat gave warning of the mammoth struggle ahead.

FOOTBALL LEAGUE — DIVISION I

**EVERTON v.
NORTHAMPTON TOWN**

SATURDAY, 21st AUGUST 1965

Kick-off 3.0 p.m.   Price 6ᴰ

EVERTON'S PACE GIVES BOWEN'S BOYS A SHOCK

By MIKE ELLIS

Everton 5, Northampton 2

IF the Government ever have a vacancy for the diplomatic corps I suggest they call in at Northampton and interview Dave Bowen.

Summoning up all the smooth-talking prose the Welsh are renowned for, manager Bowen cleverly sidestepped all the traps and pitfalls as he discussed his team's baptism into the First Division.

"We shall respect everything in this league," was his careful answer to Everton's five-goal blasting of his cinderella cubs.

"The lads found the pace even faster than they expected. Everton's ability to turn defence into attack within seconds came as a surprise."

Dave had the answers all right and he was cute to admit that Northampton won't be talented enough to hold their own.

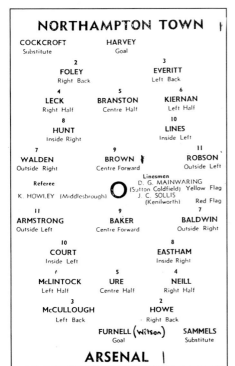

NORTHAMPTON TOWN

COCKCROFT Substitute	HARVEY Goal	
	2 FOLEY Right Back	3 EVERITT Left Back
4 LECK Right Half	5 BRANSTON Centre Half	6 KIERNAN Left Half
8 HUNT Inside Right		10 LINES Inside Left
7 WALDEN Outside Right	9 BROWN Centre Forward	11 ROBSON Outside Left

Referee
K. HOWLEY (Middlesbrough)

Linesmen
D. G. MAINWARING (Sutton Coldfield) Yellow Flag
J. C. SOLLIS (Kenilworth) Red Flag

11 ARMSTRONG Outside Left	9 BAKER Centre Forward	7 BALDWIN Outside Right
10 COURT Inside Left		8 EASTHAM Inside Right
6 McLINTOCK Left Half	5 URE Centre Half	4 NEILL Right Half
3 McCULLOUGH Left Back		2 HOWE Right Back
	FURNELL (Wilson) Goal	SAMMELS Substitute

ARSENAL 1

On Wednesday August 25th I watched the first home game. Ironically it was against Arsenal and much to the fury of visiting fans, reserve goalkeeper Bob Wilson was promoted to replace Jim Furnell. The future Scottish international, 'Double' winner and TV presenter, was subjected to a tirade of non-stop North London abuse, apparently centred upon his poor kicking ability.

"Where's your f...ing leg-iron Wilson?" is perhaps the mildest example I can recall.

The result, a 1-1 draw, was the first of a series of matches in which vital points were dropped at the County Ground.

"COBBLERS" CHATTER

The Cobblers reach the peak of 45 years league football on the County Ground when entertaining Arsenal tonight in their first home game in Division One. It is a momentous occasion indeed. The Northampton Town Football Club is very proud to have attained the top class and will do their utmost to be worthy of it.

We have climbed from Division Four to Division One in five years through teamwork by all sections of the club, and complete dedication to the task in hand. That policy will be continued in future. No effort will be spared to make the Cobblers a credit to the First Division.

During the close-season everything within our power, and the capacity of the County Ground, has been done to improve the accommodation. Work has gone on continuously to this purpose. We do ask all sportsmen in the area to give their full support, in attendance, in encouragement to the players, and to the various fund-raising efforts.

The fixture list could not have produced more appropriate opponents for the Cobblers' first home game in Division One than Arsenal because, over the years, the two clubs have had so much in common. Our manager, David Bowen, who has guided the Cobblers to the top sphere in so short a time, played for the Arsenal for nine years before returning to Northampton, his first club. He captained Arsenal, and was a very popular figure at Highbury.

Earlier the famous Herbert Chapman managed the Cobblers, taking them to the Southern League championship, at the start of a career which took him to many triumphs with the Arsenal. Both Northampton and Arsenal officials and supporters will think of Herbert Chapman tonight, knowing how delighted he would have been that the two clubs with which he had such notable associations are meeting on Northampton's entry into Division One

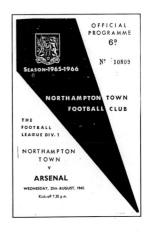

OFFICIAL PROGRAMME 6D

Nº 10809

SEASON 1965-1966

NORTHAMPTON TOWN FOOTBALL CLUB

THE FOOTBALL LEAGUE DIV. 1

NORTHAMPTON TOWN
v
ARSENAL

WEDNESDAY, 25th AUGUST, 1965.
Kick-off 7.30 p.m.

The following Saturday, the day of the British Timken Show, brought Manchester United to Northampton.

£12,000 side v Giants

Northampton T. .: ...... 1 Manchester U. 1

BEFORE THE GAME Dave Bowen. the manager who has worked the miracle of bringing Northampton from Fourth to First Division, muttered nervously: " It's a different world, this," and when Manchester right-winger, Connelly, cruised through a slack offside-trap to score after 10 minutes, it did look as if his words bore much truth.

Yet before the afternoon was over a strangely languid United had been forced to concede one point and very nearly two. Perhaps they were affected by the rural atmosphere of a ground enclosed on one side by a rope, with cricket pitch beyond.

But champions should take such things in their stride, and Manchester were easily ruffled. Law, too, was playing his first League game of the season.

Charlton, acting as link man, tried to keep his side moving with the aid of Best, but Northampton, playing with the keenness of a cup-tie, tackled them into a loss of poise and posi- tion. Their left-half, Kiernan, boldly controlled the middle of the field with his partner Leck running through intelligently, gradually pushing Manchester back to their goal area where the gliding feet of inside-left Line and the bursts of speed by his winger Robson often had Gaskell, in the United goal, groping in despair

Northampton's goal did not come until seven minutes from time, the reason being the lack of a marksman to finish off the constructiveness of Lines. At this moment, Manchester seemed to be walking their way to victory. Charlton clipped the ball across field to a non-existent right winger, and from the throw Line worked it up the left-wing before chipping it into the centre where inside-right Hunt volleyed it past Gaskell.

The rope sagged, and on rushed the crowd to greet a goal that might have won them the League Championship itself, such was the clamour It was a moral victory for Northampton, this mere £12,000 of a side meeting the £300,000 Manchester

A first league victory was achieved on October 23rd when Ron Greenwood's West Ham were beaten 2-1.

Victory preceded a run of successes in which Aston Villa, Fulham and Blackpool were all defeated.

A real boost for Cobblers

By Michael Beesley

Northampton Town 2, West Ham United 1

THE dark clouds of depression which had seemed settled indefinitely over the County Ground, lifted at 4.40 p.m. on Saturday when the Cobblers' first win of the season, and debut victory in the First Division, became a reality.

It was easy to understand the sheer jubilation of the Cobblers' fans who had waited 14 matches and 68 years for this glorious moment.

History was made and, although the Cobblers fully deserved their two points, it was ironical to recall they had played better this season and lost.

For once the Cobblers had the largest slice of the good fortune which was available, and it was obvious the long spell of waiting was finally over when Ken Leek managed to deflect a hard shot from Bobby Hunt into the net 10 minutes from the end.

However, the Cobblers fans should not have been waiting this long for their dreams to come true. The Cobblers should have sewn up this game long before half-time for West Ham put up only token resistance, and it was pathetic to see such a lethargic and dispirited display from this potentially fine team.

Moving quicker and with more determination than their opponents, the Cobblers attacked almost non-stop for the first half-hour. They always looked likely to score against the shaky West Ham defence, but somehow the vital goal eluded them.

NO MISTAKE

Then West Ham right-back Dennis Burnett presented the Cobblers with a goal when he unnecessarily tripped Bobby Hunt inside the penalty area, although the ball was fully 10 yards away. Cobblers skipper Theo Foley made no mistake with his second spot kick of the season.

Once again it was a slip by goalkeeper Bryan Harvey which allowed West Ham to get back into the game after 49 minutes. He completely missed a corner from the left and centre-half Ken Brown's header put West Ham on level terms.

This long-awaited win will give the Cobblers a terrific boost and, if it succeeds in destroying any inferiority complex which may have grown up over the past few weeks, it could herald the start of a steady climb away from the danger of relegation.

Northampton Town 1965-66 before the start of the season.

Back Row: Foley, Carr, Everitt, Bates, Kurila, Branston, Walton.
Standing: Payne, Lines, Best, Leck, Barron, Linnell, Harvey, Mackin, Cockcroft,
Kiernan, Mills.
Sitting: Walden, Hall, Livesey, Hunt, Bowen, Brown, Martin, Etheridge, Robson,
Howe, Fagan, Price, Bamford.

There were inevitable changes in personnel as Charlie Livesey, Derek Leck, Bobby Hunt and Tommy Robson moved on - Robson to Chelsea for £30,000.

New signings included infamous winger Joe Broadfoot from Ipswich and inside forward Graham Moore. The Welsh international added craft and experience to midfield alongside the hugely impressive Joe Kiernan.

As contemporary reports indicate, Kiernan relished the pace and style of the First Division, and consistently brilliant performances attracted the attention of numerous top clubs.

Bowen shrewdly noted one correspondent's comment, (reprinted below), and Kiernan stayed.

EVERTON BID £40,000 FOR KIERNAN

JOE KIERNAN, a £2,000 cast-off two years ago, could smash Northampton's transfer record this week. Everton are determined to sign the 22-year-old left half.

Northampton's board have already turned down two Everton bids—£35,000 and then £40,000. Now they are awaiting a third Everton offer and, if it reaches £45,000, I forecast that Northampton will accept.

Bowen's one shining light is left-half Joe Kiernan, once a Sunderland discard.

Kiernan strolled through this game without putting a foot wrong. He was the one touch of class in a team of honest-to-goodness workers.

Sell him, Dave, and you sell your First Division pass.

While relishing the opportunity to parade his own skills before a wider, more appreciative audience, Joe remained somewhat in awe of the opposition - particularly Manchester United and Denis Law. He recalls an incident in the Old Trafford game where he was opposed by the great man near the corner flag. As Denis lunged in to take the ball, Joe slipped it between his legs. Law recovered quickly enough to get in a second challenge only to be 'nutmegged' again. This time he responded by taking Kiernan's legs away. As Joe regained his feet, Law patted him on the head saying, "I don't mind being beaten ...... but don't take the bloody piss!"

Northampton had eleven heroes

Man Utd 6 Northampton 2: by RONALD KENNEDY

THE score-line is Soccer's understatement of the year. United got six but it could have been a dozen had there not been as many rescue acts by the woodwork.

This top-and-bottom clash was a show case of all that is best in the game—and topped by a Bobby Charlton hat-trick.

And alongside it there, was the youthful genius of George best and the gallant spirit of Northampton who refused to lie down under the fiercest barrage I have seen for ages.

United made it clear from the start what kind of mood they were in and after David Herd rattled a post Denis Law flicked a Charlton drive right out of the waiting fingers of keeper Norman Coe.

This was in the seventh minute and less than two minutes later John Connelly volleyed in a Herd centre.

The Northampton defence standied—although against a United forward line possessing so much power and magnificent footwork, it was little more than a gesture of defiance.

But if Northampton's defenders suffered agony their attack was as lively as a basket of monkeys.

Reward came their way in the 23rd minute when Barry Lines, on the half-way touchline, saw the home defence crouched together like a Rugby scrum.

His accurate lofted pass dropped into Graham Moore's stride and Gregg dived without much hope as the shot whistled past him.

Charlton began his hat-trick in the 27th minute and got the second goal in the 31st.

Bobby's final goal in the 84th minute resulted from a nod of his head after 'keeper Coe pushed out a Herd drive.

Meanwhile other people had been at it—Law, strangely over-shadowed reared up for one of those famous headers as the second half was a few seconds old. In it went.

Don Martin a "far post" raid finished off brilliant work by Joe Broadfoot for Town's second in the 56th minute.

If United had an Achilles heel it was the old warrior Noel Cantwell. Broadfoot could beat him almost but the tiny winger was reduced almost to tears at the constant appalling wastage of chances made by his bye-line dashes.

Northampton were a team of heroes. They kept going forward and left-half Joe Kiernan matched any United man in craft—and perhaps bettered them in the heart he put into his job.

But if there was a man in the Town side to top the rest it was 'keeper Coe. I faulted him—only slightly—with one goal. For the rest of the game he kept out a bundle of shots that would have beaten many another 'keeper.

A Christmas fixture with Chelsea attracted a huge crowd. Footballing friend John Sewell remembers joining twenty or so other supporters to drag a heavy roller across the cricket field to provide an impromptu grandstand from which to watch the visitors secure a 3-2 victory.

Defeat at Stoke provided spectacular revenge for John Ritchie, Kettering's centre forward back in 1961, who netted four times in his side's 6-2 victory. Charismatic George Hudson, successor to Denis Emery at Peterborough and Terry Bly at Coventry, scored on his Cobblers debut against Don Revie's Leeds United.

Yet spirited performances, including a 0-0 draw with eventual champions Liverpool, were not enough to stave off the probability of relegation.

180

As the league table shows, with just three games remaining, defeat against Fulham in the fateful St George's Day fixture would leave Dave Bowen's side needing to rely on the results of others to avoid returning to the Second Division.

A record crowd of 24,523 filled the County Ground to witness a truly remarkable game.

Although I was away in Kent on a school residential visit, spending the afternoon at Dover Castle, my thoughts were back in Northampton. Making spasmodic, surreptitious excursions to the coach I was able to keep up with the score on the radio. With goals from Hudson and Kiernan giving the Cobblers a 2-1 half time lead I joined the rest of the party inside the castle, confident that the game was safe. Then came the incident that brought back memories of the historic FA Cup match at Derby.

THE FOOTBALL LEAGUE — DIVISION I		P	W	D	L	F	A	Pts.
Liverpool	... ...	39	25	8	6	76	30	58
Burnley	... ...	38	21	7	10	74	46	49
Leeds	... ...	37	20	8	9	71	35	48
Chelsea	... ...	36	20	6	10	58	45	46
Leicester	... ...	37	18	7	12	72	57	43
Manchester United	...	35	15	12	8	66	49	42
West Bromwich	...	37	15	11	11	76	62	41
Tottenham	... ...	37	14	12	11	72	61	40
Everton	... ...	39	15	10	14	56	57	40
Sheffield United	...	38	14	11	13	51	55	39
Stoke ...	...	38	13	11	14	60	61	37
West Ham	...	38	13	9	16	64	78	35
Arsenal	... ...	37	11	12	14	60	65	34
Newcastle	...	38	13	8	17	47	57	34
Nottingham Forest	...	37	13	7	17	52	64	33
Blackpool	...	39	12	9	19	48	62	33
Sunderland	...	38	13	7	19	47	69	33
Aston Villa	...	38	13	6	19	63	72	32
Sheffield Wednesday		36	12 -	7	17	50	58	31
Northampton		39	9	13	17	51	84	31
Fulham	... ...	38	12	5	21	59	80	29
Blackb. n	... ...	36	7	4	25	51	77	18

In 1950 the opposition were gifted a crucial goal when the referee refused to consult his linesman. Sixteen years later, as George Hudson's lob appeared to cross the line before being belatedly retrieved by Fulham keeper, McClelland, referee Jack Taylor did seek guidance from the official on the cricket field side. Unfortunately for Northampton, the linesman had lost his footing as the centre forward broke free. Lying prone on the touchline yards from play, he was in no position to advise the referee, who had no option but to wave play on. The moment was lost and so, eventually was the match.

181

Returning to the bus I heard the final result with disbelief. Two goals in the dying minutes gave Fulham a 4-2 victory. From our vantage point on the Castle coach park, above a grey, bleak English Channel, I imagined the chilled atmosphere in the Cobblers' dressing room.

COBBLERS LACK KILLER SHOOTING

**NORTHAMPTON T. 2,
FULHAM 4**

Disastrous final minutes

TWO disastrous final minutes plunged the Cobblers and their supporters into the deepest gloom as Fulham right-w i n g e r Steve Earle snatched goals which might well keep his team safe, and drop North- ampton back into Divi- sion Two, writes Fred Speakman.

Both Cobblers' players and supporters will long debate how victory slipped from their grasp. Twice before the interval they led through Hudson and Kiernan. They were 2—1 up with 25 minutes to go.

Then Earle scored the first goal of a hat-trick, which sent hundreds of Fulham fans jumping joyously across the pitch at the end chanting "Easy, Easy."

But it was not easy. And Northampton will reflect that it should not have happened. Before Fulham equalised a second time the Cobblers had found enough chances in the first hour to make the game safe.

One controversial incident, which almost certainly decided this game, and probably the relegation issue, came just before Earle's first goal.

Hudson was through on his own. He lobbed skilfully, as he did at Tottenham the previous week. But goalkeeper McClelland just touched it as he leaped up. That lifted the ball which still fell into the goal. But McClelland found time to drop back and pull it away.

Northampton thought it was a goal. Referee J. Taylor waived on play. A linesman, who might have given some guidance, had slipped over. Northampton, 3—1 then, would

almost certainly have taken command and held the lead.

The Northampton players were just as convinced that Mackin's long free kick which beat McClelland should have counted. They said afterwards that the goalkeeper was not fouled or impeded, but was beaten by the swerving ball.

This "goal" also would have made 3—1. The Cobblers were convinced that a third goal would have clinched their victory. Other bad luck at this time was when two efforts were cleared luckily off the line. Earlier Moore hit the bar with a fine effort.

Goals count, though. Fulham won because they had the man in Earle, who could score readily and consistently. This 20-year-old local winger has now scored 10 goals since getting his first on February 19.

His first followed a Cohen run that found a defensive gap. This incident shook the Cobblers. They were thrown out of their stride for a time. Fulham, marshalled by Johnny Haynes, then provided some really dangerous moves.

Cobblers' results in the remaining two games had no bearing on the final outcome - Northampton were relegated with Blackburn.

Almost thirty years later Joe Kiernan still has difficulty comprehending the events that so cruelly ended his brief flirtation with First Division football. If ever a player deserved a second chance, it was he.

Discussing tactics. Walden, Kiernan, Payne, Livesey, Martin, Foley, Branston

Across the county, Peterborough too faced First Division opposition during 1965-66, in the Football League Cup. This competition, inaugurated as recently as 1960, may have lacked the glamour of its more venerable counterpart but Posh's performance in reaching the semi-finals is certainly worthy of note. The side scored four goals in each of the first four rounds, at Newcastle and Millwall, and at home to Charlton and Burnley, when the Turf Moor club was top of Division 1. Victory at Newcastle was the club's first ever in the League Cup.

GREAT WIN AT ST JAMES' PARK

WHAT suddenly makes a team, who had only a few days earlier failed to win a relatively easy home game, suddenly humiliate a respectable First Division club before their own spectators?

For this is just what Peterborough United did at St James' Park on Wednesday evening when they knocked Newcastle United out of the Football League Cup in their second round meeting.

After an incident packed game, with seven goals and a continuous stream of shots, Peterborough emerged as deserving victors.

They had the most industrious players, the hardest players and the more spirited players.

NEWCASTLE 3 UNITED 4

NEWCASTLE: Marshall; Burton, Clark; Anderson, Moncur, Iley; Hockey, Bennett, McGarry, Hilley, Knox.

UNITED: Duff; Hollow, Crawford; Crowe, Rankmore, Wright; Watson, Conmy, Beesley, Byrne, Barnes.
SCORERS: Bennett, Iley, Hilley (Newcastle); Conmy (2), Beesley, Watson (United).

REFEREE: Mr. P. Rhodes (York).
ATTENDANCE: 16,110.
WEDNESDAY, SEPTEMBER 22.

UNITED 4

BURNLEY 0

A 6-3 aggregate defeat by eventual winners West Bromwich Albion denied Peterborough a place in the final.

League Cup success compensated for a moderate Third Division campaign, 13th place, and a disappointing second round FA Cup exit at Shrewsbury. The attendance for the last game of the season, 3935, was the lowest for a league game to date.

"The greatest performance ever put up by a Peterborough United side". That was the general comment after Posh's brilliant League Cup victory on Wednesday night.

"What can I say after such a performance?" said chairman Vic Grange, whose expression spoke the words he could not find.

This was indeed a football match which puts all Peterborough's giant killing feats in the background.

Manager Gordon Clark warned before the game "This will be a much harder match than the one we had against the Arsenal last term", and there were few who, irrespective of this warning, gave the Posh the slightest chance of winning this match against the team sitting on top of the first division.

Peterborough fans, already proud of a post-war history packed with great footballing feats, can be even more proud today.

This defeat of Burnley, the biggest they have encountered this season, is indeed a tribute to those 11 players and the manager, and gives lie to the statement that no third division clubs can match their more illustrious colleagues in the higher spheres of league football.

The Internationals

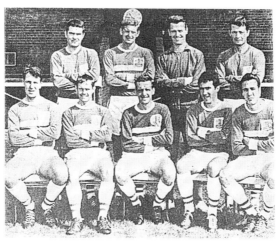

Peterborough United have eight players who have represented their country.
Back Row: Tony Millington (Wales), Derek Kevan (England), Peter McParland (Northern Island) who is training with the Posh, Willie Duff (Scotland)
Front Row: Frank Rankmore (Wales), Ollie Conmy (Eire), Vic Crowe (Wales), Ian Crawford (Scotland), John Kirkham (England)

Late season signings Derek Kevan and Tony Millington boosted the number of internationals on the club's books to eight.

Ollie Conmy, Peterborough's first player to be capped while in Posh colours. (Eire v Belgium)

Frank Rankmore, a Cardiff City colleague of Steve Gammon, is pictured here with Kettering referee Roy Reddaway before a friendly game.

Corby Town began the season with several new faces, including Tony Needham, Alan McBain, Johnny Haasz and Charlie McGlinchey. Leading goalscorer Tommy Crawley however, (109 goals in 3 seasons), had moved to Southern League Premier rivals Worcester City.

The new campaign proved to be Barrie Parson's last after injury in the first match cost him a regular place in the side.

Although the new look Steelmen were successful in retaining their elevated status, the season will long be remembered for their FA Cup performances. Kings Lynn were beaten 2-1 in the final qualifying round and, in the first round proper, Burton Albion suffered a 6-3 defeat with Maurice Goodall and Alex Garden scoring twice.

THIS WAS A CREDIT TO NON-LEAGUE FOOTBALL

CORBY TOWN 6.
BURTON ALBION 3

NINE goals, a hatful of thrills and incidents galore made this FA Cup-tie one of excitement and tension right to the very last kick, writes Steelman.

Nearly 4,000 people saw a game that sizzled, simmered and eventually reached boiling point. They also saw some wonderful entertainment from two sides who were a credit to non-League football.

EFFICIENT

But Albion were not as outplayed as the score might suggest. For almost 70 minutes they gave an efficient Corby side some trying moments and twice fought their way back into the tie after being two goals in arrears.

In the end, though, it was the confident-looking Corby outfit who triumphed. And, whatever happens between now and their Cup exit, they will surely not score a more amazing goal than Goodall's second—the one that eventually put paid to Burton's hopes of a replay.

And, to cap an excellent afternoon, the result was enough to take the Steelmen into the draw for the second round of the FA Cup for the first time in their history.

After two poor performances Corby supporters saw their side back at their best. And a lot of credit for this success must go to an attack over which hung a huge question mark before the kick-off.

However, the front line clicked—and unfortunate Burton had their hands full from the opening minutes.

Burton Albion goalkeeper Les Green makes a desperate effort to reach this shot from Maurice Goodall but he failed and the Steelmen were one up in F.A. Cup tie and on their way to 2nd Round for first time in their history. *(Photo by courtesy of Evening Telegraph).*

Victory brought a home tie with Luton Town, finalists only six years earlier. Sadly, secretary Wilf Wiseman, a founder member back in 1948, died shortly before the club's finest hour.

185

The Football League side trailed Corby 2-1 until a late penalty, awarded for a dubious handball by winger Haasz, was converted to force a replay. The referee's decision cost Haasz a place in the rematch at Kenilworth Road on Tuesday December 7th. He was replaced by McGlinchley and the experienced Dick Whittaker came in at full back for Alan McBain.

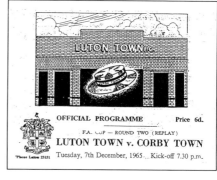

OFFICIAL PROGRAMME   Price 6d.

F.A. CUP — ROUND TWO (REPLAY)

LUTON TOWN v. CORBY TOWN

'Phone Luton 23151   Tuesday, 7th December, 1965. Kick-off 7.30 p.m.

Luton's playing staff at the time included numerous familiar names including the ubiquitous Barry Fry, David Pleat and John O'Rourke from that schoolboy international trial some years before. Also prominent were future Scottish international and current Arsenal manager Bruce Rioch and young reserve striker Howard Kettleborough.

■ *Heroes all — the 1965-66 Corby Town squad that reached the third round of the FA Cup with a memorable replay victory over Luton Town. Back from left: manager Tommy Hadden, assistant trainer Donald Johnson, Alan McBain, Dick Whittaker, Alan Alexander, George Armour, Tony Needham, Johnny Haasz, trainer David Yates. Front: Charlie McGlinchey, Maurice Goodall, Alex Stenhouse, Alex Garden, George Jagger.*

186

HERO GOODALL

THE furnaces in the steel town of Corby will be burning brighter than ever this morning as a red-hot reminder of the night Luton crashed out of the F.A. Cup.

Luton—Wembley finalists just six years ago—were melted down to small-fry size last night in a blaze of emotion and excitement.

Hundreds of fans made a mass invasion of the pitch as the final whistle signalled Corby's entry into the giant-killing ranks.

And it was 21-year-old centre forward Maurice Goodall who gave them the key of the door to a Third Round tie at Plymouth.

That goal may also give Goodall an opening into League football. Several managers were at the match to weigh up this red-haired leader.

The match-clinching goal Corby always threatened to collect during quick, thrusting counter-attacks, came in the 34th minute. It was a cracker.

Alex Stenhouse, captain of Corby and a house-painter by trade, brushed past two Luton defenders and set off on a 40-yard gallop along the right wing.

His low, swirling cross flashed to the feet of Goodall, who coolly stabbed the ball into the back of the net from six yards.

The goal rekindled the fire of a game that had been deteriorating into an undignified scramble after an action-jammed start.

Luton Town 0 Corby Town 1
F.A. Cup Second Round Replay

CLUB chairman, Mr. Fred Deeley, said: "We have now grown up. When you're into the second or third round you're playing against men. The people of the town must accept us now.

"Naturally I'm thrilled for everybody. In 29 years' voluntary service in the town and with the club this has been the crowning moment. After last Saturday I though we must be in with a great chance."

Mr. Deeley gave credit to the Luton officials for the way they accepted defeat.

"Luton were wonderful in defeat and I sincerely hope that they get promotion to Division Three as a consolation."

GOALSCORER Maurice Goodall said: "It made up for those I missed on Saturday and it felt just great. We can't hope to do more to attract the public."

Speaking of the atmosphere in the dressing room after the game, Tommy Hadden said: "Maurice was holding up the boot that brought the goal and he was shaking like a leaf, he was so thrilled."

A crowd of over 13,000 watched Maurice Goodall give the Steelmen the lead after 33 minutes. Remarkably the non-league side held on for a famous victory, although O'Rourke went close in the dying minutes.

Ironically, on the evening when a town full of emigrant Scotsmen enjoyed rare national success, Scotland were eliminated from the World Cup by Italy, thus missing a place in the 1966 finals.

The historic cup run ended at Plymouth in Round 3, the 6-0 defeat disappointing the hundreds of fans who travelled by car, coach and train to watch the match.

187

Dave Pacey

Two former U23 internationals joined Kettering in the summer of 1965. One was Dave Pacey, who had scored Luton's Cup Final goal in 1959. The other was Steve Gammon. Gammon was still serving an engineering apprenticeship at ICI when called into the Cardiff first team for his league debut in 1960.

Steve Gammon

"A reporter rang me at work on the Friday afternoon to ask how I felt, and I didn't even know I was playing," he recalls. The side won promotion to the First Division and part-timer Steve quickly earned a reputation for 'tight marking' opposing star inside forwards.

Representative honours followed when he was chosen, alongside friend and colleague Graham Moore, for the Welsh U23 side against Scotland at Wrexham. The opposing Scottish side included inside forward Denis Law.

Wales U23 v Scotland.. Steve Gammon is extreme left on the back row, Graham Moore, centre, in the front next to a youthful Mike England. The goal keeper is Dave Hollins, Newcastle keeper in the FA Cup defeat by Peterborough in 1962.

Shortly afterwards, the two players were in opposition at Ninian Park with tragic consequences for Gammon, who broke a leg in a clash with the Manchester City star.

GAMMON WILL BE OUT FOR SIX WEEKS

Cardiff City 3 Man. City 3

Wing-half star Gammon, picked to play for Wales Under-23's against England on Wednesday, was carried off eight minutes from the end after a tackle with £53.000 inside-right Denis Law.

The most optimistic forecasts give Gammon at least six weeks before he starts training again.

Disappointment was compounded when, after regaining a first team place, he suffered a similar injury and missed possible selection for the full National squad's summer tour to Brazil. Recovery was again short-lived. A freak accident in a six-a-side training game put him in plaster for a third time. New manager Jimmy Scoular decided against extending his contract and gave him a free transfer at the end of the season.

Today Gammon is philosophical about the decision.
"A couple of years earlier they wouldn't have let me go at any price. Now I was a bad risk and worth nothing. I lived in a club house, had a wife and baby, and for my family's sake I had to make a fresh start. It was a salutary experience which has since helped shape my whole attitude to life and work. With hindsight, I'm grateful."

Just weeks later, Mel Charles, who lived a few doors away, invited Steve to join him on a visit to Kettering to meet Chairman Nash, who was interested in signing the Welsh star. Gammon impressed Nash, and when Charles declined an offer to join the Poppies, the chairman was shrewd enough to give the young wing half the two year contract he demanded.

George Swindin

Gammon had only been installed in his Kettering home for a few days when 'Boss' Dick White was replaced by former Peterborough manager George Swindin - ironically, late of Cardiff City.

There was no FA Cup glory, only ignominious defeat at Wisbech. By November, relations between chairman, manager and players had soured alarmingly. The home match with Bath City on November 25th 1965 proved decisive. Manager Swindin's disarmingly honest programme notes were his last, as a humiliating reversal brought resignation.

As a part-time manager with successful business interests outside the game, Swindin had no desire to become embroiled in such distasteful happenings.

At the end of the match the famous goalkeeper walked into the dressing room, shook Gammon's hand, and said quietly, "I'm finished."

His record at Kettering was certainly impressive.

P	W	D	L
20	11	4	5

In programme notes from the next home match against Canterbury, Chairman Nash defended the board's decision not to appoint an immediate replacement.

George Swindin retains strong views on the proper role of club chairman and directors. He has not forgotten his own experience

at Peterborough in the fifties, when criticism from within the club sought to undermine his authority at a time when the team was enjoying unprecedented success. Such influence, often exerted by people with little knowledge of the game but possessing power and financial wherewithal, can make the manager's position untenable.

It was several months before matters were resolved.

On a long coach journey to Dover in early December, Nash discussed the club's future with Gammon, then team captain, who agreed to take unofficial responsibility for training and selection.

As the season progressed and club confidence grew, he was offered the post of player-manager

The appointment of Steve Gammon as team manager was not all that surprising. Gammon has done well in his role as coach since George Swindin left in November, and his two-year contract as team manager will give him a chance to look at a long-term, as well as short term policy.

The directors had no hesitation in appointing Gammon. Although the post of manager was never advertised, they received 23 applications from would-be managers, ten from Southern League clubs and the rest from players in the Third and Fourth Divisions.

and set about building the team which would restore Kettering's fortunes over the next few seasons.

190

For a Midland Floodlit Cup fixture against Worcester at the end of the season the Poppies side included local players Livsey and Evans, and a new left wing pairing of Corby youngsters Mick Goodall (brother of the Steelmen's Maurice), and Dennis Martin. The opposition team included star wingers Deeley and McParland, Tommy Crawley and significantly, Gammon's former Cardiff City colleague Trevor Peck.

Mick Goodall

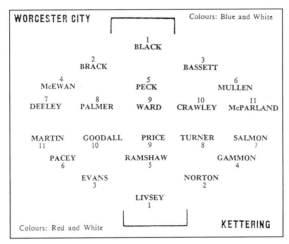

WORCESTER CITY   Colours: Blue and White

1
BLACK

2   3
BRACK   BASSETT

4   5   6
McEWAN   PECK   MULLEN

7   8   9   10   11
DEELEY   PALMER   WARD   CRAWLEY   McPARLAND

MARTIN   GOODALL   PRICE   TURNER   SALMON
11   10   9   8   7

PACEY   RAMSHAW   GAMMON
6   5   4

EVANS   NORTON
3   2

LIVSEY
1

Colours: Red and White   KETTERING

Dennis Martin

On the same November afternoon that Corby Town were disposing of Burton Albion, Wellingborough Town provided a marvellous advertisement for United Counties League football at Aldershot. Victory over Harwich and Parkeston had ensured that the Doughboys became the first post-war UCL team to reach the 1st Round proper of the FA Cup.

The 2-1 defeat at the Recreation Ground was a memorable achievement by a fine Doughboys side, for whom goalscorer Barry Daldy was outstanding. In common with many recurring peculiar quirks of fate, Aldershot's crucial second goal was scored by former Wellingborough and Corby player Peter Kearns, while Daldy had been a young professional at Aldershot.

191

Peter Kearns

Barry Daldy

A15014

ALDERSHOT (Red & Blue)   2 (LEFT

(RIGHT)

DAVIES   JONES

WALKER DEVEREUX   3 RENWICK

4 NORMAN   5 GUNTER   6 WALKER KNIGHTS

7 BURTON   8 PRISCOTT   9 HOWARTH   10 KEARNS   11 HOWFIELD

REFEREE: BALL DONOR:
N. A. S. MATTHEWS   A. V. BARRACLOUGH
(Oxford)   (Farnham)

LINESMEN :   Substitutes :
R. MITCHENER (Red Flag)   Aldershot — Davies
S. G. CHRISTIE (Yellow Flag)   Wellingborough Town—
                                 Desborough

11 FRANKLIN   10 HARPER   9 MILLER   8 CASEY   7 DALDY (B.)

6 KIGHTLEY   5 WOODING   4 DALDY (J.)

3 HAYWARD   2 PATENALL

FOSTER

LEFT)   1 (RIGHT

WELLINGBOROUGH (Royal Blue & Amber)

THE MEN FROM UCL SO NEARLY MADE THE HEADLINES

Doughboys' goalkeeper Brian Foster leaps to take this header from Aldershot's inside-right, Priscott. Also in the air is Burton, Aldershot's outside-right.

ALDERSHOT 2, WELLINGBOROUGH TOWN 1

ALDERSHOT saluted the Doughboys on Saturday. At the end of this grand Cup-tie the crowd rose to the eleven heroes of Wellingborough Town, the "nobodies" of the first round, who had come, fought, and so nearly hit the headlines, writes "Doughboy".

In a climax which defies superlatives the Doughboys strove for the equaliser which never came. There was Alec Harper discarding shin-pads and pumping life into the attack as the Doughboys hit back at the Fourth Division professionals.

There was Barry Daldy playing against his old club, and producing a five star performance and a goal for good measure. And there was Dave Wooding, who easily held Jack

Howarth, moving up with the forwards. John Daldy, shirt out over shorts, thankful he had regained fitness in time for the big game.

Although the b'd failed Wellingborough Town FC were £450 richer, and had learned a lot when Keith Hayward led his men off amid back-slapping and "Well done, bad luck Wellingborough." sentiments from home supporters.

FLAGGING

While there was no difference in the sides' fitness—and at the end the home side was flagging — Aldershot were much faster on the ball than the Doughboys.

● **B**ARRY **D**Y, Doughboys' .t winger: "They deserved to win, but we played a lot better in the second half. All we can do is learn from the game. We were much fitter."

❊   ❊   ❊   ❊

● **P**ETER KEARNS, Aldershot inside-left who started with the Doughboys: "Wellingborough played above themselves. They did very well."

● **K**EITH HAYWARD, Doughboys' skipper: "We didn't get hold of the game in the first half as we should have done. We went out determined in the second to get into the game, and did."

● **D**AVE SMITH, Aldershot manager: "Wellingborough were a bit lucky to be let off the hook. We missed some chances. Wellingborough impressed me with their fitness, and considering the league they're in they played very well indeed."

192

A Boston United side composed entirely of highly experienced former Football League players became UCL champions in their only season in the league.

Desborough Town were one of only three sides to beat them, gaining a goal advantage over the champions elect's nine men before the missing players, both no doubt used to more illustrious venues, located the Waterworks field.

In what would prove the last season when sides habitually fielded two wingers the top nine sides all scored over one hundred goals!

1965-66 Division 1	P.	W.	D.	L.	F.	A.	Pts
Boston United	36	28	5	3	132	38	61
Bourne Town	36	25	7	4	104	49	57
Rushden Town	36	24	4	8	154	64	52
Wellingborough Town	36	23	4	9	117	54	50
Bletchley Town	36	22	6	8	108	57	50
Holbeach United	36	19	5	12	104	60	43
Peterborough Athletic	36	19	4	13	108	76	42
Desborough Town	36	19	4	13	114	91	42
Rothwell Town	36	16	7	13	102	80	39
Biggleswade Town	36	17	3	16	85	70	37
Wolverton Town	36	13	11	12	79	82	37
Potton United	36	13	8	15	71	87	34
Northampton Town 'A'	36	10	9	17	73	94	29
Wisbech Res.	36	11	3	22	65	126	25
Eynesbury Rovers	36	8	6	22	52	129	22
B. Timken Athletic	36	7	4	25	61	137	18
Kettering Res.	36	7	4	25	50	135	18
S & L Corby	36	6	4	26	54	137	16
Corby Res.	36	3	6	27	41	103	12

Rothwell, including Tony Brewer, Dick White and Andy Easton looked a good bet for the title when annihilating rivals 'Ar Tarn' 8-3 in late August. Their early form flattered, however, and they finished in a disappointing mid-table position.

Rothwell Town 1965-66
One of the strongest UCL sides of the sixties yet failed to fulfil expectations.

Back Row: Kettley, White, Henson, Brewer, Easton, Peacock, Stacey.
Front Row: Jefferies, Linnett, Dawson, Kelcher, Roe.

The FA Cup final on May 14th was contested by Everton, Northampton's conquerors in the first match of the season, and Sheffield Wednesday. The referee, Jack Taylor, had officiated in the Cobblers fateful game with Fulham and one of the linesmen was Kettering's Walter Morris. The formal invitation to officiate appears curiously dated, especially in its reference to commercial interests.

Extracts from Kettering's Walter Morris' formal invitation to officiate as linesman at the Cup Final in 1966

THE FOOTBALL ASSOCIATION

Patron: HER MAJESTY THE QUEEN
President: THE EARL OF HAREWOOD
Chairman: J. H. W. MEARS

Secretary:
DENIS FOLLOWS, M.B.E., B.A.

Telegraphic Address:
FOOTBALL ASSOCIATION, LONDON, W.2

Ref: HNB/MH

22 LANCASTER GATE, LONDON, W.2

29th April, 1966.

Dear Mr. Morris,

F.A. Challenge Cup 1966
Final Tie

I have pleasure in informing you that you have been selected to act as Linesman in the above match to be played at the Empire Stadium, Wembley on Saturday, 14th May, 1966, kick-off at 3 p.m. Extra time will be played if necessary.

Last year a firm of Sports Goods manufacturers informed us that they would like to present the match officials with a complete Referee's outfit for use in the Final Tie. If you should be approached in this manner The Football Assoc-iation would have no objection to your accepting such a gift provided it com-plied with the standard type and colour of outfit. If your name is used in any way for advertising purposes you should arrange that it would only appear in desirable magazines and not in cartoon types. If you are approached by more than one outfitter, however, will you please refer the matter to me?

Yours sincerely,

Follows

Secretary.

Walter Morris, second right joins white suited Arthur Caiger 'look a like' and Jack Taylor, (hand clasping ball in typical pose).

And, of course, on Saturday 30 July England won the World Cup.

194

TRANSITION, RELEGATION AND SCAPEGOATS
1966-67

1966-67 was a lean season for most of the County's senior sides.

Peterborough reached the fourth round of the FA cup with victories over Hereford, Colchester and a Bedford team containing Denis Emery.

A 7-1 defeat at Roker Park to Sunderland's all star side, including Montgomery, Todd, O'Hare and Baxter, before 43,998, left the club free to concentrate on the struggle to avoid relegation.
Eventual fifteenth place ensured Third Division survival.

If Posh supporters were disappointed, their counterparts at Northampton must have been devastated. Few had been surprised that a First Division existence was so short-lived, but to drop straight down into the Third was little short of calamitous. Injuries, and an unhealthy amount of movement in and out of the club, militated against a settled side.
Clive Walker, Bobby Jones, Denis Brown and Bill Brown came - Bobby Brown, George Hudson, Mick Everitt, Bobby Hunt and Bill Brown left. Frank Large returned from his wanderings, and youngsters Graham Felton and John Clarke were promoted from the reserves.

There was no FA Cup glory to offset the disappointing league form - defeat by West Brom ending a brief run. The same side also put paid to League Cup hopes after the Cobblers had beaten Peterborough, Rotherham and Brighton, Don Martin netting four times in a remarkable 8-0 victory over the Sussex team.

The absence of Kiernan with cartilage problems compounded the club's misfortunes and a disastrous run-in resulted in relegation and the virtual break up of the side of 65-66. Foley, Branston, Cockcroft, Walden, Moore and Harvey all left. An era had ended.
After the heady FA Cup successes of 1965-66, Corby were eliminated in the first round by Cambridge City, whose United counterparts also accounted for the Steelmen at a similar stage of the Southern League Cup. There was little to cheer in the league either as the side struggled to find consistency. The signing of Barry Kelcher from Rothwell, however, gave

supporters a new favourite in the Tommy Crawley mould. (Kelcher had scored 4 goals in 'The Bones' celebrated victory over Desborough the previous season). Relegation was avoided, but, as at Northampton and Peterborough, transition was proving painful and the omens for the following season were not promising.

Kettering, in player-manager Steve Gammon's first season in charge, seemed certain to climb into the Southern League's Premier section. At the beginning of March 1967 the club was in second place and, with four to be promoted and a relatively easy run-in in prospect, elevation seemed assured.

Among Kettering's close season signings was a diminutive inside forward from Barry who became one of the Poppies most prolific goalscorers.

Ken Gully netted 34 times in league matches during 1966-67 including all 4 against his former Welsh team mates.

Young goalkeeper Gordon Livsey had moved on trial to Wrexham in January 1967, but a broken leg sustained after only ten minutes of the first game against Stalybridge Celtic appeared to have put paid to his hopes of making the grade at a higher level. The leg was broken in two places and the young keeper was in plaster from thigh to toe for eighteen weeks. A consultant at Kettering General Hospital, Dr Keech, worked wonders and Livsey made a complete recovery returning to Wrexham at the beginning of the next season.

Poppies should make certain of promotion

IN a tight March schedule, Kettering Town have four of their fixtures against teams languishing in the lower half of the First Division of the Southern League, and with three of these matches on their home ground they should finish the month in a very strong position.

Ken Gully

Gully hits his old club for four

**KETTERING TOWN 4,
BARRY TOWN 0.**

KEN Gully, who joined the Poppies from Barry at the beginning of the season, celebrated the visit of his old club to Rockingham Road by scoring all four Kettering goals.

POPPIES MUST LOOK FOR ANOTHER 'KEEPER

THERE was considerable concern in the Kettering camp this week when news came through from Wrexham that reserve goalkeeper, Gordon Livsey had broken his leg.

After an 8-2 Central League defeat against Tranmere Reserves on the last day of his extended trial period, Gordon was recalled to take a first team place the following Saturday. He went on to become one of the finest keepers in the lower divisions, extending his league career with Chester before returning to Kettering in 1973.

Livesey takes Schofield's place against Barnsley

WREXHAM manager Alvan Williams has dropped veteran goalkeeper Johnny Schofield for to-morrow's match against Barnsley at the Racecourse and brought in 20 years-old trialist, Gordon Live-sey (makes his debut) (writes Ron Chaloner).

Livesey, whose home is at Kettering, had the mis-fortune to break a leg last season in his first game for Wrexham Reserves when he was on trial.

He made a complete re-covery and was granted another trial period at the start of this season.

Livsey also achieved national fame when voted the week's top 'fab' footballer in a newspaper poll, gaining more votes than Georgie Best.

Despite his many league appearances, it is a Kettering reserve game from 1963-64 that features prominently in his memory. When the team arrived at Cheshunt for their Metropolitan League fixture against Spurs A, they hardly expected that the legendary Danny Blanchflower would line up against them at inside right. (The Spurs side also included Keith Weller, later to star for Leicester City and England, John Sainty and David Gillingwater, who would make a single appearance for the Poppies two years later against Banbury in the Southern League Cup).

Top Ten

ANOTHER Fourth Division player tops this week's Top Ten. Wrex-ham's cornet-playing Salvation Army goalkeeper Gordon Livesy has been the idol of teams of Round Robin vote-collectors from all over North Wales. Writes Ann Royden of Walnut Street, Rhos, near Wrexham: "When we go away from home all the girls we meet tell us how fab is Gordon. We are proud of that."

George Best, though out of the first Ten again this week, has extended his lead as the season's most attractive footballer in all ways . . . as his 31,172 votes clearly show.

This Week's Top Ten:
1 GORDON LIVESEY (Wrexham) 3,020
2 JOHN O'HARE (Derby County) 2,800
3 EDDIE GRAY (Leeds United) 2,549
4 GEORGE BEST (Manchester U.) 2,221
5 BRIAN USHER (Sheffield Wed.) 1,886
6 IAN MOIR (Wrexham) 1,749
7 BRIAN FAULKES (Northampton T.) 1,654
8 DAVE WAGSTAFFE (Wolves) 1,542
9 DANNY LIGHT (Crystal Palace) 1,434
10 JOHN KURILA (Northampton T.) 1,428

Tottenham "A" v.
Kettering Res.
Metropolitan League

Spurs "A" had Danny Blanch-flower at inside right in their Metropolitan League game with Kettering Reserves at Cheshunt (Herts) this afternoon. Danny was making his first appearance after being injured in a Reserve game some weeks ago. Kettering had Bobby Tebbutt, the old Northampton player, at outside left and Dennis Randall, the regular first team centre forward and former amateur international also at inside right.

Half-time:
Spurs 5
Kettering 0
BROWN scored for Kettering in 75 minutes, WALKER Spurs o.g. 80 mins, BLANCHFLOWER scored for Spurs in 88th minute.

Kettering's 1966-67 season ended in disappointment and, as Gammon indicates in programme notes for the final game against Bexley United, defeats at Dover and Ramsgate in late April proved crucial and promotion was missed at the death.

Desborough Town became champions of the UCL. Victory over Bletchley in early April virtually ensured that the title would return to the Waterworks field for the first time since 1949. The visiting side that Sunday afternoon included former Luton and England B wing half, Bob Morton. Comparisons in any sport are always odious. Yet I can clearly recall a game at Manor Fields, Bletchley, (in the days before Milton Keynes), when Morton, vainly seeking a well positioned team mate to whom he could pass, refused to surrender possession and, quite literally, sat on the ball. There are few matches today at any level, where players have time to stop the ball, let alone sit on it! Another notable name, which time has since rendered infamous, was also associated with the visiting club. (Note the President identified on the cover of the Bletchley programme from November of the same year).

1966-67 Division 1	P.	W.	D.	L.	F.	A.	Pts
Desborough Town	30	22	5	3	82	31	49
St. Neots Town	30	20	4	6	90	36	44
Bletchley Town	30	20	3	7	75	45	43
Wellingborough Town	30	18	6	6	67	33	42
Holbeach United	30	17	4	9	78	47	38
Bourne Town	30	16	6	8	69	59	38
Rushden Town	30	14	7	9	72	35	35
Kettering Reserves	30	14	4	12	61	54	32
Rothwell Town	30	11	6	13	69	69	30
Potton United	30	11	5	14	52	58	27
Wolverton Town	30	11	4	15	54	72	26
Peterborough Athletic	30	9	5	16	50	77	23
Northampton Town 'A'	30	5	8	17	33	74	18
Biggleswade Town	30	7	3	20	54	87	17
Eynesbury Rovers	30	5	4	21	35	89	14
Wisbech Reserves	30	2	3	25	22	92	7

Desborough collect title in fine style

DESBOROUGH 5, BIGGLESWADE 1

DESBOROUGH won the UCL championship in fine style on Saturday although there was a sad note to the game when Biggleswade's goalkeeper Paul had to be carried off on a stretcher.

Paul collided with goal post trying to save Desborough's third goal and right-winger Archer took over the keeper's sweater.

After the visitors' enforced changes, the match became a rather one-sided affair and Biggleswade were fortunate only to concede five goals.

Desborough took an early lead when in the fourth minute a curling corner from Addis was headed home by Marlow.

Biggleswade hit back and Archer centred for Dixon to equalise. Dixon was playing an outstanding game and was robbed of a certain goal when Coe dived to save at his feet.

But, playing the more controlled football. Desborough restored their lead after half an hour when Underwood scored with a chipped shot over Paul's head.

Then came the turning point of the game. Paul received his injury as he tried to save Underwood's brilliantly headed goal.

Although unorthodox in his approach to goalkeeping Archer made several good saves before Addis beat him with a difficult high ball.

Finally, after heavy pressure, Marlow completed the scoring when a shot from Underwood rebounded from a post.

Desborough's player-manager 'Charlie' Marlow had again achieved a successful blend, the January signing of midfield 'strongman' John Daldy proving crucial in maintaining an unbeaten league run which extended from mid-November to the final Saturday in April.

Desborough Town UCL Champions 1966-67

Back Row: Buckby, Daldy, Coe, Dawkins, Stacey, Wright, Pratt, Hales.
Front Row: Addis, Underwood, Young, Moore, Sellers, Marlow.

Only John Dawkins and I survived from the team of 1961, although Les Pratt, goalkeeper in 1949 was still trainer, and Bobby Wyldes, reserve team coach.

Magical memories of the season abound, many of which involve manager Marlow. His fabled mispronunciation - "We always struddle at Biddleswade" - features in the following example of his idiosyncratic style of leadership.

Duncan McGregor had proved an able deputy for injured first choice Pete Wright, but suspected that he would lose his place on the regular centre half's return to fitness. At training on Thursday evening he boldly announced his intention to challenge Charlie's selection should his fears be realised. They were. The team sheet showed that Wright had been restored. 'High Noon' arrived when the manager entered the hushed dressing room to be confronted by the towering McGregor, or 'Tam O'Tam' as Charlie called him.

Without flinching, face deadpan, Marlow looked up at the angry Scot and said, "Look Tam O'Tam, I'm not making you the scrapegoat ..." Ripples of laughter began to circulate amongst the players - even Duncan began to chuckle - until the whole room was in uproar. An ugly situation diffused. Man-management of the highest order.

Team talks were now elevated to an higher plane than those favoured by Bobby Wyldes, (or even Johnny Carey).

None bettered Charlie's, prior to an FA Cup match with St Neots. We arrived some three quarters of an hour before kick off to discover the treatment bench swathed in the green baize of a table soccer pitch. Subbuteo, or Subbuttayo, as he called it, was the manager's other passion. The pitch was populated by tiny celluloid players wearing Desborough and St Neots colours, but Charlie was nowhere to be seen. We got changed and prepared for the game. Time passed. Still no Charlie. Finally, minutes before kick off, he appeared in full kit, and presided over the Subbuteo pitch. We awaited his words of wisdom, and at last he spoke. "Today," he said, "we've gotta goo .... like f...!"

Charlie Marlow in action in a charity match - aged 49!

We obviously didn't goo hard enough, as we lost narrowly to the team that went on to emulate Wellingborough in reaching the First Round proper, (losing 2-0 to Walsall before a crowd of 15,000 at Fellowes Park).

It was out on the park, however, that Marlow's true value was realised, especially in front of goal where his instincts were predatory.

On one occasion, a huge defensive clearance sent the ball high into the branches of a tree which overhung the pitch midway inside the opposition half. Everyone was momentarily stunned, watching bemused as the ball bounced to and fro in the giant, wooden pinball machine. Except Charlie. When it finally dropped to the ground he was ready, controlling the ball instantly before speeding goalwards to beat the keeper with a searing shot.

He was particularly deadly from free kicks on the edge of the penalty area. Should anyone else be foolish enough to consider taking the kick he would brush them away derisively. "Step aside boy, there'll be murder done!" or "Just set it up and your old dad'll trigger it."

He was swerving shots round defensive walls long before Gascoigne or Le Tissier were born. "They cairnt stop me benders," he used to shout, before rushing to retrieve the ball from the back of the net in front of Desborough's faithful 'scratching shed' supporters.

The club whose name appeared on the Division 2 trophy had begun life only 20 years before. The Irthlingborough side chose its own unique appendage, the Diamonds, in deference to the famous Moscow Dynamo team which toured Britain shortly after the 2nd World War.

200

Having played for several years in the Rushden and District and Kettering Amateur Leagues the Diamonds moved into the UCL in 1964.

Barry Ellis

Fixtures were played on the Manton Road Recreation Ground, on which the team was near invincible, centre forward Barry Ellis amassing a phenomenal 200 goals in the first 3 seasons of UCL football.

Fans celebrate the Diamonds success with home made banners at the Recreation Field in Manton Road. A far cry from the modern splendour of Nene Park.

Diamonds, champions of UCL Division 2 1966-67.

Back Row: Nunn, Souster, Toms, Bosworth, Lloyd, McClellan, Byford. Front Row: Souter, Brown, Jones, Ellis, Manning

201

On October 11th 1966 Wellingborough Town had joined the growing number of clubs with floodlights and celebrated the occasion by entertaining Northampton Town. The game also marked the beginning of the Doughboys centenary year.

Wellingborough Town 2, Northampton Town 7

HAT-TRICKS by George Hudson and Jim Hall enabled the Cobblers to coast to a comfortable victory in this friendly match at the Dog and Duck ground last night. The game marked the opening of Wellingborough's new floodlights, and the start of their centenary year celebrations.

Mr. Denis Follows, Football Association secretary, performed the official switching-on ceremony—and told an enthusiastic crowd: "The F.A. applaud the initiative and endeavour of all clubs and we offer our congratulations to you on getting your own floodlights.

"I hope these lights will provide the means for many games of excellent football." added Mr. Follows.

Eight towers

The lights, which comprise eight 60-foot towers, each bearing eight special lamps, cost the club £4,000 and, although they have only been running a daily competition since April, the supporters have already paid off a quarter of the cost.

Northants lads are SO good...

NORTHAMPTONSHIRE 3, HERTFORDSHIRE 1
(Northamptonshire win on aggregate 5—4)

THREE goals in 13 minutes shattered Hertfordshire and gave Northamptonshire victory in the FA County Youth Cup Final at Peterborough on Saturday.

With a 3—2 defeat in the first leg of the final still fresh in their minds, the Northamptonshire youngsters quickly buckled down to the task in hand.

They played and tackled hard, but an all-important goal eluded them in the early stages.

Constant attacking, however, brought its just reward. Northamptonshire were able to dominate the second half and emerged as worthy winners.

A side brimming with young talent won the FA County Youth Cup overcoming Hertfordshire in the final. Several of the team were to make their mark in league football, none more emphatically than Irchester born Phil Neal.

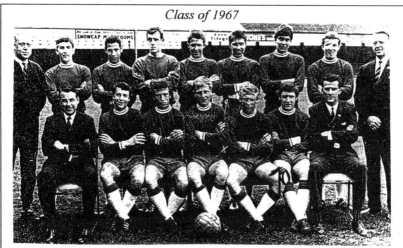

Class of 1967

Back Row: Bates, Dunkley, Jenkins, Frost, Neal, Martin, Townsend, Groom, Stratford
Front Row: Scott, Garwood, Beeby, Carnague, Adams, Foard, Vernum.

"BACK TO THOSE FRIENDLY GAMES NEXT WEEK"
1967-68

1967-68 brought relegation to Peterborough and Corby, and promotion to Kettering Town. Northampton arrested their alarming slide but local UCL sides had only moderate success.

POSH DOWN BUT NOT OUT

PETERBOROUGH are playing for RELEGATION this season. This verdict, which makes a mockery of the Third Division championship, was arrived at by the Football League Management Committee in London yesterday when, after a meeting lasting more than four hours, they decided that no matter where Posh finish in the table this season, down they go to the Fourth Division.

This is the club's punishment for two offences against League regulations. There will be no punishment for directors, players or officials.

In my opinion, the League have brought chaos to the Third Division.

If Peterborough finish in the top two, which they might do on form, they forfeit promotion and the third-placed club will go up. But the League have still to make their minds up about what happens at the bottom of the table. They have deferred any action until their next meeting on December 4.

Four or five

They could decide to relegate the bottom three clubs, with Peterborough making four and bring up four from the Fourth Division.

Or they could carry on as usual, relegating the bottom four. Then, with Peterborough joining them, there would have to be five up from the Fourth.

I asked Mr. Alan Hardaker, secretary of the Football League: "Don't you think Peterborough now have nothing to play for? Suppose they lose all their remaining matches, wouldn't this make a farce of the promotion and relegation issues?

He replied: "We considered this, and surely it won't apply. The Peterborough players have their pride. They also have an incentive bonus."

The players who stay with the club will get these bonuses: £11 when in first place; £9 in second; £6 in third place, and £4 in fourth.

Doomed

Never in the history of football has there been such a punishment for a club and I think the League are being naive if they believe the Peterborough players can maintain their performance when they are doomed before they kick the ball.

There is no appeal against the League decision.

Posh fans, bewildered at what is happening to their club, want to know what they did wrong?

The answer is that if signing-on fees to players had been written into their contracts and paid by the club and not by the Supporters Club, that would have been all right.

And offering a fee to win one specific FA Cuptie is against regulations.

Last night Jack Vernum, a director for 15 years and once a Peterborough player said: "I am heartbroken. Although there is an answer to all charges so far as I am concerned, I cannot help having a feeling of guilt.

Peterborough's demotion was extremely contentious, being punishment for allegedly making illegal payment to players. The decision came midway through a season which might otherwise have brought promotion.

Manager Gordon Clark was replaced by former skipper Norman Rigby shortly before the startling revelations of financial irregularities became public. Rigby had the task of raising club morale, but FA Cup defeat in the 3rd Round by Second Division Portsmouth prompted a much quoted response by a Posh player.

"That's it then, back to those friendly games next week."

There was some consolation for inside forward Ollie Conmy, who was selected for Eire's European Championship match against Czechoslovakia in Prague.

Posh forward Ollie Conmy has been selected to play on the right wing for Eire against Czechoslovakia in a European Nations Cup tie in Prague on Wednesday. ...

The first the former Huddersfield player knew about his selection was when he was told by a Posh supporter after Saturday's game at Torquay.

EIRE KO CZECH HOPES

Czechoslovakia 1, Eire 2

PRAGUE, Wednesday.

WEST BROMWICH'S Ray Treacy and Fulham's Turlough O'Connor — club reserves who were called up for international duty late Sunday night—today headed Eire to a smash-and-grab victory that shot Czechoslovakia out of the European Nations Cup.

The Czechs, who only needed a draw to move into the quarter-finals at the expense of Spain, were given a gift lead just on the hour when John Dempsey—another Fulham man — put through his own goal.

And that was the signal for the hard-pressed Irish to come out of defence.

The greatest

Midway through the half, Treacy headed the equaliser after a glorious movement, sparked by Peterborough's Oliver Conmy, and with five minutes to go—just after the Czechs had lost Szikora with torn leg ligaments—a mistake by the home captain Popluhar allowed Treacy to swing over the centre for O'Connor to nod a dramatic winner.

Several new names appeared in club colours during the season, notably Jim Hall, acquired from Northampton at Christmas, John Wile from Sunderland and local boys, Youth international winger Colin Garwood and full back Dick Kwiatkowski. Prolific scorer John Fairbrother, (37 goals in 69 league appearances), moved to the Cobblers for £7,000.

*Back Row: Thompson, Linnell, Millington, Wright, Noble, Maynard,
Front Row: Anon, Conmy, Rankmore, Metchick, Mason*

Peterborough's final league position, 9th, was an unhappy irrelevance.

Northampton made more early season headlines off the field than on, appointing Ron Flowers as player coach and Tottenham and Juventus star Tony Marchi as team manager. Dave Bowen moved into the background as general manager, while Frank Large joined First Division Leicester City and Don Martin, Blackburn Rovers.

John Roberts signed from Swansea and Johnny Byrne from Peterborough in exchange for Jim Hall.

The season's gloomy statistics - a first round FA Cup exit at Bournemouth, third round League Cup defeat, 5-1, at Millwall, and a final inglorious 18th league place hardly justify Tony Marchi's passing comment on his dismissal.

"They wanted the slide stopping, and I stopped the slide."

The Steelmen lost their Southern League Premier status despite the optimism of an early season magazine article.

THERE'S something different about Corby Town. The club have been in existence in their present form only since 1948, but have progressed in the football world even faster than the remarkable town they represent.

In 1933 Corby was just a village of a few hundred people with a couple of blast furnaces. In the following year the steelworks of Stewarts and Lloyds became established, and the steady development of the district has given Corby a big name on the industrial map.

With a rapidly-expanding population, many of whom were drawn from the big Soccer centres, it was soon evident to the Soccer-minded people of Corby that a senior club would thrive.

So Corby Town replaced the local works team, and speedily advanced through local senior football and the Midland League to the Southern.

Enthusiasm is the keynote at Corby. Each of the directors, under the able chairmanship of Mr. Fred Deeley, has a specific duty. And on match days Corby's directors take on extra duties. They even supervise the sale of programmes, the parking of cars and the operating of turnstiles.

"We're very democratic here," chairman Deeley told me. "Everyone works for the good of the club. The programme sellers, gatemen and tea ladies are all voluntary workers."

Mrs. Una Adams, Corby's charming and attractive secretary, also serves the club in an honorary capacity. A Scotswoman from Campbeltown in Argyllshire, Mrs. Adams is a secretary with the Corby Development Corporation.

"We have the best secretary in the League," said Mr. Deeley. "She's efficient and on the ball."

Corby have plenty of ambition. They aim for Football League status, and feel they have the resources to do well in the Fourth Division. The Corby population is around 46,000. It is expected to swell to 70,000.

That would give the live Corby board every chance to establish the club on a League footing.

Approximately sixty per cent of this steel town's population is Scottish. As you thread your way along Occupation-road to the ground on a match day, it's easy to imagine you are in Falkirk or Stirling. That's the strength of the Scottish accent in Corby!

Eric Caldow

Among the summer newcomers was Exeter City reject Dixie McNeil who, playing at half back, managed just six goals in 58 first team appearances.

EXETER'S TOP SCORER JOINS THE STEELMEN

Corby Town Manager, Tommy Hadden, has completed what he described as his toughest signing to date by capturing the signature of Exeter City's 21-year-old top goal scorer, Richard McNeil, writes Steelman.

McNeil, who began his career with Leicester City, joined Exeter after two years at Filbert Street and made 31 first team appearances last term. Converted to inside-forward by Exeter—before that he played left-half or outside-left—he was top scorer with 12 goals.

Manager Tommy Hadden left the club in late March with relegation almost certain and, in a desperate attempt to revive dwindling fortunes, former Rangers and Scotland full back Eric Caldow was appointed player-manager. It proved an unsuccessful gamble as 10 of the 13 games were lost and the side dropped into the league's First Division.

Kettering Town, ironically, were moving in the opposite direction, Steve Gammon's side compensating for the previous season's disappointment by clinching promotion with victory at Banbury.

The team was a pleasing blend of ex-league players, like Walden, Tony Needham and Gammon, and a crop of local youngsters - the Daldy brothers, Evans, Reed, Goodall, Phil Coe and a promising full back named Roger Ashby.

CHAMPAGNE FOR POPPIES

POPPIES PROMOTION

KETTERING 1, BANBURY 0

A HARRY Walden penalty goal earned Kettering both points against Banbury at Rockingham Road this afternoon and made certain they move into the Southern League Premier Division next season.

Kettering: Coe; J Daldy, Needham; Gammon, Reed, Evans; Johnson, Only, B Daldy, Goodall, Walden. Sub: Smith.

Banbury: McArthur; Cassidy, Darvell; Hynes, Page, Svenson; Ward, Sansom, Jacques, Holder, Buckley. Sub: Scott.

Referee: Mr. G. Keeble, of Burnham.

Kettering swept straight on to the attack and Johnson quickly tested McArthur with a curling shot in the edge of the area.

Gammon then put a free kick across the Banbury goalmouth and Gully just failed to get his head to the ball.

The visitors moved forward and Reed fouled Jacques, but Evans cleared Ward's free kick and the Poppies moved back on to the attack.

After nine minutes Kettering missed a penalty. Following a corner Cassidy handled Goodall's header and Gully hit the spot kick high over the crossbar.

It was a tragic mistake and Banbury answered with a period of pressure. But Reed was having the better of his duel with Jacques and Coe had little to do.

Kettering hit back and McArthur had to save a fierce shot from Goodall who had been put through by Johnson.

Needham broke powerfully down the left, beating off two tackles, but Hynes got up to cut out the full back's centre.

Banbury had a narrow escape when McArthur could only palm down Gully's shot. Walden raced in to challenge but McArthur regained possession.

The Banbury goalkeeper was soon in action again, tipping a 30 yard drive from Gully over the bar.

There was a moment of panic in the Kettering defence when Coe failed to gather Buckley's corner kick and after a goalmouth scramble Gully hacked the ball clear.

The visitors were getting more into the game as the interval approached and Jacques and Buckley both put in good efforts.

For Kettering, Johnson and Page headed off the line from Reed.

McArthur then made a fine save from Gully. Half-time: Kettering 0, Banbury 0.

Kettering started the second half at a tremendous pace and Gully moved swiftly into the Banbury area but Barry Daldy cut out a centre intended for Goodall.

Barry Daldy won possession from Hynes but there was no support and McArthur easily gathered the centre forward's cross.

Holder fouled Gully just outside the area and although Barry Daldy got the ball in the net from the free kick McArthur had been fouled.

Banbury launched a swift attack after clearing a Kettering corner and Jacques got dangerously near to Holder's centre.

Then in the 71st minute the Poppies scored from the penalty spot. Cassidy handled Gammon's header and WALDEN sent McArthur the wrong way with his penalty kick.

Result:
Kettering 1, Banbury 0
Attendance: 2,464.

Like neighbours Corby, the Poppies had suffered an early FA Cup exit, losing 3-0 at Cambridge United in the 3rd Qualifying Round.

It is interesting to note that in the previous round their replayed match at Wellingborough attracted a crowd of 4,013 spectators.

The Doughboys achieved 3rd place in the United Counties League and were the most successful of local teams.

In November a crowd of 1500 watched a game with Arsenal to celebrate the opening of the club's new grandstand, the celebrated visitors winning 5-2.

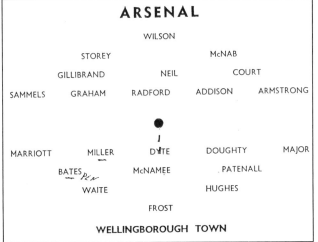

ARSENAL

WILSON

STOREY   McNAB

GILLIBRAND   NEIL   COURT

SAMMELS   GRAHAM   RADFORD   ADDISON   ARMSTRONG

●
I
MARRIOTT   MILLER   DYTE   DOUGHTY   MAJOR

BATES PEN   McNAMEE   PATENALL

WAITE   HUGHES

FROST

WELLINGBOROUGH TOWN

Irthlingborough Diamonds marked their first season in the top division by finishing a creditable fourth.

1967-68 Division 1	P.	W.	D.	L.	F.	A.	Pts
St Neots Town	32	23	5	4	96	25	51
Bletchley Town	32	23	2	7	80	30	48
Wellingborough Town	32	20	8	4	80	37	48
Irthlingborough Diamonds	32	21	3	8	83	56	45
Holbeach United	32	20	3	9	72	31	43
Rushden Town	32	19	4	9	65	34	42
Desborough Town	32	18	4	10	79	51	40
Bourne Town	32	14	8	10	62	43	36
Wolverton Town	32	16	3	13	85	58	35
Kettering Reserves	32	14	6	12	53	55	34
Biggleswade Town	32	10	9	13	57	68	29
Potton United	32	11	4	17	57	70	26
Rothwell Town	32	10	2	20	62	80	22
Northampton Town 'A'	32	4	7	21	42	93	15
Eynesbury Rovers	32	4	3	25	33	98	11
Peterborough Athletic	32	3	5	24	30	111	11
Dunstable Reserves	32	4	0	28	34	129	8

Desborough had lost John Daldy and Phil Coe from their championship side, both moving to Kettering Town and captain Ian Young joined former Wellingborough colleague Dennis Jones at Irthlingborough. The exodus continued at the end of the season as Dick Underwood signed for Bourne and I moved on to the Doughboys who, under chairman Bert Boultwood, had made the controversial decision to sever links with the UCL in search of a higher grade of football in the Metropolitan League.

UNITED COUNTIES LEAGUE Division I
WELLINGBOROUGH TOWN v IRTHLINGBOROUGH DIAMONDS
CLUB CHATTER

The fortunes of the top clubs in the league continue to sway, not the least of them is our own. Monday's game, to say the least, was unfruitful, and in my opinion best forgotten. It is indeed a pity that our motives in joining the Metropolitan League should be so misunderstood and cause so much bitterness as was evident throughout last Monday's game. For the record, the Doughboys are leaving the U.C.L. Division One, because, despite a relatively successful season, our gates are low. However difficult a pill this may be to swallow, our supporters, apart from a few teams, no longer consider the league competition sufficiently attractive to watch. The Metropolitan League application was never intended as a slur on the U.C.L.; unfortunately this seems to be the impression gained by some.

Today's game is one of the exceptions, and I would like to take this opportunity to congratulate the Diamonds on an excellent record in their first season in Division I. We all hope that today's game will rise to the heights expected of two of the top teams.

RIGHT BACK WHERE
WE STARTED FROM
1968-69

Northampton began a new season with a new manager.

Ron Flowers brought in West Bromwich Albion full back, Ray Fairfax, former Posh centre half Frank Rankmore, and striker Bob Hatton from Wolves.

It's like being in a new trade

RON FLOWERS puckered the fair brow that often headed England out of danger and answered with the decisiveness he showed on the field. "It is so different," he said. "The jobs are so apart you might almost be in another trade."

He was replying to the question: How does it feel to be a manager with a Third Division side after serving so long in soccer's high society with Wolves and England?

And after just two months in charge at Northampton, Flowers is beginning to learn. Even better, he is willing to learn despite his years at the top.

He thinks before he speaks. So when he says something, you know he means it.

Flowers thought a while and then went on: "When you are playing everything is more or less done for you. The boot is on the other foot when you are managing.

says RON
FLOWERS

"As a manager I must think of the others. The players are my responsibility and if I want the best out of them, I must have their respect. It is no good expecting them to run until they drop for you if you don't play the game with them."

At Christmas there was little hint of trouble ahead. The club was in a comfortable mid-table position and through to the third round of the FA Cup, having recorded its first victories in the competition since beating Kettering Town in 1961.

Defeat at Bolton ended cup hopes and league form deteriorated so rapidly that relegation became a distinct possibility. One point from the last five games ensured that matters rested upon the outcome of Gillingham's final game with Shrewsbury. The Kent side gained the point required to stay in the Third Division, condemning the Cobblers to the fourth relegation place.

In nine years Northampton had gone full circle. From Fourth to First and back.

At the beginning of the same season Peterborough were already contemplating life at the bottom, following enforced relegation. A strong feeling of injustice prevailed at London Road. New signings Pyatt and Price from Liverpool and Ritchie Norman, Leicester City's experienced and stylish full back joined the staff, most of whom had remained loyal to the demoted club, and hopes were high for a quick return to the Third Division. John Wile took advantage of Rankmore's departure to Northampton to became established at centre half.

The team's two internationals, goalkeeper Tony Millington and forward Ollie Conmy, expressed their reaction to 'life in the Fourth Division' in contemporary magazine articles.

A bearded Ollie Conmy lines up with his Peterborough team mates.

Ollie Conmy talks of Life in the Fourth at Peterborough

Ollie says life in the Fourth Division is undoubtedly tough.

'You've got to take some knocks. Teams come here and play eight or nine men back, and you can't get by them. Then someone pops in a goal and the net tightens for the rest of the game. Peterborough supporters can't seem to get used to this. There was a time when we were in the old Midland League and the players used to go out and win by six or seven goals to nil. They were league champions for two years running. Then they get into pro soccer and what happens, you start winning by one nil if you're lucky. Old-time supporters are still looking back five or ten years. It'll take a new generation of young supporters, the sort of lads I coach in schools, to come along and appreciate modern football as it has to be today. I bet if we were back in the Midland League we'd get more supporters than we do now.'

Ollie is a slight young man, just over five feet tall, and looks like a typical, underfed Irishman. He seemed nervous and carries the cares of Fourth Division football heavily. I asked him if demotion had demoralized the players.

'Of course we were upset, blamed the club more than anything I suppose. And in this division it's hard to get back. We're like Fulham. I remember talking to my mate John Dempsey just after they went down. "We'll be back," he said. But look at them now – all last season struggling in the bottom half of the Second Division. We're the same. We've just had a bad run and the boss has had us all back for afternoon training. Some of the lads have got coaching jobs and they have to go by the board. They're not easy to get in this town – not enough schools and they insist you're fully qualified.'

210

TONY MILLINGTON—A JOKER
WHO CAN'T STOP CLOWNING

THEY CALL him "The Joker!" Tony Millington, Peterborough and Welsh international goalkeeper, who cannot stop clowning whether it is in the dressing-room, at training, or at the Posh Club in the ballroom under the main stand where supporters go for a night out.

Then Tony talked about the reason behind his delay in signing for Peterborough this season. "I've never been as happy at any club as I am at Peterborough, but I've got to think about making a living for my family. If I don't move this year, they are getting close to school age, and I don't want to be moving around then.

"Providing the terms are right at Peterborough I'm happy to stay. How could I be any other way? When Peterborough were demoted, people stopped me in the street and even came round the house to ask me not to walk out on them.

"That sort of thing gets through to you and if the supporters will stick behind us in the Fourth, Peterborough can do great things."

If Peterborough is the best time he has had, what was the worst?

League Cup victories over Queens Park Rangers and West Bromwich Albion rekindled memories of the giantkilling past and a brave performance in a single goal defeat at White Hart Lane earned widespread praise.

Early FA Cup exit at Bristol Rovers and poor league performances eventually led to the resignation of 'Mr Posh', manager Norman Rigby, who resigned in January after an association which began back in 1951. He was succeeded by former Newcastle and Spurs defender Jim Iley, who became the club's first player-manager since George Swindin in 1954.

Peterborough United

(Back) Iley (Manager), Pyatt, Wile, Millington, Wright, Crawford, Walker (Trainer).
(Front) Downes, Price, Thompson, Hall, Conmy, Robson.

Performances continued to fluctuate, but the humiliation of seeking re-election was avoided and the side completed the season in eighteenth place - its lowest ever league position. Centre forward Jim Hall maintained his goalscoring form, netting 20 league goals, Price scored 11 and former Cobblers' winger Tommy Robson, signed from Newcastle for £20,000 shortly before Rigby's departure, hit 10.

Kettering Town enjoyed a successful return to the Southern League Premier Division, finishing ninth, but the season is memorable for a lengthy FA Cup run and particularly the manner in which it came to an end.

No fewer than five matches had already been won before the Poppies met Dartford, conquerors of Aldershot, in the Second Round.

KETTERING TOWN 5, DARTFORD 0

THE Poppies shrugged off the frustrating failure of a fruitless first half and roared into the third round of the FA Cup for the first time with this incredible five-goal romp over giant-killers Dartford on Saturday.

Admittedly glory-hunting Kettering were helped by an unfortunate own goal from Dartford's centre-half, Alan Lillis, with the second half only three minutes old — a goal that ended the stalemate.

It's also true that three goals came in the last five minutes when the visitors had caved in under the Poppies' pressure. But neither fact can detract from a superb Kettering win that put them among the big names of soccer in today's draw.

Kettering Town players Mick Goodall, Roger Ashby, Barry Daldy and Tony Needham relax after beating Dartford 5-0.

Reward for victory was a trip to Eastville, scene of Kettering's valiant display in 1951, to meet Third Division Bristol Rovers.

Centre half Mick Reed's goal earned Kettering a draw although Mick Goodall might have snatched victory in the dying minutes.

KETTERING TOWN FOOTBALL CLUB

Wednesday 8th Jan. F.A. CUP (3rd ROUND REPLAY)
BRISTOL ROVERS
OFFICIAL PROGRAMME 6D.

MICK Goodall, who was robbed of a winner by a uaring save from Rovers' goalkeeper, Laurie Taylor: "If the ball had gone in I'd have jumped so high I don't think I would have come down!".

ROVERS	V.		KETTERING
(Blue)			(Red)
Laurie TAYLOR	1		Bryan HARVEY
Lindsay PARSONS	2		Roger ASHBY
Tom STANTON	3		Tony NEEDHAM
Stuart TAYLOR	4		Steve GAMMON
Larry LLOYD	5		Mike REED
Johnny PETTS	6		Ken EVANS
Ray GRAYDON	7		Barry DALDY
Bobby JONES	8		Ken GULLY
Ray MABBUTT	9		Dick SMITH
Wayne JONES	10		Mike GOODALL
Harold JARMAN	11		Harry WALDEN

The replay took place on a frosty January night, which became decidedly bleaker as the game went into its final dramatic stages. Barry Daldy maintained his remarkable FA Cup goal scoring record giving the Poppies the lead in the thirty third minute.

With only twenty minutes remaining it appeared certain that Kettering would meet Bolton Wanderers in the Fourth Round when Rovers centre half Larry Lloyd brought down Daldy for a penalty. The usually reliable Harry Walden missed the chance to provide a two goal cushion, but, so superior were Kettering, that few realised the significance of goalkeeper Taylor's save until his wing half namesake headed past Harvey for a seventy ninth minute equaliser.

Then, as we all prepared for extra time, came the final twist of the knife. The impeccable Steve Gammon attempted to steer Bobby Jones cross away with his chest, only to see it skim from his head into the corner of the net.

Inevitably Poppies fans relived the Peterborough replay of 1958 - and like Brian Reynolds before him, Gammon's marvellous contribution would be forever blighted by an unwarranted stroke of ill fortune.

Kettering's team included no less than seven local lads!

KETTERING TOWN . . . . last non-League club left in the Cup

Back Row: Tite, J Daldy, Lawman, Walden, Harvey, Goodall, Reed, Needham, Smith.
Front Row: Gully, B Daldy, Gammon, Evans, Johnson.

HEARTBREAK END FOR STEVE

KETTERING TOWN 1 BRISTOL ROVERS 2

IF soccer's medals were handed out for bravery and hard luck Kettering Town's eleven gallant men would be the first in line to have the awards pinned on.

Victory and the glamour and glory that go with it were snatched away from the Cup-fighting heroes of Rockingham Road in 11 action-packed minutes of drama at the end of last night's nail-biting replay before a bumper 9,000 crowd.

And two of the men that have steered Kettering Town to the greatest FA Cup run in the club's history trooped to the dressing room with the inescapable knowledge that their ill-luck had been the main causes of the Poppies' exit from the Cup.

With the game 70 minutes old the Poppies were leading by a single goal scored by Barry Daldy in the 33rd minute. Goalscorer Daldy was chopped down by desperate centre-half Larry Lloyd, Welsh referee Mr. I. P. Jones pointed to the spot and Harry Walden, penalty king and darling of the Rockingham Road crowd, prepared to take the kick.

PAID OFF

A well-timed piece of gamesmanship by Rovers' goalkeeper Laurie Taylor kept Walden waiting for nearly three minutes to take the kick. And Taylor's delaying tactics paid off. Walden's tame spot kick was saved by the Rovers' keeper and the Third Division club were still in with a shout.

Kettering were just 11 minutes away from the fourth round and a trip to Lancashire to meet Bolton when Bristol grabbed an equaliser. They were awarded a free kick just outside the penalty area. Giant wing-half STUART TAYLOR outjumped the Poppies' defence and headed Parsons' cross wide of Bryan Harvey for the equaliser.

But the fighting Poppies were far from finished. They pushed Rovers back into their own half and twice came close to regaining the lead before the Cup's biggest tragedy hit the non-Leaguers.

HOME AND DRY

Talented Rovers' skipper Bobby Jones got the better of Tony Needham and tried to pull the cross back for his on-rushing forward colleagues. Kettering boss STEVE GAMMON, the inspiration behind the Poppies great Cup run, flung himself full-length in a desperate effort to cut out the centre. But the ball glanced off his head wide of Bryan Harvey and Rovers were home and dry.

So Kettering's finest Cup run is over. There is no place in the Hall of Fame for hard luck, but the Poppies had their heroes even in defeat.

Player-manager Steve Gammon was a driving force behind the industrious Kennie Evans covered nearly every blade of grass; and up front man-of-the-match Barry Daldy was a constant thorn in the Rovers' side.

Kettering: Harvey; Ashby, Needham; Gammon, Reed, Evans; Daldy, Gully, Smith, Goodall, Walden. Sub: Johnson.

Bristol Rovers: L Taylor; Parsons, Stanton; S Taylor, Lloyd, Petts; Graydon, Barney, R Jones, Ronaldson, Jarman. Sub: W Jones.

Attendance 9,050.

An amazing postscript was provided some days later when the Kettering Supporters Club received a strange request from Bristol based reporter Roger Malone.

Dear Mr Yates,

     I wonder if you will be so kind as to see if you can locate a pipe I left behind at your ground during last night's epic Cup tie, concerning which you have the sympathy of so many people for the unlucky way you lost in the end.

     I covered the match from the glass-fronted building which looked down over the corner-flag which would be nearest to that part of the penalty area in which Rovers committed the tackle which led to your penalty — sorry for using that penalty to pinpoint my seat !

     The pipe is one of those rather-expensive ones with a metal stem and metal-lower-bowl which screws off.

Unfortunately I've been unable to discover whether there was at least one happy ending to the story of the match.

214

Kettering gained some consolation at the end of the season when defeating local rivals Northampton Town in the Senior Cup Final.

COBBLERS CRUSHED IN COUNTY CUP FINAL

KETTERING TOWN 2, NORTHAMPTON TOWN (

THE Poppies are county champions! Amid scenes of wild enthusiasm, as jubilant supporters swarmed over the Rockingham Road pitch, Kettering Town received the Northants Senior Cup for the first time in nine years after they had destroyed the Cobblers in the final last night.

Northampton, balanced between the Third and Fourth Divisions, were crushed by the enthusiastic Poppies, who not only deserved their win—but made the Cobblers look second-rate in achieving it.

The man behind Kettering's biggest night for years was ex-Cobbler Harry Walden, scorer of the first goal and maker of the second.

Whatever their fate in the relegation stakes, Ron Flowers' men can have no complaints about this one. For, although they pushed the Poppies back into their own penalty area for long spells in the second half, they never looked like beat-ing one-time County Ground hero Bryan Harvey in the Kettering goal.

WORTHY

Kettering, conquerors of Peterborough in the semi-final, were worthy champions, and Northampton—suffering from the lack of punch that has sent them to the fringe of relegation—had no answer.

With Goodall having one of his best games for months, in attack, and Barry Daldy a non-stop terrier, who worried the life out of Neil Townsend, the Poppies attack functioned effectively for the first time for several games. The

defence, almost inevitably, were superb. And if Northampton had any ideas of wiping out Walden's first goal on the half-hour they were shattered by the red-shirted men at the back.

This was Kettering's night—a night on which everything their Third Division opponents had to offer wasn't enough!

Kettering went in front following a blunder by Townsend. WALDEN snapped up the chance, cut into the penalty area and beat Morritt with a shot that sent the home fans among the 4,152 fans wild.

ANXIOUS

Northampton's efforts to pull back an equaliser caused a few anxious moments in the crowd—but not in the Kettering defence. Even when Harvey dropped a cross from Knox at the feet of Felton, the Northampton winger, and young centre-forward Hawkins made a mess of it.

The best was kept until last —for Kettering's second goal had a touch of real class about it. Barry Daldy robbed Neal, took the ball wide of Townsend, sent a pass out to Walden and darted goalwards for the returns. The former Cobblers' winger's chipped centre was spot-on and Daldy rose to nod the ball past a bewildered Morritt to make certain of the trophy.

The final whistle went a minute later and, amid chants from jubilant Kettering youngsters, Steve Gammon received the cup from NFA president Mr. Harry Sykes.

Kettering: Harvey; J. Daldy, Ashby; Gammon, Peck, Gully, Goodall, Lawman.

Northampton: Morritt; Clark, Fairfax; Neal, Townsend, Kiernan; Felton, Weaver, Hawkins, Hatton, Knox. Substitute: Worthington for Hatton, 83 minutes.

Attendance: 4,152.

My old infant school pal, Kettering Youth United and Desborough Town colleague John Lawman, emulated our childhood hero Bert Henley by hitting the goalscoring headlines in a midseason game against Margate.

LAWMAN GOAL A TONIC FOR POPPIES

KETTERING TOWN 4, MARGATE 2

IT'S amazing what a difference a goal can make. And Kettering Town fans, for so long starved of this basic ingredient of the game, were given a real taste of what it's all about by a fine Poppies recovery that sent troubled Margate towards the brink of relegation,

Until substitute-turned-hero John Lawman dived in to head the Poppies' equaliser on the stroke of half-time Kettering never looked more than an ordinary mid-table outfit with the same problems that have dogged them all season—lack of finishing.

Avondale Infants School, Kettering Youth United and eventual Poppies winger John Lawman, with fellow traveller the 'Friar'. Mascot, Tug Wilson was also renowned for his rendition of 'Rawhide' complete with tin tray percussion at the Working Men's Club in Wellington Street.

215

PRE-SEASON FRIENDLY

Corby Town

v

Glasgow Rangers xi

at Occupation Road Ground

Saturday, 3rd August, 1968

kick-off 3.00 p.m.

OFFICIAL PROGRAMME 6d.

A Message From The Manager

It is with great pleasure that I welcome my old club Glasgow Rangers to Corby this afternoon. I had the good fortune to captain and play for Rangers for 15 years, and today I am particularly looking forward to meeting my old friends and colleagues such as Norrie Martin, Alex Willoughby, and Roger Hynds and of course, the legendary Bob McPhail, who holds the Scottish record for Scottish Cup winner's medals.

We are looking forward to a first-class match this afternoon, and naturally, the players especially would like to send the Rangers home defeated - this would really give them something to remember non-League Soccer by!

I know I can rely on you to give both teams a real Corby Town welcome; Rangers' first visit to Corby has already created a great deal of interest and I hope that what you see this afternoon will whet your appetite for more matches of this class.

Arrangements are already in hand to bring some of Soccer's big names to Corby during the season for friendly matches throughout the season, and I am sure I can look forward to ever-increasing support for the club both for these matches and for our Southern League and other matches in the season to come, which promises to be an important one in the history of this club.

ERIC CALDOW.

Eric Caldow's Corby Town began with a pre-season victory over the manager's former club, Glasgow Rangers.

New signings included Harry Fallon (York City), Jimmy McGeorge (Cambridge City and Sunderland) and Scottish League cap Bertie Black (Ayr United and Kilmarnock). The striking partnership of Black and McNeil provided 68 goals, but despite such prolific scoring the season proved unsuccessful.

Caldow returned to Scotland in the new year and was replaced by former Peterborough and Poppies manager George Swindin. Promotion was missed, despite achieving eight wins from the final ten matches, and defeats against St Albans in the FA Cup and Rushden in the Senior Cup contributed to the disappointment.

However, Dixie McNeil's rehabilitation was complete, his 47 goals leading to a return into league football with Northampton Town the following season.

Wellingborough Town entertained a star-studded Tottenham 'A' side in their opening Metropolitan League fixture which attracted a crowd of 1,180.

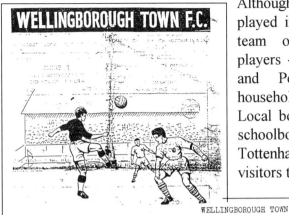

WELLINGBOROUGH TOWN F.C.

1968-69 SEASON

Although centre half Ron Henry played in the Spurs double winning team of 1961, several younger players - Daines, Naylor, Neighbour and Perryman - were hardly household names at the time.

Local boy Paul Shoemark, a former schoolboy international, played on Tottenham's right wing helping the visitors to a 2-1 victory.

```
            WELLINGBOROUGH TOWN
               (1) WILSON
          (2) HAYWARD        (3) MARRIOTT
         (4) BATES   (5) HUGHES    (6) JEFFERIES
     (7) MAJOR (8) MILLER (9) KETTLEBOROUGH (10)ADDIS (11) ROBBINS

   (11) NEIGHBOUR (10) PERRYMAN (9) GILROY (8) BUNKELL (7)SHOEMARK
        (6) NAYLOR T.  (5) HENRY    (4) EDWARDS
           (3) BISH        (2) CUTBUSH
               (1) DAINES
            , TOTTENHAM HOTSPUR
```

Howard Kettleborough

The Doughboys struggled to make an early impression, defeats including a five goal blast from West Ham's Clyde Best, but under former full back Keith Hayward, who had replaced manager Mac McCormick midway through the season, eventually attained a respectable mid-table position.

METROPOLITAN LEAGUE
Final Table

	P.	W.	D.	L.	F.	A.	P.
Bury Town ..	30	20	3	7	55	23	43
Tottenham ..	30	17	8	5	68	38	42
Bletchley	30	16	6	8	47	25	38
Metro Police .	30	16	5	9	72	52	37
Braintree .. .	30	12	11	7	36	26	35
West Ham	30	14	6	10	50	41	34
Wellingboro .	30	15	3	12	57	49	33
Chelmsford C.	30	11	9	10	56	45	31
Stevenage Ath	30	11	9	10	50	44	31
Romford	30	11	9	10	59	60	31
Sheppey U	30	12	7	11	53	54	31
Cray Wands .	30	11	5	14	49	49	27
Arsenal	30	9	4	17	34	59	22
Hatfield T	30	4	9	17	37	65	17
Wimbledor ..	30	6	3	21	30	70	15
Bedford T	30	5	3	22	28	81	13

Leading goalscorer: Kettleborough (Wellingborough Town) 31.

had replaced manager Mac McCormick midway through the season, eventually attained a respectable mid-table position.

Centre forward Howard Kettleborough, previously at Luton and St Neots, was the league's leading scorer with 31 goals.

1968-69 Division 1	P.	W.	D.	L.	F.	A.	Pts
Bourne Town	32	27	2	3	135	33	56
Holbeach United	32	20	6	6	75	40	46
St Neots Town	32	20	2	10	94	51	42
Desborough Town	32	18	6	8	69	48	42
Spalding United	32	19	3	10	82	53	41
Irthlingborough Diam.	32	18	4	10	102	60	40
Rushden Town	32	15	10	7	55	35	40
Biggleswade Town	32	14	7	11	90	68	35
Wolverton Town	32	13	7	12	66	65	33
Northampton Town 'A'	32	13	4	15	62	58	30
Kettering Res.	32	12	5	15	64	61	29
Potton United	32	11	6	15	53	71	28
Rothwell Town	32	9	8	15	58	59	26
Kempston Rovers	32	10	5	17	64	81	25
Eynesbury Rovers	32	5	5	22	39	106	15
Dunstable Res.	32	3	3	26	35	137	9
Corby Res.	32	1	5	26	33	127	7

County UCL sides trailed points behind champions Bourne in Division 1.

But a new team appeared at the top of Division 2. Northampton Spencer, formerly Spencer School Old Boys, in their first season in the UCL under manager Brian Faulkner, lost the championship on goal average to Bletchley Reserves in their first season in the United Counties League.

1968-69 Division 2	P.	W.	D.	L.	F.	A.	Pts
Bletchley Res.	36	27	4	5	117	36	58
Northampton Spencer	36	26	6	4	123	40	58
Wellingborough Res.	36	21	10	5	91	52	52
St Neots Res.	36	24	2	10	103	51	50
Wootton Blue Cross	36	21	6	9	92	48	48
Ampthill Town	36	16	9	11	63	55	41
Irthlingborough Res.	36	14	9	13	66	62	37
B. Timken Duston	36	13	10	13	63	74	36
S & L Corby	36	14	7	15	80	96	35
Raunds Town	36	12	9	15	54	57	33
B. Timken Athletic	36	12	5	19	54	61	29
Rushden Res.	36	10	9	17	53	75	29
Desborough Res.	36	10	8	18	50	63	28
Higham Town	36	11	6	19	68	88	28
Rothwell Res.	36	11	6	19	52	90	28
Olney Town	36	10	7	19	62	86	27
Wolverton Res.	36	8	8	20	52	101	24
Biggleswade Res.	36	7	8	21	60	108	22
Bedford Avenue	36	7	7	22	46	106	21

218

APPROACHING
HALF TIME
1969-70

Back in the Fourth Division the Cobblers were led once again by Dave Bowen, who replaced Ron Flowers, the former England wing half moving into non-league football with Telford United.

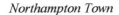

Northampton Town

Back Row: McCormick, Neal, Large, Townsend, Clarke, McParland, Book, Brookes, McNeil, Kiernan, Felton, Bowen.
Front Row: Knight, Fairfax, Fagan, Fairbrother, Rankmore, Hawkins, McGleish, Smith, Weaver, Ross.

Striker 'Dixie' McNeil had arrived from Corby Town, linking up with John Fairbrother in attack. Frank Large re-signed for the third time, joining a side which included local boys, John Clarke, Neil Townsend, Graham Felton and Phil Neal.

There were occasional re-unions with old faces from the club's more successful era - Billy Best and John Kurila at Southend, Laurie Brown and Graham Carr at Bradford. The FA Cup First Round brought Brian Etheridge back to the County Ground with non-league Weymouth, who held

Old lion Frank Large, young blood Phil Neal

Northampton to a goalless draw before succumbing 3-1 in the replay. Three games were required to beat Exeter in round 2, before a single goal accounted for Southern League Brentwood. Tranmere fell next, to Frank Rankmore's headed winner. And so to the plum draw of round 5. A home tie with Manchester United.

Rankmore heads the winner against Tranmere Rovers in Round 4.

Only Joe Kiernan remained from the side that had last entertained the famous visitors back in 1965. 21,771 supporters crowded into the ground, many sharing Dave Bowen's hopes that a major cup shock was imminent.

NORTHAMPTON ARE BACK IN THE CUP BIG TIME

JOE KIERNAN, pure foot-balling wing-half in the pure Scottish tradition and the last survivor of North-ampton's ill-fated brush with the First Division aristocracy in 1965-66, is one of the few people in the game who don't reckon mighty Manchester United have the next best thing to a push-over when they descend to Fourth Division depths to take on Northampton.

Says Kiernan, who has known more tragedy than triumph in his seven eventful years at the County Ground: "Sure, I reckon United are a great side, and it will be the thrill of a lifetime to face them again.

SKILL

"But the ways the lads are feeling about the Cup we don't have to fear any side on our own ground.

"We've got more football in our team than most people give us credit for and John Fair-brother and Frank Large are both capable of snatching a goal out of any chance.

"Look at our defensive record, too. Before Tranmere got that equaliser in the replay here, we'd gone five matches without conceding a goal.

"All that's not bad consider-ing we went nine matches at the start of the season before we got our first win.

"We've tightened up a lot since then and over the last three or four months our record must be as good as any club in the top four."

Anything can happen — Bowen

CUP football has an atmos-phere all its own and it is a wonderful feeling for any club to earn the title "giant-killers" and prepare to take on one of the most respected football clubs in the world.

I well recall the trepidation we felt at Arsenal in 1958 when we had to come to Northamp-ton for a third round tie and our fears proved well founded when the Cobblers stormed to a deserved 3—1 victory.

This is the first time since I took over as manager of the Cobblers that we have enjoyed a successful FA Cup run, and I would like to pay full credit to the players for their great effort in the past few months.

Even with their reputation and tremendous individual skill, United have all the pressure on them. They are expected to win and cannot afford to make a slip. We have nothing to lose, and everything to gain.

Football is such an unpredict-able game that anything can, and often does, happen. The lads are thrilled to get this chance to pit themselves against United, and given the same kind of support as the team received in the Tranmere replay, we shall go flat out to give United the same kind of upset that Arsenal experienced 12 years ago.

Instead, the game was memorable for a virtuoso performance by the great George Best, who was returning to the United side after a lengthy suspension.

A combination of supreme skill, luck and bad defending brought the winger a double hat-trick, inspiring his side to a remarkable 8-2 victory.

Yet Kiernan remains adamant that Best's performance was but a shadow of that four years earlier, in United's 6-2 First Division success.

BEST TOO GOOD

NORTHAMPTON TOWN 2, MANCHESTER UNITED 8

DESTROYED by the individual brilliance of the incredible George Best, who returned after a month's suspension to score six goals, the Cobblers' dreams of reaching the quarter finals of the FA Cup were buried in the mud at the County Ground today. The Cobblers' defence simply had no answer to the genius of Best who would have annihilated any team in the country on this form. Although skipper Frank Rankmore missed a penalty, the Cobblers were never really in with a chance after half time although Dixie McNeil and Frank Large scored late in the match to provide some small consolation.

F.A. Cup 5th Round   Saturday, 7th February, 1970

CHRONICLE & ECHO — The Parade Northampton

Match ball donated by

Kim BOOK	1		1	Alex STEPNEY
Ray FAIRFAX	2		2	Paul EDWARDS
Eric BROOKES	3		3	Francis BURNS
John CLARKE	4		4	Pat CRERAND
Frank RANKMORE	5		5	Ian URE
Joe KIERNAN	6		6	David SADLER
Graham FELTON	7		7	Willie MORGAN
Eric ROSS	8		8	Carlo SATORI
Frank LARGE	9		9	Bobby CHARLTON
John FAIRBROTHER	10		10	Brian KIDD
Richard McNEIL	11		11	John ASTON
B in KNIGHT	12		12	

The cup game so dominates memories of the season, that events after Saturday February 7th seem almost an irrelevance, however, John Fairbrother's 23 league goals, the club's highest individual tally for seven seasons, helped the side to an eventual fourteenth place.

Peterborough, Northampton's Fourth Division colleagues once more, lost goalkeeper Tony Millington, who returned to Wales and Swansea Town during the close season. Former youth player Mick Drewery contested the position with newcomer, Dick Dighton from Coventry, while apprentice centre half Chris Turner signed professional forms and would make his first team debut later in the season.

Player-manager Iley's team began the season well, a nine match unbeaten home run generating promotion hopes. The sequence ended in defeat by Chesterfield but in the next home game, against Oldham on November 26th, history was made with a record breaking 8-1 victory. Inconsistency destroyed any chance of league success however, and as so often in

November 26, 1969

Biggest League win

Posh 8, Oldham 1

"United were irrepressible. They churned Oldham into pathetic stragglers with eight great goals. It could easily have been a dozen."

Team; Drewery; Potts, Noble; Conmy, Wile, Wright; Moss, Price; Hall, Holliday, Robson. Sub: Garwood. Scorers: Hall 4, Price 3, Moss.

Attendance: 4,796.

the past, supporters looked to the FA Cup for consolation. Victories over Falmouth, Second Division Plymouth, and Rotherham brought a possibility of further glory especially when drawn against Gillingham in the fourth round. Sadly, supporters witnessed a below par performance resulting in a 5-1 defeat and, like their County rivals Northampton, watched the season peter to an undistinguished conclusion. Jim Hall, with 27 goals, could retain considerable pride in his contribution to the side's eventual ninth place.

DIVISION 4	P	W	D	L	F	A	W	D	L	F	A	Pts
Chesterfield	46	19	1	3	55	12	8	9	6	22	20	64
Wrexham	46	17	6	0	56	16	9	3	11	28	33	61
Swansea T	46	14	8	1	43	14	7	10	6	23	31	60
Port Vale	46	13	9	1	39	10	7	10	6	22	23	59
Brentford	46	14	8	1	36	11	6	8	9	22	28	56
Aldershot	46	16	5	2	52	22	4	8	11	26	43	53
Notts Co	46	14	4	5	44	21	8	4	11	29	41	52
Lincoln C	46	11	8	4	38	20	6	8	9	28	32	50
Peterboro' U	46	13	8	2	51	21	4	6	13	26	48	48
Colchester U	46	14	5	4	38	22	3	9	11	26	41	48
Chester	46	14	3	6	39	23	7	3	13	19	43	48
Scunthorpe U	46	11	6	6	34	23	7	4	12	33	42	46
York C	46	14	7	2	38	16	2	7	14	17	46	46
Northampton T	46	11	7	5	41	19	5	5	13	23	36	44
Crewe A	46	12	6	5	37	18	4	6	13	14	33	44
Grimsby T	46	9	9	5	33	24	5	6	12	21	34	43
Southend U	46	12	8	3	40	28	3	2	18	19	57	40
Exeter C	46	13	5	5	48	20	1	6	16	9	39	39
Oldham A	46	11	4	8	45	28	2	9	12	15	37	39
Workington	46	9	9	5	31	21	3	5	15	15	43	38
Newport Co	46	12	3	8	39	24	1	8	14	14	50	37
Darlington	46	8	7	8	31	27	5	3	15	22	46	36
Hartlepool	46	7	7	9	31	30	3	3	17	11	52	30
Bradford	46	6	5	12	23	32	0	6	17	18	64	23

Kettering Town's FA Cup campaign came to an early end with a 2-0 First Round defeat at home to Swansea. The Poppies now included England international centre forward, Ray Crawford, who had represented Ipswich in the inaugural floodlit match in 1961. Crawford became the team's top scorer netting 18 league goals as the Poppies struggled to 15th place. Brothers Maurice and Mick Goodall, and Barry and John Daldy appeared together in numerous league matches - a distinction denied the Websters, as on John's only first team appearance at Yeovil, brother Ray was unusually absent from the line-up.

Ray Crawford

A crowd of 3,534 watched the 3-0 defeat by Chelmsford in the third round of the FA Trophy - the new competition for senior non-league clubs.

At Occupation Road, Steelmen manager Swindin had brought in former Peterborough full back Ron Cooper and restored popular goalkeeper Alan Alexander for the 1969-70 campaign. It was a lack of fire power, however, that proved decisive in a disappointing season, strikers Gregory and Wilson amassing 30 fewer than counterparts McNeil and Black in the previous year. Nevertheless promotion appeared likely until the final weeks when a disastrous sequence of results brought only one victory from the last nine matches.

A champagne win—now Doughboys must wait

WELLINGBOROUGH T. 4, CRAY WAN. 0

CHAMPAGNE flowed freely in the Doughboys dressing room after the match. But it will be Wednesday night before we know whether the celebrations were for winning the Metropolitan League championship—or the consolation runners-up spot.

For victory in this, their last match of a fine season, puts Wellingborough back on top of the table one point clear of rivals Stevenage Athletic.

Now all the Doughboys can do is sit back and wait anxiously for the result of Stevenage's final fixture, away to Sheppey United on Wednesday. A draw will give Stevenage the title on goal average.

It seems incredible that this should be the case after the Doughboys have scored 12 without reply in their last two matches. "It is very disappointing considering the odd goal here and there during the season would have given us the championship comfortably," said manager Keith Hayward after Saturday's win.

CAUTIOUS

The Doughboys began cautiously with Cray making it obvious that they were not going to be such an easy sacrifice as Brentwood in midweek.

Gradually the Doughboys got on top and after 31 minutes KETTLEBOROUGH gave them a 1—0 lead with a superb shot from the edge of the penalty box.

Seven minutes into the second half Dave LOVELL ran in to head a centre from the dynamic Tony Sabey into the net to make it 2—0.

DECEPTIVE

Kettleborough sent over a deceptive cross from the right wing in the 63rd minute for DYTE to guide the third past Cray goalkeeper Jensen.

Five minutes later Dyte took over in the back four for the second successive match, this time when centre half David Williams was helped from the field after a foul by Waghorne.

Positions

Substitute Marriott, making his farewell appearance for the club, joined the attack.

Sabey found the back of the net in the 74th minute after a neat movement with Lovell but the "goal" was disallowed with referee Ingram ruling him offside.

FOURTH GOAL

However the fourth goal came five minutes later when Dorey misjudged a long ball down the middle and KETTLEBOROUGH raced through to lob the ball over Jensen's head and over the line before Dorey managed to retrieve it.

Wellingboro' Town: Knibbs. Hughes. Claypole: Sabey, Williams, Waite: Lovell, Casey Kettleborough. Dyte. Miles. Sub: Marriott (for Williams).

Cray Wanderers: Jensen: Ford. Baker: Fitzpatrick Dorey. Wolley: Crooks. Walker Waghorne. Wissenden. Wiltshire. Sub: Howe (for Walker)

Attendance: 313.

The FA Trophy provided the best opportunity for cup success. Wisbech, Holbeach, Basingstoke and Premier League Yeovil were all beaten, before a 2-1 home defeat by Hillingdon ended interest in the competition.

Wellingborough Town completed a second season in the Metropolitan League as champions. Victory over Cray Wanderers in their last game was not enough to guarantee the title, but when rivals Stevenage inexplicably lost their final game to bottom club Sheppey, the Doughboys finished on top.

The side included former Cobblers, Claypole and Knibbs, Mick Dyte from Rushden, and Denis Casey, sole survivor from the UCL championship side of 1962-63.

Attendances disappointed however, and only twice, for Senior Cup matches against Kettering and Northampton, did crowds exceed 1,000.

Rothwell Town, under manager Ken Burton, were runners up in the UCL.

Ken Burton receiving a gift from Poppies keeper Smethurst on leaving Kettering Town in 1965,

The former Poppies trainer had taken over at Cecil Street during the previous season and his unique combination of charisma and the supreme coaching skills that would eventually bring international recognition, produced a young team of rare quality.

Second spot for Rothwell

**ROTHWELL TOWN 5.
IRTHLINGBORO' DIA. 1.**

ROTHWELL Town made certain of the prestige runners-up spot with a final great display to finish a wonderful season.

Irthlingborough were perhaps a shade fortunate to lost by such a margin but there can certainly be no dispute about the result for Rothwell's determination was evident throughout the game and two goals in the tenth minute set Rothwell on the way to victory.

In the opening minute Walpole had crashed a shot against the upright and then at the other end Ellis had a great chance to put Diamonds ahead. But then came the two sensational goals from a free kick from Aldwinkle. WALPOLE ran in to score with a glancing header that left Bosworth stranded and then within seconds came another goal when HORNBUCKLE rose above the Diamonds' defence to send in a fine header from Walpole's centre.

PENALTY

Further chances were made and missed before the third goal came in the eighth minute of the second half when, following a disputed penalty award, FOWEATHER gave Bosworth no chance from the spot kick.

Rothwell were now rampant and in the 68th minute HALL made it 4-0 when he headed home from Blount's centre.

Following this goal, the Diamonds rallied and had their only success of the game when ELLIS headed in from close range following a right wing corner.

But Rothwell were soon on to the attack and eight minutes from time scored again when following a low hard centre from Foweather a Diamonds defender, harrassed by Walpole and Hornbuckle, deflected the ball into his own net.

This result capped a remarkable sequence of results for Rothwell. Their last defeat was on November 29 at Ampthill. Since then they have played 19 games, twelve won 13 and drawn six scoring 41 goals and conceding 12.

Previous to this, they had played 13 won five drawn three and lost five scoring 20 goals and 24 scored against.

The final league record is: played 32 won 18 drawn nine lost five and goals for 61 and against 36 points 45. Their home record reads: only two games lost and in all, eight points dropped. Goals scored 37 for and 11 against.

1969-70 Division 1	P.	W.	D.	L.	F.	A.	Pts.
Bourne Town	32	23	7	2	105	30	53
Rothwell Town	32	18	9	5	61	36	45
Rushden Town	32	19	6	7	76	35	44
Irthlingborough Diam.	32	19	2	11	85	43	40
Desborough Town	32	15	10	7	69	46	40
Northampton Spencer	32	16	6	10	61	51	38
Wolverton Town	32	17	3	12	71	54	37
Holbeach United	32	15	4	13	72	75	34
Potton United	32	14	5	13	74	71	33
Biggleswade Town	32	13	3	16	70	68	29
Kempston Rovers	32	9	8	15	40	62	26
Ampthill Town	32	10	5	17	39	66	25
Spalding United	32	9	5	18	55	71	23
Bletchley Res.	32	9	5	18	45	73	23
Kettering Res.	32	10	2	20	60	88	22
Corby Res.	32	7	6	19	42	86	20
Eynesbury Rovers	32	4	4	24	34	94	12

Despite the heavy defeat against Rothwell, Irthlingborough Diamonds maintained their remarkable progress, finishing fourth behind neighbours Rushden Town.

The Diamonds had begun the season by fulfilling an earlier promise by club secretary Tony Jones. Speaking to 'Chronicle and Echo' reporter Brian Barron shortly after the purchase of a piece of wasteground from the local water board he outlined his plans for the site.

Spectators will also be looked after. Attached to the dressing rooms will be a stand. Tony envisages that it will be standing room only,

although they may add a small seating section.

Players will have a separate training area, with lights, and a large car park is to be built at the entrance of the ground.

He emphasises that it will be an enclosed ground. "We intend to segregate the ground from the other land, which we do not own,"

Top priority, of course, is being given to the playing surface and dressing room facilities. Two firms have been called in to level the pitch and re-seed it.

The club have in mind large brick dressing rooms, which will accommodate a treatment room and committee room.

The first game on their new Nene Park ground was a match against a UCL representative side.

6-45 p.m. Opening Ceremony

Speakers: A. C. JONES (Secretary of Diamonds), L. UNDERWOOD (Chairman of Northamptonshire Football Association), Coun. DR. I. J. R. MUSSON (Patron to Club), C. E. BULLER (President of United Counties Football League).

7.00 p.m. KICK-OFF

Irthlingborough Diamonds

I. G. BOSWORTH
2. S. WISMAN
3. D. HOWITT
4. R. ALLEN
5. R. FIELD
6. R. GREEN
7. C. SMITH
8. B. ELLIS
9. R. HORSFIELD
10. L. CAMP
II. P. GARLEY
Subs.: W. Douglas, R. Manning, S. Brown

United Counties League Representative Team

I. FROST (Rushden Town)
2. PATENELL (Rushden Town)
3. BUSHELL (N. Spencer)
4. EZRA (Ampthill Town)
5. BINGE (Eynesbury)
6. STEERS (N. Spencer)
7. SISSONS (Bourne)
8. EYETT (Bourne)
9. MARLOW (Desborough)
10. KANE (Rothwell)
II. JOHNSON (Bourne)
Subs.: McLaughlin (Ampthill), Addis (Desborough), Gee (Higham Town). Dalton (Eynesbury Rov.) C. Notley (Bourne)

I recently visited the new Rushden and Diamonds stadium for the FA Trophy semi-final match against Woking. Few amongst the 4,500 crowd gathered for that game were aware of the debt owed to the men of 1969, whose vision and commitment initiated that first, bold move to Nene Park.

Peter De Banke

How appropriate that the West Stand terrace should be dedicated to Peter De Banke, an Irthlingborough Youth team player in 1949, skipper of Rushden Town, UCL champions in 1964, and active Diamonds committee man until his untimely death in 1994.

Desborough, in fifth place, were one of the few teams to bring back a point from double UCL champions Bourne. Yet it is the 3-2 home defeat which provides the more vivid memories.

A heavy overnight blizzard had put the match in considerable jeopardy, and I drove over to the Waterworks Field on Saturday morning fully expecting to learn of postponement. Drifting snow several feet deep covered the pitch, but where the centre circle might have been, stood a forlorn figure resembling an extra from 'Dr Zhivago'.

I shouted more out of politeness than expectation.

"It's off then Charlie!"

Player manager Marlow looked across the white wilderness, and I felt the withering glare from behind thick pebbled lenses from fully fifty yards.

"Course it's not," he retorted incredulously. "I'm getting John Dawkins to bring a tractor and we're gonna roll it. You be here at two o'clock."

The game went ahead on a near perfect surface of hard packed snow but, as at Rothwell in 1961, all his efforts proved fruitless as we surrendered a two goal interval advantage to the runaway league leaders.

Champions of Division 3 were Long Buckby, who had entered the league two seasons earlier from the Central Northants Combination.

Manager Pete Smith's side included the nucleus of the team destined to prove so successful in the higher divisions in the near future.

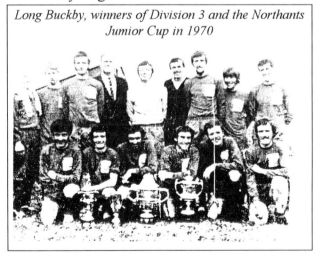
Long Buckby, winners of Division 3 and the Northants Junior Cup in 1970

1969-70 Division 3	P.	W.	D.	L.	F.	A.	Pts
Long Buckby	34	28	3	3	125	24	59
Kettering Park Wanderers	34	25	4	5	91	27	54
ON Chenecks	34	22	5	7	113	49	49
Geddington Montrose	34	22	4	8	75	41	48
VS Rugby	34	17	12	5	69	23	46
Wootton Reserves	34	19	3	12	74	54	41
Deanshanger Athletic	34	16	8	10	105	59	40
Diemers	34	14	8	12	78	72	36
Irchester United	34	13	6	15	68	73	32
Higham Rovers	34	10	8	16	50	70	28
Ampthill Reserves	34	9	10	15	49	94	28
Kempston Reserves	34	11	4	19	60	92	26
S & L Corby Reserves	34	11	3	20	48	89	25
Aspley Guise	34	9	6	19	54	99	24
Raunds Reserves	34	9	5	20	58	97	23
Brit. Timken Duston Res.	34	7	7	20	54	88	21
Olney Reserves	34	6	4	24	59	119	16
Higham Reserves	34	7	2	25	48	108	16

In second place was a side formed only ten years earlier from one of those Sunday morning gatherings so fondly recalled in an earlier chapter. The venue, Kettering's Rockingham Road park, lent its name to Roger 'Bo' Patrick's team, which competed in the local Amateur League before moving into the UCL in 1968.

Other newcomers to the league, ON Chenecks and Geddington Montrose quickly made their marks, occupying the other top four places.

POSTSCRIPT
(INJURY TIME)

The 1969-70 season drew to a belated close with the
World Cup finals in Mexico.

Huge disappointment as England lost their quarter final match with
West Germany turned to pure delight when a marvellous
Brazilian side won the Jules Rimet Trophy.

Their performance in the final against Italy, full of attacking flair and
tactical sophistication, demonstrated the 'beautiful game' at its very best,
especially when Carlos Alberto scored his side's fourth goal.

Footballing purists might have felt such brilliance could never be surpassed,
and that the world should have ended at that precise moment.

But then there would have been no Volume Two.

BIBLIOGRAPHY

100 Years: NFA Centenary Souvenir, Editor David Thorpe.
Forty Years On Corby Town FC History, Editor Derek Waugh.
A Strange Kind of Glory, Eamon Dunphy, (Heinemann).
The Observer on Soccer, Tony Pawson, (Unwin).
McIlvanney on Football, Hugh McIlvanney, (Mainstream).
English League Football, R C Churchill, (Sportsman's Book Club).
Illustrated History of Football, (Sunday Times), (Nawrat and Hutchings).
FA Cup Giantkillers, Geoff Tibballs, (Collins Willow).
FA Book for Boys 1951-52, (Naldrett Press).
Football is My Business, Tommy Lawton, (Sporting Handbooks).
Rothmans Football Yearbook 1991-92, Jack Rallin, (Macdonald).
Boys Book of Soccer 1951, (Evans).
Peterborough United Football Club: The Posh, Groom and Robinson,
(Yore Publications).
The Cobblers: The History of Northampton Town FC, Frank Grande
A Century of Football 1895-1995 (United Counties Football League),
Editor J Biggs